CW00832044

WHAM!

The Death of a Supergroup by Johnny Rogan

CONFIDENTIAL

Omnibus Press
LONDON/NEW YORK/SYDNEY/COLOGNE

Exclusive distributors:
Book Sales Limited
8/9 Frith Street, London W1V 5TZ, UK.

Music Sales Corporation
24 East 22nd Street, New York,
NY 10010, USA.

Music Sales Pty. Ltd
GPO Box 3304, Sydney,
NSW 2001, Australia.

To the Music Trade only:
Music Sales Limited
8/9 Frith Street, London W1V 5TZ, UK.

Edited by Chris Charlesworth
Designed by Pearce Marchbank Studio
Picture research by Johnny Rogan

© Copyright 1987 Johnny Rogan
This edition © Copyright 1987 Omnibus Press
(A Division of Book Sales Limited)

ISBN 0.7119.1120.7
Order No. OP 44346

All rights reserved. No part of this book may be reproduced
in any form or by any electronic or mechanical means, including
information storage or retrieval systems, without permission in
writing from the publisher, except by a reviewer who may quote
brief passages.

Typeset by Hourds Typographica
Printed in England by
The Camelot Press Limited, Southampton.

Contents

Introduction

At its simplest level, the Wham! story was an innocent tale of two school leavers attempting to achieve chart glory in the perilous world of pop. There was the customary paraphernalia of million selling records, endless interviews, unrelenting merchandising and screaming hordes of barely teenage fans, all of which contributed to what Fleet Street termed "the Wham! phenomenon". Journalists love phenomena of all kinds, but on this occasion, the cliché had more truth than any caption writer could have conceived. In many respects, the media's fascination with Wham! was far more interesting than the actions of the group itself. The extent to which the tabloids and music press fashioned our view of Wham's sexual, political and musical relevance is examined in chapters fourteen and fifteen.

Wham! both benefited and suffered from the intensity of their public relations mongering, but none of this would have happened without the clever manipulative skill of a back up team worthy of a Cabinet Minister. The group effectively transformed their own innocuous biography into a tale of high drama by bringing together some of the most powerful figures in the music industry to oversee their management, publishing, record company and legal affairs. It was rather like collecting immensely large sticks of dynamite. Great for scaring off the enemy, but one spark in the wrong place could mean catastrophe. The explosive side of the Wham! story was evident in a series of political manoeuvres, personality clashes, high handed gambles and timely accidents which accompanied their rise to the top and eventual demise. Their true power lay less in their own talent than the remarkable effect they had on their business circle. I first noticed it in 1983 when co-manager Simon Napier-Bell boasted, with more verbosity than usual, how he could take them to heights unscaled since the days of The Beatles. I recorded every word and was there again the following year when "Wake Me Up Before You Go-Go" gave them their first number 1. By this time, Napier-Bell's early confidence had been replaced by empire building arrogance. I returned again after the grand fall in 1986 to find him puzzlingly pleased by the dreadful outcome. I remember Napier-Bell's partner, Jazz Summers, weeks before the split, confident and enthusiastic, and later philosophical and resigned. Then there was Mark Dean, wise after the event, like a prize-winning school kid who has been abruptly expelled. And there were many more comings and goings involving backing singers, photographers, producers, musicians, lawyers – so much mini-drama in so few years. And finally there was publisher Dick Leahy, all knowing but tight lipped, who somehow emerged unscathed from it all. And, of course, there were the boys themselves, not always consistent in their views and comments, but reasonably sincere and disarmingly likeable nonetheless. The boys were never traditional music business pawns but occasionally resembled over-protected and invaluable chess kings, watching disinterestedly while more mobile and powerful pieces fought it out at the centre of the board. More than any other British group of the 80s, they symbolized New Pop politics at its apogee. The following is an account of what happened beneath the comfortable veneer of pop star propaganda and public relations bluster. It is a cautionary tale for managers and pop artistes alike.

Johnny Rogan
December 1986

The Triumph Of Suburbia

The early lives of England's great pop stars seldom make riveting reading, but they often have the ingredients of a reasonably good story. Childhood deprivation, illegitimacy, parental bereavement, juvenile delinquency and adolescent rebellion have all played their part in shaping the great heritage of British rock 'n' roll and transforming mediocre and malcontented youths into burning icons of pop star immortality. It is usually quite easy to dramatize a particular trauma or freakish trait that separates the future teen idol from his less distinguished contemporaries. In the case of Wham!, however, the formative years are a barren period, remarkable only for their dullness. Theirs was a childhood bereft of incident and so excrutiatingly tedious in its suburban normality, that it is scarcely believable that either member had the imagination or arrogance to proclaim himself a pop singer. For those who maintain that Wham! personify the bland nadir of mild mannered 80s pop, the unremittingly prosaic circumstances of their yawningly well-adjusted upbringing provides the perfect prelude for further critical scorn and abuse.

Their story begins amid the splendour of that eventful year 1963, a golden era for pop music, politics, crime, scandal and tragedy. One week after President De Gaulle had voiced his traditional festive message that Britain was still unfit to join the Common Market, the eldest of the Wham! duo awoke to the world in a Windlesham, Surrey hospital. Andrew John Ridgeley, who now spends most of his time chasing the sun, was born on 26 January in a country suffering the most severe winter of the century. A blanket of fathomlessly deep snow stretched disconcertingly across the length and breadth of the British Isles, driven inexorably by blinding blizzards and a numbing coldness which had already succeeded in freezing the Thames, demobilising public transport, raising the unemployment rate to a staggering 3.9%, marooning a family on a Dartmoor farm for 60 days, escalating the tragic incidences of hypothermia among the poor, aged and infirm, and encouraging eccentric religious prophets and failed meteorologists to herald the imminent arrival of an apocalyptic Ice Age.

In pop music, the incongruously titled *Summer Holiday* reminded cinema audiences of warmer days, and the all-conquering Shadows enjoyed their penultimate number 1, unaware that the cosy instrumentals which had kept their career at the top flight since 1960 were about to be rendered obsolete by a new phenomenon. A record breaking viewing audience, barricaded in their homes by the merciless climate, had just seen a young, mop-haired musical quartet whose chirpy effervescence provided a warmth of spirit and melodic infectiousness that momentarily rendered the weather irrelevant.

Six months after The Beatles' first appearance on *Thank Your Lucky Stars*, the younger member of the Wham! duo, Georgios Panayiotou was born in the North London borough of Finchley on 25 June 1963. The brief interim between the two Wham! births had seen Britain emerge from an arctic winter intent on re-establishing its lost status in a world dominated by social and political change. Harbingers of the cult of youth rightly observed a gradual erosion of the old order through a series of newspaper headlines which grew more dramatic and fantastical as the summer months whizzed passed. The great humanitarian Pope John XXIII had died at the age of 81 and his canonization was pre-empted by a miracle which strained the credulity of even the most devout and optimistic Catholic. Northern Ireland journalists noted incredulously that his death had been mourned in staunch Protestant households in which the papacy was previously perversely perceived as synonymous with apostasy or diabolism. Across the world, in the racially torn United States, the beatific Martin Luther King announced that he had a dream and inspired a new generation of kids to demonstrate publicly against institutionalized injustices which threatened the heart of American democracy. On the day of Georgios Panayiotou's birth another contemporaneous champion of the oppressed, John Fitzgerald Kennedy, was making his famous freedom speech at the Berlin Wall. Within a matter of months, he would be killed by an assassin's bullet in a city already renowned for its ostentatious wealth and barely disguised bigotry.

Back in Britain, politics also provided one of the great sensations of the year, though it was scandal rather than tragedy which characterized the Profumo affair. The embarrassing spectacle of a Cabinet Minister's sordid liaison with a prostitute might normally have passed unnoticed were it not for her exclusive clientèle which included Captain Evgeni Ivanov, a prominent naval attaché from the Russian Embassy. Profumo at first denied the charge but under scrutiny from the Secret Service later confirmed his indiscretion and promptly resigned. The scandal proved sufficient to focus attention on the Tory Party as a whole and the newspapers were full of wild stories concerning a network of organized prostitutes busily servicing various Members of Parliament, wealthy landowners and even High Court judges. The Profumo outrage reinforced the view among British youth that their elders were not necessarily their betters. The vestiges of Victorian respect for politicians and statesmen who hid private vices behind cant denouncements of juvenile delinquency and adolescent promiscuity gradually gave way to an insidious cynicism consciously summed up in a phrase which rapidly became a teen and twenty watchword: "Never trust anyone over 30".

The historic events that coincided with George Panayiotou's first few weeks of life continued with the Great Train Robbery, an event so preposterous in its execution that it further enlivened the traditionally dull English summer to a pitch of media hysteria. Meanwhile, the popular music scene was mirroring Britain's social and political upheavals with the most spectacular and rapid changes since the advent of Elvis Presley and rock 'n' roll. The phenomenon that had accompanied the winter birth of Andrew Ridgeley had since developed into a full scale movement conveniently dubbed the Beat Boom. The Beatles' chart topping conquests had opened the gates of the Hit Parade to a legion of groups including Gerry and The Pacemakers, Billy J. Kramer and The Dakotas, The Searchers, The Hollies, Freddie and The Dreamers and The Rolling Stones. The beat route traversed across the British Isles and for a time each major city boasted its own version of the original Merseybeat. Groups came and went, but the best of them, The Beatles and The Rolling Stones, continued to dominate the news headlines and the top of the chart for the remainder of the decade.

The revolutionary year of 1963 not only celebrated the apotheosis of the post-war British teenager, but set in motion a series of social, political and cultural changes which transformed the era. As the years passed, epoch was mounted upon epoch and Britain's sepulchral isle glorified in its revitalized status as the music and fashion capital of the world. Even in the unlikely area of international sport, England inexplicably emerged as global champions, audaciously lifting soccer's 1966 World Cup in a parodic equivalent of real wars past. And so it went on. Callow youths were awarded prestigious political honours, *enfant terrible* entrepreneurs infiltrated the stuffy boardrooms of British industry, and piratical broadcasters in garish floral shirts and psychedelic ties invaded the hallowed corridors and sanctified airwaves of the BBC. Everyone, or so it seemed, paid gratuitous homage at the apparently inviolable altar of youth.

For Andrew Ridgeley and Georgios Panayiotou, the 60s were evanescent moments of time containing half-remembered incidents of questionable significance. Their decade was to be the 70s, that time after the Fall when each successive year underlined all that had been lost, when each budget provoked fears of a probable imminent economic collapse, when Harold Macmillan's optimistic rejoinder to the British public "You've never had it so good" echoed down the years with an irony that even a newly elected Conservative government could not disguise with obfuscating political argument.

The two future pop stars were not destined to meet until as late as 1975 when the peripatetic Panayiotou family moved to Radlett. Superficially, the pre-teenage duo shared a similar family background in both having immigrant fathers and English mothers. There, however, the comparison ended, for beneath the polite upper middle class aspirations of the Ridgeley and Panayiotou clans lay distinctly contrasting family histories.

Albert Mario Ridgeley was born in Alexandria but it was only the colour of his skin that betrayed his Egyptian/Arabic origins. Educated at public school, he quickly assimilated English middle class values and found his Shangri-la in Suburbia with a schoolteacher wife Jennifer and two sons, Andrew and Paul, separated by only thirteen months. It was a nuclear family remarkable only for its unerring conventionality. Andrew's upbringing was free from trauma and blessed with the patient solicitude of a mother whose career had taught her the importance of keeping children happy, but firmly under control. Andrew learned quickly how to be charming and popular among his family and peers. He excelled in sport, particularly football, and from an early age revealed an awareness of his above average looks. His was the type of precociousness usually associated with child models and pre-pubescent British television stars. A revealing colour photograph, taken on the occasion of his fourth birthday, portrays the boy consciously remoulding his image for the prying camera lens, his disarming puppy dog eyes and white toothed smile ingeniously disguised behind a studied frown and moody macho cowboy pose, borrowed from a favoured Western T.V. hero. From his earliest appearance in the school playground Andrew Ridgeley was always the kid who wanted to be famous.

Fame was not a word usually associated with the sleepy picturesque parish of Bushey. Although its history stretched back to the Domesday Book, the village boasted nothing of note until as late as the nineteenth century when Dr Thomas Monro, a specialist in mental illness, founded an academy of painting which influenced several young artists including Girton and Turner. Fifty years later, in 1873, Bushey's cultural credibility was further enhanced by the arrival of the Bavarian painter Hubert Von Herkomer who later opened a school which attracted 150 art students to the village. That, however, was the extent of Bushey's claim to fame and even two World Wars failed to disturb its suburban somnolence. Although the population had increased by a third during the 50s and rapidly topped the 20,000 mark, Bushey retained its air of self-satisfied, quiet rural affluence.

The Panayiotou family's journey to suburban mediocrity took a more circuitous route via Cyprus, Finchley, Burnt Oak and Edgware. Kyriacos "Jack" Panayiotou was one of seven brothers from an aspiring working class family in Greece. In emigrating to London, his ambition was to transform hard work into comfortable affluence. The embourgeoisement process took a couple of decades during which Jack rose from a lowly waiter to a respected *restaurateur*. Like most successful entrepreneurs, Panayiotou placed his faith in dynastic power, but his determination to progenate a male successor proved as tortuously time-consuming as his lengthy occupational strategies. Following the birth of two daughters, Melanie and Yioda, Jack Panayiotou was finally rewarded with a son, Georgios.

In spite of his Greek ancestry, the young Georgios immediately fell under the influence of his quintessentially English mother. They developed a close relationship which continued throughout his junior school education. While other working mothers trusted the fate of their offspring to subliminal homing instinct or the vagaries of public transport, Lesley Panayiotou put her secretarial work aside and dutifully appeared at the school gates each afternoon to collect her precious only son. Such maternal solicitude was beyond the scope of Jack Panayiotou whose business interests demanded an insatiable industry. Throughout Georgios' infant years he seemed a benignly omniscient but distant presence. George recalls those childhood years of the 60s in which he lost the chance to assimilate his ancestral culture: "My father was the typical Greek who comes to London and works 24 hours a day, so his views were never impressed on me when I was very young. I always saw it through my mother's eyes in terms of what I should be after, and it wasn't money".

Indeed, with such a hard-working father, financial fears were banished permanently and Georgios grew up amid the security of a close knit family highly attuned to his every need. Only occasionally did the cosseted child reveal a flash of wayward behaviour or eccentricity. At the age of 7, he displayed brief signs of over activity, occasionally rising at 6 am and wandering out into the garden to collect insects. A neighbour spotted him one morning sauntering around the shrubbery, jar in hand and pyjama clad, merrily singing half-learned pop songs. Lesley Panayiotou was so amused by this revelation that she bought the child a tape recorder. From that point on, Georgios luxuriated in childhood fantasies of becoming a pop singer and, for a time, his family proved remarkably sympathetic and supportive towards the notion. Sensing the possibility of a genuine musical talent, Lesley Panayiotou encouraged the boy to attend extra-curricular lessons in classical violin. Her unselfish support was typical of an ever-attendant mother who, ten years later, would be found loudly cheering in the incongruous company of two thousand teenage Wham! fans at the Lyceum ballroom. Even today, Georgios looks back at his primary school years as a time of hugs and kisses from a family whose unity was unscathed by the amoralistic dictates of the new 60s Britain.

1974 was not the most memorable year to start a secondary school education in Britain. The country was embroiled in political turmoil and the electorate seemed as confused and indecisive as the warring politicians. A state of emergency was replaced by a three day week when the National Union of Mineworkers decided to call an all out strike. The intransigent Conservative Prime Minister Edward Heath held firm and called a general election which resulted in further deadlock. With no overall majority, a coalition government soldiered on and another general election took place later in the year. Labour increased their short lead, but failed to win a clear majority. After losing two elections, Heath's leadership was subject to debate among Tory high office but as yet there was nobody sufficiently charismatic to depose him. Even in British politics, the nadir had become the norm.

Georgios Panayiotou completed his first year at Kingsbury High School before life was disrupted by another family move. Their new destination was an oak-lined avenue in the opulent district of Radlett, Hertfordshire. This meant another change of school and Georgios soon found himself on a coach destined for nearby Bushey. At that moment, he was indistinguishable from his fellow commuters dressed uniformly in dark green blazers, bottle green pullovers, charcoal grey trousers, white shirts and black shoes. Georgios's parents had obtained his new school tie and stag encrested blazer badge from the Bushey Meads matron who had sternly warned that "plimsolls and similar canvas footwear are unacceptable on medical grounds". It all sounded rather like Tom Brown's Schooldays, but before the day was out, Georgios was in for some pleasant surprises.

In spite of its strict uniform regulations and in-house matron, Bushey Meads School had rather humble origins as a secondary modern in the prehistoric tripartite days of 1957. Up until the late 60s, it played second academic fiddle to the rival grammar school, but comprehensive reorganization rapidly altered the ethos and reputation of the institution which gradually attracted more able pupils from the local community. When Georgios Panayiotou enrolled on 9 September 1975, he discovered a school whose atmosphere was unexpectedly relaxed and caring despite distinctly paternalistic undertones. Pupils were referred to by their Christian names and considerable stress was placed on "social education", most notably in the grandly named "Preparation For Life Course", which was obligatory for all members of the upper school. With its twice weekly youth club and active school council, Bushey Meads maintained a healthy relationship between staff, pupils and the community, but its adherence to comprehensive ideals was far from all-embracing. Rather than introduce mixed-ability teaching to replace old-fashioned streaming, the school took a safe middle course by banding pupils in three divisions. However, the egalitarian etnos behind this system was somewhat undermined by the self-defeating decision to retain the familiar A-B-C grading classification. The result was tantamount to self-fulfilling quasi-streaming.

The school's tendency to uphold outmoded "traditional values" was, and still is, most blatantly evident in the retention of that controversial sanction, corporal punishment. Banned throughout London, the cane is still wielded at Bushey Meads in exceptional circumstances as an "appropriate disciplinary measure". It seems all the more remarkable in view of the school's commendable pastoral concerns and pleasantly relaxed atmosphere. Like everything else in suburban Bushey, school professes a willingness to assimilate sudden change while clinging firmly to old and familiar ways.*

The rigid banding system employed in the school in 1975 fortunately worked in Georgios Panayiotou's favour. The news that he had been allocated to Form 2-A1, the top band, was a clear enough indication that they expected him to do well. He only hoped that his new classmates would prove equally welcoming. Whatever reservations he may have had were allayed at 10.25 when 2-A1 were dismissed for morning break. It was then that Panayiotou first encountered Andrew Ridgeley in a fifteen minute scenario that would not have been out of place in the pages of a boys' comic. Long before Georgios passed through the school gates, Andrew had established himself as the most popular boy in his form. His natural pushiness, combined with an astute awareness of the importance of stylish Saturday clothes and athletic prowess, betrayed the qualities of a precocious lady-killer and future sports captain. Georgios, by contrast, was the embodiment of adolescent awkwardness, a podgy, gangling figure whose intimidating height was immediately rendered irrelevant by the comic shock of curly hair and the thick-rimmed spectacles which perched precariously on his nose. While Georgios took his first tentative steps across the school playground, Andrew was establishing his authority in a hardy game known as "king of the wall", the purpose of which was to secure a specified peak against rival invaders. As Georgios passed this noisy assembly, he noticed his future partner gleefully jettisoning all comers and immodestly proclaiming himself "king of the wall" before the entire playground. It was clear that the game served merely to reinforce Ridgeley's already inflated ego by emphasizing his undoubted physical superiority and athletic dexterity. Seeking further attention, the irrepressible Ridgeley goaded an embarrassed Panayiotou into taking part in the proceedings, much to the amusement of his fellow pupils. Their sarcastic gibes soon turned to astonished silence as the unfancied Panayiotou abruptly unseated the erstwhile king and sent him spiralling towards the ground where he landed in an ignominious heap. Some observers claimed the upset was caused by Andrew's over-confidence and lack of effort, others suggested he had underestimated the awkward style of his opponent but the rest realized that the fat kid with the glasses was a powerful figure in his own right. For the dethroned Andrew, such reasoning was academic. Dazed and humiliated, he looked up to discover Georgios Panayiotou overseeing his former playground realm. The formative incident that introduced the duo was destined to be played over in later years for far greater stakes. From that day forward, Ridgeley would assume the role of nominal leader while Panayiotou perfected the art of quiet usurpation.

It says much for Ridgeley's self-confidence and beneficent nature that he immediately forgave his vanquisher and resisted any temptation to seek revenge by exposing Panayiotou as a flash-in-the-pan pretender. Instead,

*In August 1987, the cane was finally banished from British schools, effectively forcing Bushey Meads into line with their more liberal counterparts.

he insisted that his playground rival sit alongside him in the classroom of
2-A1 and thereafter they remained inseparable. Visually, they appeared an
odd couple, though anyone familiar with adolescent classroom dynamics
recognized the sight of a vainglorious peacock bestowing his presence on
an ugly duckling. It was to prove a remarkably successful partnership.
Panayiotou's physical shortcomings and reserved nature accentuated
Ridgeley's good looks and eloquent charm but not to such an extent that he
ignored the needs of his partner who benefited greatly by association with
such a fashionable Lothario.

Ridgeley's adoption of a new friend had another important consequence
which proved particularly attractive. Since childhood, Andrew had experienced a vague desire to achieve an undeserved fame, but the means to this
extravagant end remained elusive. Although he fantasized about life as a
football star, his skills on the sports field and temperamental disposition
towards hard training left several question marks against future success.
What Georgios provided was a far less strenuous route to the fashion house
of fame through that alternative teenage indulgence, pop music. Although
Ridgeley was essentially a non-musician at this stage, a brief glimpse at the
national competition must have proved extremely heartening. The pop
charts had been abandoned to a motley collection of pre-pubescent teen
idols whose anodyne wholesomeness made even the pre-Beatles balladeers
seem radical and rebellious by comparison. For anyone who valued the
singles charts as a barometer of teenage taste, then the first half of the 70s
indicated that the new generation had failed to progress beyond the mental
age of eight. The short-lived deification of The Osmond Brothers was
proof positive that the spirit of Pat Boone had outlived Elvis Presley as the
primary influence on the psyche of modern youth.

The rise of the innocuous Osmonds was paralleled by another teenage
fad – glam-rock. The impact of this latest phenomenon was measured
largely in layers of make-up and yards of tinsel. The historically overrated
glitter craze proved particularly pernicious since it provided a spurious
credibility for a number of rather average acts led by T.Rex, Slade, Sweet,
Gary Glitter and an attendant brigade of brightly plumaged followers.
Even a commentator as sober-blooded as disc jockey John Peel could be
heard suggesting, without a hint of irony, that The Slade and The Sweet
were The Stones and The Beatles of the 70s generation. Apparently, this
meant that their 45 rpm offerings transcended po-faced critical snobbery
from killjoy elder brothers and 60s nostalgists. The argument, of course,
was fallacious for the comparisons were both odious and imprecise. The
Slade/Sweet contingent recorded a handful of strong singles but on the
graph of popular music they were probably closer to the Freddie and The
Dreamers/Herman's Hermits division than the exalted company of The
Beatles and The Stones. For all their promise, neither Slade nor T. Rex
approached greatness. What was self-evidently lacking in the glitter
phenomenon was any sort of confrontation with what used to be called

"intelligent pop".

By the time Ridgeley and Panayiotou met in their school playground, the notion of intelligent pop had been absent for so long that Doubting Thomases, united in a mass crisis of confidence, convinced themselves that they could no longer recognize the form. Since the glitter boys were not as transparently awful as The Osmonds, David Cassidy or other aural assailants, and even released records whose quality occasionally approximated 60's beat groups on a bad day, they were accepted or patronized as the inheritors of quality pop. The fact remained that they lacked totally the originality, ingenuity, adventure and eclecticism of their 60s pop counterparts. Quality and innovation in the teenage singles market was declining at an alarming rate and had reached the lowest ebb since the darkest days of 1961. The disease was precipitated by the expansion of the albums market which had literally drained the singles chart of original or innovative material. Elder statesmen, such as The Stones and The Who, who had done so much to refine and perfect the quality of the three minute 45, now indulged themselves in overblown operatic pastiches or albums laced with dubious fillers. For the majority of self-professed "intelligent" musicians, the single served merely as a cheap advertisement for their next album and record companies were assigned the onerous task of choosing commercial LP tracks for radio consumption. In short, the crucially important singles market was surrendered to philistines content to churn out easy listening fodder. This regrettable policy effectively alienated older listeners who came to regard the 45 as an outmoded form rather like their parents' 78s. Since virtually nobody of note was producing songs for the singles market *per se*, the new teenagers found themselves caught in an unhealthy musical generation gap. Important artists, who would once have served an apprenticeship in the singles charts and educated their teenage audience while growing alongside them, now dived headfirst into album projects. In such a climate, it was small wonder that Slade and their ilk so easily achieved teenage superstardom. The distance between pap, pop and progressive could not be broached in a single leap particularly when everybody was ignoring the importance of quality pop as an aesthetic object in itself. Several artists briefly attempted to bridge the gap, most notably David Bowie, 10cc, Roxy Music and Wizzard, but their releases were too sporadic and seemed geared inevitably towards more important money-spinning albums projects.

The state of bastardised early 70s pop was of particular importance to the genesis and development of Wham! One of the reasons Ridgeley and Panayiotou indulged in schoolboy pop star fantasies was because the contemporaneous competition was so unintimidating, both in style and substance. A glimpse at the previous few years provides a harrowing discography. 1971 began with Clive Dunn's "Grandad" at number 1 and concluded with Benny Hill's tale of "Ernie (The Fastest Milkman In The West)"; 1972 commenced with a Coca-Cola jingle dominating the premier spot and ended with an oblique anachronistic paean to The Beatles' home town from the latest pubescent phenomenon, Little Jimmy Osmond; 1973 provided a brief respite with seasonal chart toppers from Slade and Sweet and impressive singles from 10cc and Wizzard, but by 1974 we were back to The New Seekers who epitomized the new Eurovision mentality of so many British singles artistes. The day that Ridgeley and Panayiotou met, pop radio was broadcasting non-stop mind-rotting pap. The most commercially successful chart artistes of the 1974-1975 period were The Wombles, Mud and The Bay City Rollers. British pop had reached its all time nadir.

In 1975, teenage pop heroes of quality were so scarce that Ridgeley and Panayiotou felt obliged to place their faith in the eldest honorary member of the glitter establishment. At that point, England's most celebrated 70s pop star was a balding, pot-bellied, myopic, self-confessed bi-sexual fop who favoured ludicrously stacked high heels and oversized spectacles as a theatrical distraction from his all too noticeable physical shortcomings. Ironically, it was this embarrassingly unfashionable singer who was to have the greatest influence over the musical direction of the yet to be formed Wham! With twelve Top 10 hits already under his belt, Elton John had at least demonstrated that good melodies and memorable hooks counted as much as good looks in the hunt for long term international chart success. Like everyone else in the early 70s, however, Elton was haunted by a 60s heritage which emphatically underlined the relative paucity of his talents and achievements.

The two decades met head-on during a hot summer day in June 1975 at an open air performance rightly publicized as the concert of the year. In the spacious grounds of Wembley Stadium, where Elton's uncle had played in an FA Cup Final 17 years before, the archetypal 70s pop star sat backstage while his American support acts, The Beach Boys, The Eagles and Joe Walsh, brazenly transformed a quiet English suburb into a Californian colony. The Beach Boys appeared to be intoxicated by the rejuvenating rays of the sun and effortlessly drained every last accolade from the 72,000 strong audience merely by careering through an inspired but familiar medley of 60s summer anthems. By the time Elton John took the stage, a sizeable section of the already sated audience was heading swiftly towards the exit gates. Those that remained felt the uncomfortable sting of anti-climax. The following week the *New Musical Express* headline said it all in a well chosen epithet: "Beach Boys Cup Runneth Over – Elton John Left To Pick Up the Empties". It was surely the most embarrassing moment of John's performing career. Neither Ridgeley nor Panayiotou felt old enough to attend a big concert in the city, and so missed their hero's humiliation. Their trip to mediocrity was saved from the horrors of premature disillusionment.

The blandness that was destined to pervade the recorded output of Wham! can be traced back to their unfortunate adolescence when genius was measured in the length of Elton John's pigeon steps towards his imaginary Yellow Brick Road. Deprived of an inspirational and uplifting musical culture, Ridgeley and Panayiotou were further hampered by conservative, middle-class aspirations and a geographical location synonymous with dullness and inertia. From the vantage point of 80s superstardom, the boys can afford to look back with puzzled nostalgia at their embarrassing ordinariness. Panayiotou is disarmingly modest about his uneventful youth and has frequently reminded journalists of his once plain looks, bashful innocence and inexperience in amours. He likes to present an unattractive portrait of a lad racked with growing pains who is studiously ignored by legions of pretty, unattached girls. Deflated by his physical blemishes, the poor boy eventually invests in a pair of contact lenses and an elaborately permed Kevin Keegan haircut. The self-conscious re-grooming process improves his self-confidence, and he becomes a "bit of a lad", but the girls still stay away in droves. That portrait of Georgios Panayiotou as a teenage nonentity may read like the self-effacing biographical imaginings of an over-paid publicist, but enough key witnesses subscribe to its veracity. Ridgeley and the Panayiotou sisters have frequently testified to Georgios' drabness as a schoolboy and occasionally marvelled at his remarkable transformation into an 80s sex symbol.

Georgios' oft-repeated tales of homely adolescence are qualified by one rather odd admission of a sexual encounter at the tender age of 12. The unfortunate surrendering of his virginity to an elder girl whom he refers to rather ingraciously as "a right old dog" sounds scarcely believable in the context of his teenage history. The story may well be apocryphal since at the time of the revelation Wham's youthful escapades were in sore need of a spicy revisionism. It is quite plausible that an established pop star, hounded by the press, might playfully fabricate a sensationalized parody of Sunday newspaper style pre-teen sex. Alternatively, one can only sympathize with a shy, fat boy who, for indeterminable reasons, felt obliged to indulge in sexual congress and lose his precious virtue at such an awkward and embarrassing age. What this supposed loss of virginity actually constituted in strictly biological terms, the singer has chosen not to reveal. Suffice to say, it remains the one eccentric action of an otherwise unerringly normal childhood and represents such a seemingly traumatic loss of innocence that the reader suspects that the word 'virginity" may have been seriously misused in the context.

At home, Georgios continued to receive support and extravagant displays of affection from his *nouveau riche* parents. On his twelfth birthday, the lad received an expensive drum kit, a gift that most parents would have blacklisted without a second thought. If Georgios seemed capable of getting his own way, he also displayed a cautious respect for his parents' conservatism. It was not until his thirteenth birthday, a full school year after enrolling at Bushey Meads, that he finally introduced the notorious Andrew Ridgeley into his Radlett home. Mrs Panayiotou was preparing her customary elaborate birthday tea when she first encountered the self-proclaimed trendiest person in the second year. Ridgeley was nauseatingly fashion-conscious for a 13 year old and displayed a cocky macho image supported by an impressive list of sporting injuries. The well-bred Mrs Panayiotou immediately recognized a potentially disruptive presence and patently gave Andrew the cold shoulder. Undeterred by his frosty reception, Ridgeley rapidly won over the Panayiotou clan with his undoubted charm as a raconteur. Nevertheless, he failed to assuage their concern over his dangerous unruliness and received a curiously ambivalent response, particularly when school examinations drew near.

Lesley Panayiotou was proved correct in her summation of Ridgeley's character. He did prove a distracting influence over her beloved son, insidiously undermining his commitment to school work with lurid fantasies of pop star fame and its attendant trappings: women, clothes and money. For all their flash talk, however, the twosome lacked the burning commitment usually associated with adolescent musical prodigies and pop parvenus. Ridgeley desired fame minus industry and technique, while his partner seemed content with mere proficiency. Their attitude was far removed from that of the classic young rock star stereotype whose teenage years are surrendered to the monastic seclusion of a tiny bedroom, where immortality is weighed in the flow of blood from aching fingers agonizingly seeking to emulate the impossibly dexterous chord changes of long dead bluesmen and godlike guitar heroes. As if predicting the musical barrenness of the computerized 80s, they spent their leisure compiling tapes from assorted radio programmes featuring the sounds of their favourite artistes, Elton John and Queen, juxtaposed alongside inappropriate jingles and adverts from different stations. Their childishly clever musical montages betrayed the same lazy ingenuity of those disc jockeys who would soon transform the plagiarism of rap into a pseudo-art.

Panayiotou's increasing interest in pop coincided with the completion of a music block at Bushey Meads School. Georgios was keen to take advantage of the new facilities and was seen frequently emerging from the practice room with a violin case. Although he studied music theory up until A-level, he was not entirely comfortable with the subject preferring the anarchic fun of experimental home taping.

While the suburban duo were barricaded in their bedrooms enjoying the innocuous strains of chart music, a radically challenging underground movement was rearing its ugly head from the clubs of London. Punk rock, spearheaded by the incendiary Sex Pistols, had attracted the attentions of a new breed of teenager, totally different from the screaming hordes that followed The Bay City Rollers. They adopted a confrontational uniform of torn clothes, safety pins and outlandishly spiked hair. Following the lead of their anti-hero spokesmen, they spouted nihilistic politics, proclaiming the advent of anarchy in the UK. The blank generation, as media observers conveniently dubbed them, provided the perfect antidote to the anodyne pre-pubescent pretty boys who had dominated early 70s pop. The new breed were ugly, dangerous, irreverent, challenging and, above all, newsworthy. Moreover, in Malcolm McLaren, the self-proclaimed creator of the punk movement and manager of The Sex Pistols, they boasted a proselytizer whose situationist subversiveness ensured that playful, and sometimes serious, havoc would inevitably ensue. The violence that erupted in London clubland during the summer of 1976 momentarily forced punk underground, but its impact was too strong to be ignored. When record companies entered the fray waving cheque books punk was on its way to the front pages of Fleet Street. The simplistic yet incandescent début single from The Sex Pistols, "Anarchy In The UK", caused a mild controversy, but it was their use of obscene language on Thames Television's *Today* programme which finally lifted them into the nation's consciousness. The tabloids sensationalized the event with banner headlines ("Off . . . Off") leaving McLaren wringing his hands in glee. A subsequent attempt to ban The Sex Pistols' nationwide tour effectively succeeded, but in doing so merely increased their popularity among the newly radical music press.

For Ridgeley, Panayiotou and their school fellows, the punk phenomenon still seemed a seasonal joke which would wilt as quickly as flower power had done ten years before. However, unlike previous youth subcultures, punk highlighted some crucially important social issues, most notably the uncertain future of a disillusioned youth, trapped in a nation plagued by unemployment. As The Sex Pistols hopped from record label to record label, the bad joke gradually grew more earnest. It was not until one year later, during the eventful summer of 1977, that the full impact of the movement was realized. The release of "God Save The Queen", during Jubilee Week, not only poured scorn on the country's most sacred cow, but tore mercilessly into the heart of British Nationalism in a macabre fashion which came close to a genuine act of situationism. From their original vacant sullenness, the Pistols had introduced a comic sense of anarchy into the lives of their doleful supporters.

The negative aspects of The Sex Pistols' brief life, and there were many, were partly qualified by the positive achievements, not least the release of a spontaneous rush of unexpected youthful enthusiasm resulting in the establishment of new groups, fanzines and fashions. With their own standards and DIY labels, the new kids strongly influenced the direction of British popular music and effectively ended the careers of several already redundant rock stars. The Bushey boys no doubt breathed a sigh of relief when their hero Elton John skilfully managed to survive the purge.

Punk, for all its dynamic effect on the teenage generation, found few converts in the leafy environs of Hertfordshire. The suburban kids generally found punk too urban, too anti-authoritarian and too outlandish in its execution. Ridgeley and Panayiotou held their ground in the increasingly barren area of straightforward chart pop where true talent such as Abba was now largely submerged by such pretenders as The Brotherhood of Man, Showaddywaddy, Pussycat and even The Wurzels. Not surprisingly, the boys sought fresh inspiration in uncomplicated dance music, particularly the Philly Groove, featuring the work of Philadelphia's prolific and talented producers, Kenny Gamble, Leon Huff and Thom Bell.

The determined exploration of dance music coincided with the first stirrings of troubled adolescence. Andrew's rebelliousness began to intensify from the age of 14 onwards. As he moved higher up the school he became more and more adept at flouting its dress regulations, a habit Georgios noted with mischievous envy. Although extremely impressionable, Panayiotou took considerable coaxing before he was ready to follow in the footsteps of his insubordinate classmate: "I was very shy and quiet. I looked up to him really. He was good looking and one of my favourites. I've always admired him for the fact that he bothered with me at a point when who you're with is as important as who you are."

Ridgeley's loyalty was duly rewarded when Panayiotou emerged from his awkward shell half-way through the first term of the fourth year. October 1977 was the eventful month when Georgios embarked on his first proper date. The girl was another pupil at Bushey Meads, though the pair had seldom conversed in the disconcertingly public school yard. It was the more intimate surroundings of a house party that had brought them together and even then it was the girl who did most of the talking and courting.

The bashful Georgios eventually accepted her hints and asked her out. From all accounts, he conducted himself as a gentleman throughout the relationship, even betraying an endearing streak of romanticism. After four weeks, the puzzled girl was pleasantly surprised to receive a copy of Chic's "Dance Dance Dance" in commemoration of their first "anniversary". The title of the song effectively summed up their major mutual interest, as Georgios fondly recalls: "We both liked dancing a lot, and we often used to go down to a disco in Harrow, which we managed to get into because I looked quite a bit older than I really was. Going out with a girl for the first time in my life made me even more conscious of my appearance than I had been previously, and I used to make sure I was always very well dressed – or, at any rate, what I thought was well dressed at that time".

The qualification is not without significance for during this period Panayiotou began wearing brightly coloured clothes in a brave attempt to match the snazziness of his ever fashionable classmate. These questionable forays into sartorial loudness do not appear to have effected the romance adversely, though it gradually fizzled out after an impressive five months. By that time, Georgios and Andrew were enmeshed in a new musical craze which was to have as profound an effect on their lives as punk had had for innumerable unemployed youths in the capital.

The disco fever that permeated the British and American charts during 1978 was largely a by-product of a hit musical based on pop writer Nik

Cohn's magazine story "The Tribal Rites of Saturday Night". Financed by the Australian entrepreneur, Robert Stigwood, the film soundtrack of *Saturday Night Fever* spawned several Top 10 singles during the spring including Yvonne Elliman's "If I Can't Have You", Tavares' "More Than A Woman" and no less than three hits for the revitalized Bee Gees: "How Deep Is Your Love", "Night Fever" and "Stayin' Alive". By the time the Bushey boys saw the movie, it had grossed more than 81 million dollars and, according to music business statisticians, a copy of the soundtrack double album could be found in one of every seven American homes. Although its appeal was less pervasive in Britain, both the film and the music claimed substantial converts particularly among that sector of the teenage population for whom punk and its attendant outrage had seemed dull or irrelevant. For Panayiotou and Ridgeley, the rhythmic writhings of male lead, John Travolta, provided sufficient inspiration to develop a new code of cool based on the one-upmanship of superior dance techniques. Like many of their friends, they immediately retired to closeted bedrooms and put themselves through painful and exhaustingly physical workouts until their tired limbs grew supple and acutely sensitive to the peculiarly moronic rhythmic patterns of the disco beat. Meanwhile, a number of clubs and discotheques opened in Hertfordshire, eager to transform the disco craze into late night profit. Ridgeley and Panayiotou frequently attended these dark, subterranean establishments where blindingly strong flashing strobe lights and horrendously loud and repetitive disco riffs bludgeoned the sardine-packed throng into a robotic series of pre-rehearsed gyrations which grew systematically more elaborate and athletically dangerous as the night wore endlessly on. They became what is condescendingly known as "soul boys", another youth sub-culture devoted almost exclusively to the music of black performers. Enthusiasts were generally recognisable by their absurdly loud clothes with deliberately clashing primary colours. Like most "soul boys", the Bushey duo enjoyed showing off their garish dress and indulgent dance routines at house parties or, preferably, in the sterile surroundings of exploitative nightclubs where all forms of artifice and narcissistic posturing are regarded as worthy human expressions.

The fascination with all things pop and soul allowed the more musical Panayiotou to walk tall alongside his fashion-conscious mentor. At times, however, Georgios discovered to his cost that late night partying held hidden horrors, even for the constitution of a sturdy 15 year-old. On one occasion, he plied himself with so much alcohol that he became violently sick on the way home, vomiting over those luminous green trousers that symbolized his status as a sartorial soul boy. As he inspected the nauseating damage, the lingering after effects of an unfamiliar spirit worked like a truth serum, involuntarily loosening his tongue until he had confessed all his secret fears to the astonished Ridgeley. It rapidly transpired that contact lenses and boutique clothes had proven insufficient to distract the boy from adolescent worries about his unattractiveness. Ridgeley listened sympathetically, no doubt aware that his colleague was the worse for drink and prone to exaggeration, yet fully realizing the vast chasm between their respective self images. For Andrew John Ridgeley, such self-depreciating admissions would have been anathema. Unlike his best friend, self-confidence was to remain the single, necessarily inviolable trait in a personality intent on winning public approval.

Throughout the fifth year, Panayiotou was badgered with requests to leave school from his increasingly impatient partner. At 16, Ridgeley already felt the pangs of fame, but his appetite was not to be sated for some time yet. With fatidical parental warnings still ringing in his ears, Georgios insisted that they complete their O-levels before even considering a musical career. For the moment, Ridgeley would have to be content with impromptu practice sessions in the front room of their respective homes. This eminently sensible arrangement actually provided dividends for both parties. The more studious Panayiotou predictably sailed through his O-levels while his ever restless colleague surprisingly held his own with an impressive five passes.

The pressure of the examination dominated third term coincided with a sudden change in musical tastes and fashions. A strong jazz funk influence swept into the clubs around Bushey transforming the once revered soul scene into a minority cult. Georgios and Andrew stood helplessly still as those elaborate dance steps that they had perfected the previous summer were rendered redundant by an awkward, unchallenging mid-tempo rhythm which mockingly prohibited the pyrotechnic movements that they so loved. What they now coveted was a revival of old-fashioned soul or, alternatively, the discovery of a new musical genre dedicated to snappily dressed lads with a penchant for choreographical athleticism.

The Executive Experiment

The restless duo found new inspiration in ska, a West Indian sub genre that had first come to national attention in the early 60s. A late 70s mod revival had encouraged many groups to adopt ska as their predecessors had done fifteen years before. Although Panayiotou and Ridgeley tended to follow the fashions with typical suburban sluggishness their interest in ska was impressively precocious. When they arrived for the new school term in September 1979, their conversation was littered with exclamations extolling the virtues of 2-Tone, a movement which had yet to achieve chart prominence. The Specials had hit the Top 10 with "Gangsters" in July, and Madness crept into the Top 20 with their paean to Prince Buster during the first week of September, but it was not until the late winter that 2-Tone heavily infiltrated the playlists of influential disc jockeys. Nevertheless, Ridgeley was so taken by the vibrancy of this revitalized movement that he urged Georgios to leave school and form a group immediately. Although the once shy Panayiotou now betrayed a cockiness and ambition capable of accepting this challenge, the pressure of his family background remained as pervasive as ever. Parental admonishments concerning the importance of educational qualifications convinced Georgios that he must complete the two year A-level course which he had begun with a mixture of boredom and trepidation. In short, he would not be free to embark on a professional musical career until July 1981 *at the earliest*.

For Ridgeley, the prospect of another two years at school was unthinkable. He felt oppressed by the standard school regulations concerning uniform and punctuality, and found to his dismay that his rebellious presence was not always appreciated by fellow pupils. The school librarian still recalls with a smile that "Andrew just couldn't stand still!" After some consideration the restless pupil decided to transfer to a nearby sixth form college which offered the possibility of achieving the same academic qualifications in a more relaxed atmosphere. "College", he argued, treated you like a responsible adult and was blissfully lax in enforcing petty regulations concerning unorthodox dress, smoking and non-attendance. Implicit in that idyllic environment, however, was the ever present temptation to avoid the disciplined work rate and formal routine that a comprehensive sixth form demands as a matter of course. Andrew's A-levels were virtually doomed from the day he walked out of Bushey Meads Comprehensive, but his decision was both inevitable and irreversible.

With self-conscious grandeur, Ridgeley had chosen November 5 as his final school day. While younger kids were preparing for the traditional fireworks night display, Andrew and Georgios were still discussing the merits of all things 2-Tone. In a determined attempt to ensure that his leaving represented the beginning of a new epoch, Ridgeley convinced his partner that they should form a pop group that very evening. It was a ludicrously impromptu decision born of a need to prove that they could act the part of musicians while keeping one foot lodged in the educational door. That same afternoon, the duo recruited two school friends, David Mortimer and Andrew Leaver and, against the odds, persuaded them to play a short set at a scout hut during the bonfire night celebrations. Later that day, Andrew's younger brother Paul, an aspiring drummer, added his musical weight to the proceedings and by the evening the group had found a name, The Executive. The quintet had never previously played together but since they would merely be performing before a bunch of young schoolkids, the majority of whom had never seen a live pop group, competence was barely necessary. All they needed was a handful of three-chord songs, some parodic pop star poses and a few vivacious acolytes to shout encouragement. Even if their performance was abysmal, the audience could always wander off to inspect the dying embers of the bonfire. In effect, it was one of the most comfortable débuts that a pop group could ever wish for.

The Executive felt pleased enough by their Guy Fawkes Night extravaganza to continue playing the odd gig throughout the remainder of the first term. One of their more memorable performances took place at Bushey Meads School's Christmas party where they helped raise a couple of hundred pounds for charity. At a superficial glance, they seemed an exceptionally close-knit unit but as the months passed the shifting group dynamics proved particularly interesting. Contrary to popular belief, Georgios and Andrew were not inseparable soul brothers whose every living moment was spent nurturing their legendary friendship. Since moving to Cassio College, Ridgeley had discovered a new set of friends and began to act in a self-consciously condescending manner which Panayiotou denounced as pretentious. It was only their musical involvement in The Executive which prevented them from growing irrevocably apart. At that point, few observers would have tipped Georgios and Andrew to form a long-standing musical partnership for Panayiotou clearly preferred the company of David Mortimer, a more proficient musician whom he had known since the age of two. It was this duo that could be found rehearsing together most frequently, occasionally venturing into London during the school holidays to try their luck busking in the portals of Leicester Square tube station. With their brief repertoire of Elton John and Carly Simon golden hits, the duo resembled nothing less than adolescent sentimentalists publicly displaying the hopeless dreams of would-be bedsit superstars.

Andrew Ridgeley's circle of college friends ensured that his social life was more eventful than ever. During one of many pub crawls around the watering holes of Watford and Bushey, his bleary eyes focused upon a girl who was destined to play an integral part in the Wham! story. Shirlie Pauline Holliman was another Bushey Meads School alumna, though she had only vague, unflattering memories of the music-loving boys from the form one year below. Like most girls of her age, she was considerably more mature than her male contemporaries and paid scant attention to the activities of younger boys. Her opinions of Panayiotou and Ridgeley were largely determined by half-recollected visions of two unattractive youths who overestimated their own importance. On one occasion, she and her friends had ridiculed Georgios after he had emerged from the music block carrying an expensive violin case under his arm. Even the self-satisfied Ridgeley had not escaped her scornful eye and found himself dismissed as "small and foreign". Her pubescent xenophobia was forgotten on the memorable evening when she and her brother Danny came face to face with Andrew across the tables of a local bar. Recognizing the senior girl, Ridgeley respectfully introduced himself and immediately blotted out her negative recollections. The tiny foreigner had miraculously metamorphosed into a confident, hunky youth, with charm, style and a sense of fun not dissimilar to Holliman's own bubbly personality. After several further meetings, the pair found themselves embroiled in a volatile relationship which was to last two years.

The Executive wasted no time in dragging Ridgeley's girlfriend into their circle. Her possession of a driving licence ensured instant popularity and she was swiftly commandeered as their official chauffeur. The acquisition of free transport extended The Executive's performing radius by several miles but their gigs remained few and far between. Throughout this period, Georgios and Andrew wrote a handful of ska-influenced compositions, but with titles such as "Rude Boy", it was clear that originality was not their forte. Georgios now admits that those early songs were blighted by poor arrangements but could have been developed and magically transformed by an imaginative producer. Like most other teenage groups, however, The Executive were judged on a badly recorded, low quality tape which was hawked around numerous small record labels without success.

By early 1980, The Executive found themselves running behind a pack of other ska-influenced groups and appeared little more than well-meaning imitators. A rejection slip from Go Feet, home of The Beat, seemed to end their fleeting hopes of a recording contract, though they continued playing on an occasional basis. In a final act of desperation, the impatient Ridgeley turned to a local acquaintance, three years his senior, who had recently secured a post with a prestigious London music publishing company.

Mark David Dean was another precocious Bushey boy undergoing the subtle processes of embourgeoisement. His working-class father still drove a van for the *Evening Standard* but had made enough money to set up a comfortable home in middle class Suburbia. Dean rapidly adopted second generation *nouveau riche* aspirations and after leaving school chose the music business as his passage to entrepreneurial achievement. His street wise confidence won him a post at And Son, a company administering the publishing affairs of the chart-topping Jam. As a sharply dressed teenager, Dean was particularly impressive when communicating with mod groups and established a good working relationship with The Secret Affair. Living only a few doors away from Dean's parents in Chiltern Avenue, Ridgeley heard all about the exploits of their mogul-minded son and coveted the music business contacts he had already made. Dean's interest in mod and ska convinced Andrew that he would give The Executive a fair hearing and perhaps win them a publishing deal. At that point, however, Dean was infatuated with London clubland and blithely dismissed The Executive as a bunch of well-meaning, amateurish schoolkids. Although Ridgeley eventually thrust a tape into his hands, a single hearing convinced Dean that it was "dreadful" and, in spite of further solicitations, he never managed to see the group rehearse or perform before a live audience. A further two years would pass before Dean received the opportunity to revise his hasty judgement.

The Executive struggled on through 1980 but failed to reach the end of the year intact. Like most school based groups they eventually lost their initial motivation and drifted into other pursuits. When Leaver and Mortimer departed, Ridgeley and Panayiotou elected to perform some final dates as a duo. Musical impoverishment and technical imperfections were cleverly disguised by the simple act of appearing onstage in fancy dress. For Ridgeley, at least, those gigs confirmed the extent to which style, image and theatricalism could sell a barely competent act.

Following the demise of The Executive, Andrew and Georgios reverted to their original dance stance as flashily attired soul boys. The disc which brought them back to the fold was "Burn Rubber On Me", a Christmas hit for The Gap Band. During the festive season and beyond, Panayiotou, Ridgeley, Mortimer and Holliman established themselves as an insepar- able clique at clubs and discos throughout the area. Any thoughts of reforming The Executive were thwarted by the ominous imminence of Georgios' summer A-level examinations. In the months preceding that epoch, the sole concessions to pop star aspiration were to be discovered in occasional impromptu musical get-togethers and the handful of blue-eyed soul songs which Georgios and Andrew composed during rare moments of inspiration.

1981 was a disconcerting period to be contemplating the end of school life and the beginning of a long-term career. Great Britain found itself in the grip of a new conservatism, so grim and austere that there was talk of turn- ing back the clock one hundred years. The incumbent Prime Minister, Margaret Thatcher, resembled nothing less than a stern and inscrutably benevolent Dickensian governess, encouraging thrift, orderliness, self-discipline and anti-permissiveness. Her antidote to the moral malaise among modern youth was the metaphorical equivalent of several mouthfuls of syrup of figs to be followed by numbingly cold showers and a quick run around the block. Her dream of restoring dear Blighty to the ideals of a hopelessly lost golden age apparently required an economic policy so stringent and incisive that it threatened to amputate the Welfare State from the body politic and replace the offending limb with some unsteady age concern crutches and a near complete reliance on the Victorian vagaries of a few privileged philanthropists. Across the Atlantic, an even more fierce conservatism gripped a continent revelling in a distasteful orgy of consumerist greed, jingoistic pride and boorish "You've never had it so good" back-slapping. In keeping with the national mood, the leader epitomised the fantasy values of the celluloid American West where complex ethical issues were reduced to the simplistic white and red morality of cowboys and Indians, the goodies and the baddies.

Rather fittingly, the chief "goodie" controlling US affairs was himself a former cowboy and Hollywood idol. On 20 January, 70 year-old Ronald Reagan was invested as president and began his administration with a surge of unprecedented nationalist fervour. By some Almighty providence, the day of his investiture coincided with the long-awaited release of US hostages following 444 days incarceration in Iran. In the months that followed, it was hard to dispute the theory that Reagan had appointed some deific scriptwriter to transform his presidential office into a barely credible partisan B-movie.

In a year threatening to eclipse 1963 for political news headlines, the US president almost re-enacted the events of 20 years ago by falling victim to an assassin's bullet. John Warnock Hinckley, a deranged obsessive suffering the pangs of an unrequited passion for actress Jodie Foster, had decided to demonstrate the depth of his infatuation by writing his name large in the annals of American history. On 30 March, he succeeded in unloading his gun into the lungs of Ronald Reagan, missing his heart by mere inches. Remarkably, the aging president not only survived the assassination attempt but was back at work in the White House within twelve days. This was the stuff of Hollywood movies, in complete contrast to the real life tragedies of the Kennedys, Martin Luther King and, only a few months before, John Lennon. Reagan's survival and visibly indomitable spirit effectively rendered his dubious political stratagems irrelevant. Overnight, he had been transformed into a national hero and it was now clear that he would not be dislodged easily.

Four days before Reagan's flirtation with oblivion, Britain had given birth to a new political party forged from the disillusionment of four breakaway Labour Cabinet members, David Owen, Shirley Williams, William Rodgers and Roy Jenkins. The confusingly titled Social Democratic Party was launched with a firm promise to "depolarise society". The internal strife within the Labour Party allowed the Conservatives to continue their radical market-orientated policies, which had yet to reverse high inflation, let alone decrease unemployment which rapidly soared to three million.

The harrowing unemployment figures were merely of passing interest to Georgios Panayiotou as he sat in a school hall poring over his A-level scripts. In spite of all the musical distractions of the past year, his academic work rate was to prove just sufficient to scrape two low grade passes, thereby enabling him to gain entry to a polytechnic, teacher training college or a selection of respectable professions. The only problem was that Panayiotou, in common with the less qualified Ridgeley, was evidently not interested in doing anything except singing. For the past two years, Georgios' pop star fantasies had been frowned upon by his concerned parents as school work was time and time again sacrificed to indulgent hours spent dancing, writing songs and rehearsing with the ill-fated Executive. Along the way, there had been some spectacular flare-ups and reluctant compromises. The ever supportive Lesley Panayiotou had discovered that her son possessed a stubborn streak and could prove uncharacteristically temperamental when roused. On one occasion, she innocently suggested that he should spend less time playing with Ridgeley, but instead of acceding to her wishes, he threatened to leave school immediately. From that moment on, she tended to take his musical ambitions a little more seriously, only daring to betray an occasional detached scepticism. Jack Panayiotou showed no such ambiguity in his response. From the outset, he was against Georgios' pop star affectations and took every opportunity to drag the dreamy singer back to earth with a cynically resounding bump. Incensed by his son's erratic school progress, Jack even banned the boy from purchasing records and Georgios was reduced to smuggling 45s into his bedroom or glibly explaining that the offending discs were borrowed from friends. The thorny subject of Georgios' pop star fantasies had temporarily died down in the run up to A-levels, but as summer holidays and unemployment beckoned, some familiarly uncomfortable questions were recapitulated across the Panayiotou breakfast table. The tone, if not the exact words, echoed the immemorial conundrum presented to every confused and indecisive teenager: "What are you going to do with your life?"

While Georgios suffered troubled debates on the subject of unemployment, the country witnessed mayhem and serious rioting in Liverpool and Southall. Even the distracting spectacle of a Royal Wedding could not assuage the feeling that Britain was going to the dogs. While the Royal Family feasted themselves at a wedding banquet, a fifth hunger striker expired in the appallingly primitive Maze Prison in a vain attempt to win recognition as a political prisoner. Since the self-martyrdom of Bobby Sands, just two months earlier, the intransigence of the Prime Minister had been transformed into a startlingly effective propaganda weapon for the Bold Boys, who celebrated an unprecedented number of electoral victories in Northern Ireland. Violence born of political and religious differences reached alarmingly pandemic proportions during those eventful summer months: Pope John Paul II emulated Reagan's miraculous recovery following an assassination attempt by Mehmet Ali Agca; tensions in the Lebanon increased with bitter and bloody clashes between Israel and Iraq and the world learnt of the puritanical ferocity of another fanatical leader, Ayatollah Khomeini. The summer ended on a further pessimistic note with Ronald Reagan's grand plan to build a neutron bomb.

In the light of contemporary global events, Panayiotou's future hardly seemed worth contemplating. Nevertheless, he chose not to follow Ridgeley's example and sign on the dole while waiting to become a star, but accepted a series of demeaning part-time jobs. For the remainder of the year, the closest he got to breaking into the music business was working as a disc jockey in the unlikely setting of a restaurant and sports complex. He was by now also known as George Panos, an anglicized approximation of the unpronounceable Greek name which had occasionally muddled teachers and prompted Ridgeley to nickname him "Yog". Between jobs, Panos continued working on his music, writing songs and playing the soul boy routine with Ridgeley. For a time, they thought seriously about forming another group and even rehearsed a few musicians, but the candidates seemed like old men and not one professed the remotest interest in soul.

Throughout the winter of 1981 George continued to suffer life as a cinema attendant by day and a disc jockey by night. Disagreements with his industrious father became more frequent as career prospects receded with each passing month. Jack Panayiotou was determined that his son should not waste his education on frivolous pop and for a time the youth felt so pressurized that he considered leaving home. The work-shy Ridgeley was receiving similar criticism and just before Christmas he flew the nest and moved to a flat in Peckham, South London. Within a month he scurried home, unable to resist the domestic comforts that his supportive family provided without complaint. The brief spell in Peckham had at least encouraged the boys to write some songs together. While discussing life on the dole in Andrew's dingy kitchen, the duo adapted their mildly sardonic musings to a catchy hummable tune. The rather infantile ad-libbed chorus rhyming "Wham!", "Bam" and "Man" persuaded them to name the song "Wham! Rap". Their dearth of imagination was further demonstrated when they threatened to name themselves "Wham! Bam!" before eventually settling on the abbreviated Wham! It was an odd group title, with a distinctively dated charm. "Wham" conjured up visions of flashy 60s American comic book super heroes and recalled a television pop programme broadcast three years before Andrew's birth.

The original "Wham!" was the brainchild of Jack Good, a flamboyant American producer who had already revolutionized the presentation of pop on television in such innovative shows as *6.5 Special, Oh Boy* and *Boy Meets Girls*. He had intended to continue that tradition by establishing "Wham!" as the first great pop programme of the 60s, but after only three months the show was removed from the air. Unaware of the unfortunate history of their chosen group name, Wham! set about recording a cut-price 4 track demonstration tape in Andrew's front room containing fragments of their most recent compositions.

The Deals Forged
In Heaven And Hell

The New Year brought no peace to the Panayiotou household. George's insistence on pursuing a recording career had strained his father's patience to breaking point. Frequently, Jack chided his boy with benign condescension: "All 18 year-olds want to be pop stars". His impish son would arrogantly retort: "No, all *14* year-olds want to be pop stars. This is different". The exasperated patriarch would then resort to statistics pointing out, quite correctly, that success in the pop world was largely a matter of luck, while failure was commonplace. George's weary riposte was the bland conviction that good songs transcended bad fortune. The rhetorical arguments solved nothing apart from reinforcing George's resolve to secure a record deal without delay.

The focus of attention now turned back to the previously dismissive Mark Dean, whose recent exploits were causing considerable comment at the Three Crowns pub in Bushey. Having assimilated some knowledge of publishing, Dean had secured an a'n'r post at Phonogram and immediately proved his worth by winning the rights to Stevo's celebrated *Some Bizzare* compilation. Stevo (Stephen Pearse) was one of the more eccentric figures on the pop scene, specializing in electronic music and arcane talent. Most record company executives found his unpredictable nature and short temper difficult to handle, but Dean was young and enthusiastic enough to earn his trust. The success of the *Some Bizzare* album led to the signing of one of its principal participants, Leeds duo, Soft Cell. That Dean could accommodate some of Stevo's rather odd demands, such as a regular supply of sweets for the entire duration of the contract, was deemed no small feat. The ability to communicate effectively with a new breed of temperamental artist and McLarenesque management was tested further when Dean bagged Sheffield hopefuls, ABC. Within months, Phonogram was scoring hits with two of the more critically fashionable groups of the day and enjoying an exceedingly rare hip credibility. Suddenly, observers noted that their *wunderkind* a'n'r representative walked with the swagger of a prize-winning greyhound breeder. Before long, record business headhunters were actively wooing the new boy with promises of higher wages and greater power. A tempting offer from Warner Brothers became resistible only after CBS entered the fray with a keenness which Dean was convinced could be manipulated to his advantage.

When George heard the local rumours about Dean's successes and, more especially, his weakness for blue-eyed soul, he urged Andrew to step up the Wham! promotional campaign. The boy Ridgeley needed little prompting. Already, he was camping on the doorstep of Dean's parental home, urging the occupants to pass on a tape. For some time, young Mark resisted his mother's infrequent admonitions on behalf of the Wham! boys, but Andrew's presence at his local pub gradually eroded his steely resolve not to get involved. Eventually, he agreed to take home the demo tape which Andrew had proffered with a mouthful of public relations bluster. The pathetic four track recording which Dean expected to consign to the dustbin without delay contained enough surprises to assuage even his cynical ear:

> I heard the tape and the songs were so good, and yet the backings were so bad. It was about twenty seconds per song. "Wham! Rap" literally just had a guitar and a few words and "Careless Whisper" had six chords and a couple of lines. I thought "God, they've got talent".

After hearing the remaining snatches of "Come On" and "Club Tropicana" Dean realized that a potential talent lay undiscovered on his own manor. Yet, he needed a second listen to convince himself that he was not daydreaming. "You never think anything is going to happen next door to you. How possibly could it?"

Dean's lingering doubts evaporated following his first professional meeting with Wham! in mid-February. Initially, he had assumed that the 20 second song fragments represented the sum total of their creative output up until that point. He was floored when the exuberant Panos revealed that the songs had long been completed and were only presented in abbreviated form to attract the listener's attention. So far, no record company had expressed interest and the boys were anxious to make a record. Mark hastily arranged a second more professional demo session and preliminary negotiations concerning a record contract began in earnest between Wham!, Dean and his accountant/secretary Shamsi Ahmed.

Ridgeley and Panos were intrigued to learn that Dean's prospects had markedly improved in the last couple of months. He had refused to join CBS Records as an employee but posited the idea of forming an independent label backed by the corporate. It was an arrogant request from a 21 year-old kid whose record company experience totalled a mere ten months. Remarkably, however, Dean received a sympathetic response from CBS managing director Maurice Oberstein who favoured the idea of launching satellite labels to seek out new talent which could be commercially exploited by the financial power of the major. Accordingly, Innervision Records had been formed on 25 November specifically for this purpose. The company had an authorized share capital of only £100, which was divided into 100 ordinary shares, 99 of which had been allocated to Mark Dean. The remaining share was taken by Dean's solicitor, Paul Henry

Rodwell, a man with considerable experience of the music business, whose involvement as co-director and professional adviser to the infant entrepreneur was not insignificant. Rodwell had extensive knowledge of CBS and, indeed, was instrumental in recommending Dean to Maurice Oberstein, with whom he had worked closely while engaged as the company's lawyer. Rodwell's acceptance of a directorship no doubt quelled any possible misgivings concerning his client's rather alarming youth. In the circumstances, Oberstein's generosity was commensurate with Dean's inexperience and the deal negotiated between CBS and the newly created Innervision Records erred on the side of financial caution. The precise terms of that agreement were to have a profound effect on the career of Wham! and it is necessary to look closely at the figures and percentages to understand the limitations that were placed upon Dean in his subsequent negotiations with Ridgeley and Panos.

In return for worldwide rights to Innervision product for an optional term of up to five years, CBS agreed to pay the company a first year nonreturnable advance of £150,000 rising to £150,500 (year 2); £165,000 (year 3); £181,500 (year 4) and £199,650 (year 5). A separate document provided a facility loan to assist Innervision with its working capital and capital expenditure requirements. The sums involved were £75,000 (year 1); £75,000 (year 2); £82,000 (year 3); £90,750 (year 4) and £99,825 (year 5). In return, Dean agreed not to use this loan either to produce master tapes or pay advances to artistes contracted to Innervision or invest in anything else not referred to in cash flow projections. Notwithstanding these restrictions, Innervision was obliged to repay to CBS the entire loan plus outstanding interest and costs at the end of the fifth year. Although Dean now maintains that the contract was "extremely tough", his mixed feelings ultimately convey the sense of a rather small company forced to run a very tight ship:

> We were working on £150,000 which is basically enough budget for one album a year, including signing the act. And we were looking to sign three to four. So Innervision wasn't that stable. Financially, it wasn't bad, but it couldn't have gone on long term. It was inevitable what was going to happen. We'd have been OK for two years with £150,000 per year. As long as we played it correctly, we could have lasted.

In the long term, however, a bigger problem for Dean lay in the cumulative royalties and numerous restrictions contained in contractual sub clauses. As with all recording contracts, the breakdown of royalties was lengthy and specific. For single recordings, Innervision was allowed a surprisingly small 8% in respect of the US, and 11% in respect of the UK and Rest of the World. That wasn't a lot of percentage points to play with.

The more lucrative sums generated by albums sales inevitably involved a more complex series of escalating royalties, varying considerably in different territories. During the first three years of the agreement,

Innervision was promised 15% in respect of UK sales; 13% in respect of US, Japanese and German sales, and 12% for the Rest of the World. For year 4 those percentages increased to 16%, 14% and 13%, respectively. Rising royalty rates for albums came into operation in the various territories as follows:

UK
100,001 to 150,000 sales: $15\frac{1}{2}$%
150,001 sales and above: 16%

Japan
100,001 to 150,000 sales: $12\frac{1}{2}$%
150,001 to 250,000 sales: 13%
250,001 to 300,000 sales: $13\frac{1}{2}$%
300,001 sales and above: 14%

Germany
100,001 to 150,000 sales: $12\frac{1}{2}$%
150,001 to 250,000 sales: 13%
250,001 to 300,000 sales: $13\frac{1}{2}$%
300,001 sales and above: 14%

USA
250,001 to 500,000 sales: $13\frac{1}{2}$%
500,001 to 750,000 sales: 14%
750,001 to 1,000,000 sales: $14\frac{1}{2}$%
1,000,000 (sic)* sales and above: 15%

Rest of the World
350,001 to 500,000 sales: $12\frac{1}{2}$%
500,001 to 750,000 sales: 13%
750,001 to 1,00,000 (sic)* sales: $13\frac{1}{2}$%
1,000,001 sales and above: 14%

From the above percentages, Innervision was responsible for paying both artiste and producer royalties as well as those of any union officials attending a recording session. In certain circumstances, the royalty rate payable to Innervision could be cut by 50 per cent. This clause covered (a) any record with a retail price less than 25% of normal Innervision "top line" recordings (b) any disc manufactured from coloured vinyl, other than black (c) any "two for the price of one" record sets or double albums issued at less than twice the single retail price (d) records sold for charitable fund raising purposes or for sale through military exchanges (e) records pro-

---

* Interestingly, the minor anomaly concerning the millionth copy of any US Innervision album (which according to the contract was *both* $14\frac{1}{2}$% and 15%!) remained unaltered, as did that non-existent figure of "1,00,000".

duced on a custom or non-catalogue basis for CBS clients (f) any cheapo subsidiary labels, (g) sales on records promoted by a substantial† television advertising campaign, in both the four months following the campaign and the two months preceding it.

Furthermore, Innervision was due no royalties whatsoever for cut outs and promotional records, and received no payment for 12″ singles until at least 30,000 units were notched up in each respective territory. Most of these clauses were standard at the time for such a small licensing deal, though several of the percentages have improved considerably since then. For Dean, the most important clauses in the short term were the UK rates for albums and singles, which seemed just about workable. The excessively harsh terms offered for 12″ singles reflected the dinosaur mentality of a company which still assumed such items were largely promotional gimmicks. It was a fair general argument but held little water in late 1981 when exclusively 12″ disco cuts were selling in staggering numbers. As a champion of blue-eyed soul, Dean should have realized that a large proportion of Innervision's future sales would stem from the 12″ boom. His decision to allow that clause to remain unaltered was to prove a regrettable and costly oversight.

With hindsight, Dean accepts that it was a mistake to sign such a tough contract, though he claims to have been fully aware of its limitations from day one. Overall, he concluded, the positive aspects of the deal outweighed any reservations concerning particular percentage points. For a young kid anxious to make a name for himself in the music business, the ego gratification of running a record company proved irresistible:

> At 21-22 years of age, you don't really care about the deal, you care about getting recognized. You feel you can make money anytime. I felt I just wanted to get recognition for my talents and that's what happened.

In his naivety, Dean sounded remarkably like a pop artiste too eager and self-obsessive for his own financial good. But the innate confidence which made him covet a company directorship also soothed his worst fears. Whatever happened, no matter how badly the deal turned out, Dean seemed set for greater things. CBS was effectively funding his apprenticeship and their various options lasted only five years. By that time, Dean would still be in his mid 20s with enough experience, courtesy of CBS, to hit the big time as a fully fledged independent. For the moment, he had merely to prove his ability to discover and nurture young talent on a relative shoe-string.

The executives at CBS probably expected Dean to unearth a few oddball minor league groups, a couple of whom might reasonably be expected to

---

† It is not clear from the contract what constitutes a "substantial" as opposed to "insubstantial" television campaign.

scrape a Top 40 hit, thereby turning over a small profit. It was a calculated corporate gamble. The possibility of Dean hitting the jackpot, however, and signing an artiste of greater commercial potential than a top act of the mother company remained preposterously low. His economic resources alone precluded that likelihood. No doubt in his wild mogul fantasies, Dean believed himself capable of turning the law of averages to his own advantage. Maybe Innervision could establish a reputation for picking winners, and after a couple of years and several duff signings, they might even discover a major talent. In that case, CBS would possibly renegotiate the Innervision contract so that Dean might pass on more substantial incentive rewards to his star signings. This, however, was a matter of long-shot odds and board room political manœuvring. Alternatively, Dean could persuade his dark horse winner to stick with Innervision until the CBS contract expired and then thrash out a mutually acceptable renegotiation. Such logic left one question unanswered: what would happen if Innervision found a megastar in its first year of operation? It was a notion so far-fetched that it commanded little attention but, in retrospect, the implications were alarming.

The Innervision set-up was designed to benefit short-term up-and-coming acts, but an instant megastar could unwittingly cause organizational chaos. CBS would inevitably encourage the satellite company to put their budget entirely behind the hit act rather than gambling on new talent, a move which Dean would obviously resent. Meanwhile, a massive act signed to a long-term contract would gradually become distraught by the relatively small percentages that a company of Innervision's size and resources could offer. This would force Innervision into a corner where they would be fighting their own act or arguing with CBS for a bigger slice of the cake. Yet, there was nothing to prevent CBS from refusing to restructure the original deal and, in such circumstances, the act would be left with whatever terms they had agreed with Dean's company. It was an unlikely equation, but in March 1982 a series of star-crossed deals were to transform fanciful theory into hard fact.

The controversial contract which united, and later separated, Wham! and Innervision Records was despatched in draft form from the offices of Halliwell Rodwell on 5 March 1982. A facing letter added, quite correctly, that the boys should seek independent legal advice before accepting the terms offered. In fact, Wham! had already found a solicitor following the unlikely recommendation of a customer at Jack Panayiotou's restaurant. Fortunately, Sims, Muirhead and Allan proved a reasonable choice and Wham's adviser, Robert Allan, was later described by no less a personage than Mr. Justice Harman as "a solicitor who had extensive experience in this particular field and has an expertise nobody questioned for a moment". Allan put his unquestionable expertise to work immediately and replied to Rodwell indicating that Wham! were willing to accept the main terms of the contract but required certain changes. Chief among these were the exclusion of merchandising rights and a clause which allowed Innervision to deduct producers' fees from Wham's record royalties. Both these points were wholly conceded by Dean, who also agreed to pay George and Andrew an advance of £500 each. That left a series of less important, but still significant, amendments which Allan felt were necessary to protect his clients' interests. At this point, things began to go disastrously wrong.

As Mr. Justice Harman later noted, ". . . all the young men were in a hurry". Andrew Ridgeley had long dreamed of recording a hit single and was anxious to conclude the deal at the earliest opportunity. His more cautious partner also revealed an uncharacteristic impatience, having recently suffered criticism from his ever solicitous parents. With his father breathing down his neck, George felt an urgent need to prove his worth without delay or face the prosaic prospect of abandoning pop in favour of the family business. The pauses during the negotiating process had proved so tortuous to George that he actually telephoned his solicitor and briefed him to negotiate "on legal points only". His request was all the more remarkable since both Rodwell and Allan had dealt with matters extraordinarily speedily. George, in fact, was betraying the insecurity of a novice negotiator who dreads rocking the boat for fear of irrevocably upsetting the deal.

What followed can only be described as a comedy of errors. The over eager Dean, understandably desirous of concluding his first Innervision deal, obtained a draft contract from Rodwell which included some, but not all, of Allan's amendments. Apparently, Rodwell assumed that the document was to be taken to Allan for further negotiation before being passed over to the boys for signature. Dean, on the other hand, claims that he was labouring under the mistaken assumption that the contract contained all the proposed amendments. Clearly, he saw no reason not to present the papers to the boys for their immediate signatures.

On 24 March, Wham! was rehearsing at the Halligan Band Centre in Holloway when they received a telephone call from Dean explaining that the contracts were ready to be signed. Two hours later, the Innervision director appeared at the rehearsal studio and after some initial discussion with Wham!, all three adjourned to a nearby cafe. According to Dean, Ridgeley was eager to place his signature on the document immediately and Panos needed no persuading either. After flicking through the contract, George noted some marginal amendments and, like Dean, assumed that everything was in order. For better or worse, all three signed an agreement, the contents of which would later provoke a High Court action.

The precise clauses which remained unamended may never be revealed publicly, but even Dean admits that the boys had little opportunity to earn a good living from the deal. In order to protect the interests of Innervision Dean had effectively translated the toughest terms and percentages offered by CBS into an even harsher standard artistes contract. Quite apart from the small advance, Wham! was due no royalties whatsoever from the sales of 12″ records (Innervision at least earned money if sales exceeded 30,000) and saw their royalties halved for any product advertised on television for three months preceding a substantial campaign up until the end of the second accounting period following the final advertisement. Other severe terms, such as 50% reduced royalties on coloured vinyl and marginally discounted albums, accurately reflected the restrictions placed upon Innervision by CBS. Here, at least, Dean could hardly be blamed for offering terms which he had himself accepted as workable.

On the credit side, Robert Allan's exclusion of the merchandising rights and refusal to allow Wham! to pay producers' royalties were to prove invaluable. The latter was a particularly tough blow to Innervision reducing their profit margin to a pittance. From the 11% royalty offered by CBS for single recordings, Dean's company agreed to pay Wham! 8% and foot the bill for the producer's royalty which was between 2-3%. Thus, they could look forward to receiving a 1% profit, if they were lucky. Dean effectively offset that loss against the more fruitful royalties accruing to Innervision from possible album sales. Here again, Wham! accepted 8%, but Innervision was receiving 15% which meant that they could reasonably expect a 4-5% profit after deducting producers' royalties. Dean could afford a smile about that, at least.

Innervision also covered themselves with astute care in computating the rising royalty rates offered to Wham! under the terms of the contract. Whereas the CBS/Innervision package contained a detailed breakdown of percentages relating to various territorial markets, the Wham! contract revealed a straightforward 8% in respect of UK sales, and 6% for the Rest of the World. Only after the third year did those rates increase to 9% and 7%, respectively, and it was not until year four and later that Wham! could boast a respectable 10% and 8% slice of the cake. In short, they would have to sell an awful lot of albums over a long period before affluence replaced factory floor pocket money.

Clearly, Wham's decision to sign the draft contract without first consulting their solicitor was reckless beyond reason. They were the first, and not the last, victims of this contractual comedy of errors. Their failure to report back to the faithful Robert Allan underlined how insecure and pressurized they felt throughout the negotiating period. They later admitted their fear that Dean would lose his patience, terminate negotiations and seek another unknown act on even easier terms. They also suspected that the release of their first single might be delayed for several months if they did not sign to Innervision post haste. Dean expressed perplexity at these suggestions and emphatically denies that he took advantage of the boys' naivety by cajoling or pressurizing them into an onerous agreement:

> They were begging *me* to sign them. There was no pressure on them to sign. While going into the demo studios I said, "Look, if you want to take more time about this and you don't want to sign, we'll go into the

studio in three or four weeks time, but I can wait". I've waited on many contracts since then . . . It wasn't as if I went in there and said "Listen boys, here's the contract, sign it or I'm throwing you out".

You've got to remember that Andrew Ridgeley and I had a close relationship for quite a few years. Not buddy buddies, but we did know each other. There wasn't a lot I could pull on Andrew even if I wanted to. He's far from stupid and George Michael is far from stupid. He did a company search quite independently several days before he talked to me. For an 18 year-old innocent boy that was astute enough.

Contractual complexities aside, Dean argues that George Michael went into the deal with his eyes open, though he accepts that both parties were guilty of over enthusiasm and incautious behaviour:

George Michael knew that I was probably the best person for the job. He knew that I was going to get the backing and he also knew that I was going to break him before I broke anybody else. He also knew that I was completely in love with his music. It was a perfect partnership. But the way we signed, we should never have signed that way. That's the honest truth. We both made a mistake. A classic mistake. We were both very stupid. I shouldn't have approached the matter that way and neither should he. It should have been done properly through the lawyers.

Wise after the event, Dean failed to realize the extent to which that unfortunate contract would place his own future in jeopardy.

One odd coincidence that sticks out a mile is that both the CBS/Innervision and Innervision/Wham! contracts were dated 24 March. This conjures up a vision of the indefatigable Dean concluding a deal with Maurice Oberstein over lunch and then sashaying across to Holloway in the afternoon to pull off his first signing as a record company mogul. In reality, the signing had no such dramatic overtones, as Dean explains:

I was negotiating with Wham! before that. I was negotiating with them in February. I'd already done my deal with CBS and got the money. I was just signing. As far as CBS was concerned it could have been any band. They'd never heard of Wham! We needed new demos to get the producer. It was the availability of the producer that allowed us to get the record out, not the availability of my record company. CBS can turn records around in one month.

The contractual enigmas did not end with that controversial coffee bar signing on 24 March. The following day, Dean drafted an addendum letter, the contents of which reiterated the terms of the standard artistes contract and confirmed his willingness to be bound to the enclosed document. However, the letter also outlined terms, recording commitments and advances which modified the previous day's provisions and concluded:

In the event of any conflict between the standard artists conditions attached hereto and made part hereto and the provisions of this letter then the provisions of this letter shall prevail. Please confirm you (sic) agreement to and acceptance of the provisions of this agreement by signing below as indicated.

Panayiotou and Ridgeley duly signed.

The letter outlined a specific breakdown of advances for albums as follows:

a. £2,000 upon delivery of the first album
b. £5,000 upon delivery of the second album
c. £7,500 upon delivery of the third album
d. £10,000 upon delivery of the fourth album
e. £12,500 upon delivery of the fifth album
f. £15,000 upon delivery of the sixth album
g. £20,000 upon delivery of the seventh album
h. £25,000 upon delivery of the eighth album
i. £30,000 upon delivery of the ninth album
j. £35,000 upon delivery of the tenth album

An additional clause provided Innervision with the power to release an indeterminable number of singles from these LPs after prior consultation with the group.

The erudite journalist, Simon Garfield, has expressed his own horror at the far reaching implications of these sub-clauses arguing ". . . Innervision were entitled to one album (annually) and could ask for another if they wished, making a possible ten in all. If the duo broke up, each member could be bound to Innervision for a further ten albums, even if the split occurred towards the end of the band's ten album period. If this happened, each member would only receive three quarters of the agreed royalty". What is interesting about the letter of 25 March, however, is that in spite of detailing the ten album advances, its provision for the minimum recording commitment covers only four options and four annual albums. During their first year as Innervision artistes, the group are required to produce only "two sides" (one single) with an option to record one more if Dean demanded. The first album, moreover, is not required until the second year of the contract. The optional terms detailed in the letter are far fairer than those outlined by Garfield, though it is unclear whether they were intended to modify the *stricter* provisos of the standard agreement.

The precise contents of these contracts remained a mystery to Robert Allan until 29 March, when he received a letter from Paul Rodwell explaining the details. Allan was acutely embarrassed and understandably indignant at Wham's failure to notify him of their intentions prior to signing. Accordingly, he wrote a strongly worded letter to George Michael, pointing out the error of his ways. On the same day, he despatched a second letter to Innervision alleging that the contracts which Wham! had signed were binding. Although one might have expected a letter arguing the opposite point of view, Allan evidently felt an urgent need to protect his clients' interests by at least ensuring that Innervision was fully aware of its contractual obligations. Several days after his exchange of letters, George wrote to his solicitor explaining his anxiety about the deal and revealing that he had signed in order to secure a recording contract immediately. He added that, as far as he was concerned, the contract was binding. It was a pity that the dubious document could not have been nullified and renegotiated there and then, but the comedy of errors concluded with the parties agreeing that it should subsist.

Club Shambolic

1982 was an important pivotal point in the history of the so called "New Pop". Adam Ant, the punk turned pantomime clown, had already demonstrated how a colourful image and catchy tune could produce a string of sizeable hits. While he topped the charts, a new generation of fashion-obsessed youths congregated in London clubs and celebrated the parochial triumph of peacock vanity over dreary post-punk ennui. The delightfully eclectic Blitz Kids, or New Romantics, or Futurists, as each movement was alternatively dubbed, created instant media stars from inveterate poseurs, who hid musical impoverishment behind programmed synthesizer pop. The early recordings of Spandau Ballet, Visage, Ultravox! and Duran Duran demonstrated the clever but limited charm of 80s electronic experimentation. However, the most careerist of these new groups understood the need to move into mainstream pop if lasting success was to be assured. That point had been punctuated most forcibly by Sheffield's Human League who had split in half overnight, only to re-emerge as a surprisingly high gloss pop act. Their Christmas 1981 chart topper "Don't You Want Me", and attendant million selling album *Dare*, set the tone for the New Year. The message was singular and clear – the pop song, irrespective of fashionable trappings, was back in vogue with a vengeance.

When the Human League emulated their chart topping success in the US, all hell broke loose. Previously, it was generally accepted that since the entire UK punk movement had failed to make an impression in the adult-orientated Stateside rock market, these flashy new pop groups would fare little better. After all, even our most consistently successful young chart acts of the late 70s, The Jam, The Boomtown Rats and Madness, were virtually unknown across the Atlantic. Nor had the myriad of flash-in-the-pan revivalists from mod to rockabilly fared much better. The conservatism of US rock radio had produced a cultural chasm between the US and UK youth markets which some pessimistic commentators felt might never be bridged again. What changed that unhealthy situation overnight was a miracle greater than any single UK pop group could have achieved.

The launch of MTV with its non-stop selection of pop videos enabled UK record companies to overcome the puritanical programming of stuffy radio stations and reach young purchasers through a previously unexploited medium. The classic "Don't You Want Me" video, along with several others, started a chain reaction which saw regional disc jockeys picking up on the video boom and actually playing UK pop songs that would normally receive little or no airtime. Before long a select bunch of androgynous UK singers and groups took the US by storm.

Although the much publicised gender benders stole the headlines, it was the music itself which was more important. Suddenly, the Blitz Kids and their contemporaries looked terribly grown up. It was, as George Panos had predicted several months before, the age of the well-crafted pop song. Word was out that ABC were threatening to complete an album full of classic pop songs to be titled *Lexicon Of Love*. Others would follow that trail with a sharpness and perspicacity scarcely evident in their early work. After two middling singles, Culture Club would virtually establish themselves as brandleaders with a song which seemed destined to become a standard – "Do You Really Want To Hurt Me". Spandau Ballet left synthesizers and Brit funk behind and attempted to push Tony Hadley as a junior Sinatra. They too would find a chart topping standard with "True". Before long, even aging Doubting Thomases were forced to concede that the New Pop consisted of a lot more than frivolous fashion horses gallivanting around London nightclubs.

The competitive element among these precocious new pop songsmiths augured well for the development of George Panos and the future success of Wham! The greatest beneficiaries of these recent trends, however, were those fortunate music publishers whose catalogues contained the complete works of the latest budding Lennon/McCartneys. With the prospect of inestimable American sales on the horizon, the UK publishing fraternity were more receptive than ever before to the untutored demo tapes of fledgeling performers.

It was in this climate that Wham's demo tape was despatched to a number of prominent music publishers. Several quickly spotted one song that had the word standard written all over it: "Careless Whisper". That songwriters as young and untested as George Panos and Andrew Ridgeley could produce such a melodically infectious ditty prompted immediate investigation. Eight publishers expressed interest in the boys but fortune favoured a relatively new firm, Morrison/Leahy Music.

Bryan Morrison was a hard-nosed survivor of the mid 60s British Beat Boom. Once manager of the controversial Pretty Things, he had successfully moved into agency work and publishing, achieving considerable success along the way. During the late 70s, he administered The Jam's publishing, a potential goldmine of a catalogue, spoiled only by the group's absolute lack of success in the US market. These credentials alone made Morrison a worthy candidate for the Wham! catalogue, but it was his choice of employees that weighed more heavily in his favour. For Bryan Morrison had once shown the foresight to take on a young kid named Mark Dean.

Dean knew enough about Morrison to respect his pedigree in the music industry and he hadn't forgotten that the middle-aged, cigar-smoking publisher had given him his first break. The news that Bryan had recently established a new company with an equally intriguing partner increased the odds in his favour still further.

Dick Leahy's music business history also stretched back to the golden era of the mid 60s, when he worked for Philips Records. Coincidentally, the company was enjoying a periodic upswing in its fortunes during Leahy's period of tenure and boasted some sizeable hits from such perennial favourites as Dusty Springfield, The Walker Brothers and Dave Dee, Dozy, Beaky, Mick & Tich. Leahy bathed in the reflective glory of those 60s artistes and rapidly ascended the record business ladder until he was in a position of considerable power. As managing director of Bell Records, during the early 70s, Leahy achieved the kind of success record that many company men would willingly die for. Although lacking the financial clout of its rivals, Bell Records dominated the UK market in the early 70s with an incredible ratio of hit singles from such artistes as Dawn, David Cassidy, Gary Glitter, The Drifters, The Delfonics, Johnny Johnson and The Bandwagon, Barry Blue, Showaddywaddy and Slik. Leahy's eagle eye for chart potential focused mercilessly on dance floor hits and bedroom wall pubescent pin-up stars. In 1971, he signed the biggest UK teen phenomenon of the era, The Bay City Rollers. Marketing consistent hits for ephemeral weenybop stars is no easy task, and the experience that Leahy gained in forwarding the Rollers' impressive chart career was to prove invaluable.

The Leahy history came almost full circle in the late 70s when he ran GTO Records, one of whose artistes was the reformed Walker Brothers last seen during his days with Philips in 1966. With a roster which included disco queen Donna Summer, GTO was a significant addition to Leahy's already impressive *curriculum vitae*. If Wham! were to succeed as club favourites or pretty boy pop stars, they could not have hoped for a more experienced backroom adviser than the hit spotting Dick Leahy.

The combined power of Bryan Morrison and Dick Leahy greatly impressed the young Mark Dean who himself harboured ambitions of achieving long term success as an independent record company mogul. Confronted by the perpetually tanned Leahy, he perceived an older role model whose cynical worldliness was couched in an engaging approachability. Their rapport was strengthened by Leahy's evident distaste for CBS Records. Dean urgently needed somebody to advise him about the internal workings of the company and the most effective ways of cutting through the red tape of middle management. Leahy was so frank, accommodating and forthright in his views about the parent company that Dean convinced himself he could turn that knowledge to Innervision's advantage at a later date. Not surprisingly, he wholeheartedly recommended Morrison/Leahy to the Wham! boys who were sufficiently impressed to conclude a publishing deal, with the able assistance of their solicitor, Robert Allan.

In the succeeding months Dean came to rely heavily on the advice of Dick Leahy, whom he appeared to regard as a father confessor figure. Believing that the great Leahy could help him "operate the system" at CBS he actively encouraged his involvement with Wham! on both a business and personal level. For a kid who prided himself on street-wise caution, Dean was proving unusually trusting. The degree to which his reverential attitude towards Leahy affected the behaviour of George Panos is unclear, but the young songwriter always showed a willingness to listen attentively to the words of his sagacious publisher. In moments of indecision or career crisis, Leahy's opinions carried considerable weight and he was destined to play as important a role in the Wham! story as any single figure in this book. Taking a wider view, Mark Dean maintains that the quiet, understated power of Dick Leahy consistently inspired and influenced George Michael far more than anyone dares admit: "Leahy has *always* controlled that band. Always from behind the scenes". Even assuming there is an element of hyperbole in Dean's opinion, it is still a remarkable statement, implying that beneath the throne lay powerful ministers whose mastery of Wham! remained unmeasured in column inches.

In spite of their naïvety and innocence, Wham! were far from traditional music business puppets and Leahy was certainly no Svengali. He always remained out of the limelight and seemed content to prove his worth as a professional adviser and energetic publisher. In that sense, he certainly administered the group's affairs. For their part, Wham! showed strong signs of independence, unusual in a unit so new to the music business. They had stubbornly resisted appointing a personal manager, mistakenly believing that they could control their own artistic and economic destinies while avoiding the pitfalls of the biz. In effect, they had already blundered by signing a recording contract which a Svengali-minded professional manager would have resisted with steely contempt.

Whatever their failings as young businessmen, Wham! continued to maintain an admirable grip over the professional and artistic direction of their group. That fact was demonstrated with administrative acumen when they hit the road during the early months of 1982.

Rather than falling into the rut of the morale-sapping rock'n'slog pub/disco circuit, Wham! embarked on a series of "personal appearances" at selected nightclubs in and around Watford. This meant that they did not have to suffer the antics of hard drinking jack-the-lad rock musicians or sap their energies lugging heavy p.a. equipment half way across the country. Instead, they used pre-recorded backing tapes which enabled them to concentrate on their showmanship. Nightclub audiences were far more interested in snazzy dressers and pyrotechnic dance displays than skilled musicianship, and George took advantage of this prejudice with the confidence of a seasoned stage director. In order to put more glam into Wham!, the boys incorporated a couple of blonde female companions whose choreography added a new dimension to their embryonic musical performance. The bubbly Shirlie Holliman, Andrew's girl friend and Executive roadie, suddenly found her bedroom dance steps had become an integral part of the show. Her partner, Amanda Washbourn, was another local girl whose dolly bird looks and love of discos greatly impressed the star-spotting George.

The foursome underwent a rigorous but pleasurable period of rehearsal, perfecting their routine on the dance floors of local clubs and, equally often, in the front room of the Panayiotou residence. According to Washbourn, the exuberant Panos frequently spun her around in the air like a John Travolta stand-in, before completing a dangerously ambitious splits routine. His boundless energy was partly motivated by an understandable desire to reduce his 13 stone bulk to more manageable proportions. The fearful gyrations, fuelled by a fat reducing bran diet, worked small wonders on the star's sizeable girth. Satisfied with his stage persona, George began to take a greater interest in the deportment of the girls. With an almost feminine solicitude, he encouraged them to restyle their hair and dress as provocatively as good taste would allow. One of his colourful ideas was getting the girls to dress in tight fitting frocks which flared at the pleats so that their legs would be teasingly uncovered during the more frenzied dance displays. This subtle eroticism ensured that the posing patrons did not pay too much attention to the group's still undeveloped musical repertoire.

In one respect, these selected club gigs were good confidence boosters. As long as the backing tapes played at the right speed, the foursome had only to concentrate on their lip synching and synchronized choreography. If they timed their entrance punctually, they could complete their act in about 20 minutes, and sometimes take in up to five different club appearances in one evening. The most exhausting part of the gig was rushing from one club to another and finding an empty dressing room to change into their stage clothes. It was all good fun and enormously gratifying as long as they played the local circuit. When they ventured into unfamiliar territory, however, shambolic scenes were always likely to ensue.

One evening, the boys found themselves booked into a gay disco and George was so taken aback by the sight of openly homosexual displays of affection that he found it difficult to concentrate on his miming. His prudishness was later expressed in an audible sigh of relief in the car on the road back home to Radlett. The star elect was to suffer even greater embarrassment during a prestigious appearance at London's fashionable Stringfellow's club. Here was a golden opportunity to mime before some of the richest and most glamorous night people in the capital. Limbering up in the dressing room, Wham! were ready to knock them dead with some startling dance routines, invigoratingly perfected over the previous few months. What George hadn't reckoned on, though, was a glass dance floor, specially shone to ease the movement of tired feet. When the stocky singer attempted one of his John Travolta styled kicks, he accelerated so fast that he completely lost balance and his right shoe went flying into the audience.

For the remainder of the song, the unfortunate Panos was reduced to dancing with one shoe and a glaringly bright red sock, which matched the colour of his face. His humiliation was completed later in the evening when he could be found furtively scrambling around the dance floor on his hands and knees in search of that missing shoe. It was some time before he dared show his face in Stringfellow's again.

The happy-go-lucky days of Wham's apprenticeship effectively ended after signing their recording and publishing contracts. The all-consuming ambition to break into the charts and hit the big time inevitably encouraged a strict professionalism and the first signs of an expediency which was to mark several of Wham's business decisions hereafter. The unhappy victim of their first righteous purge was the new girl, Amanda Washbourn, who completely underestimated the seriousness with which they were conducting their professional affairs. Her departure from the group was as sudden and unexpected as her recent recruitment.

The mini-drama began when Wham! were requested to play before a select gathering of CBS executives. For George, this gig was crucially important, for a good impression might well encourage the parent company to use their considerable corporate clout to break the group at national level. Unfortunately, the CBS bash coincided with a court appearance that Amanda Washbourn was making on behalf of a friend in need. When George learned that she was unavailable for Wham's most important engagement to date, he was far from pleased. Although the performance went ahead, the absence of Washbourn was frowned upon and led to some serious discussion about the practicality of the present line-up.

Amanda's greatest weakness was not her unreliability, but extreme youth. At 16, she was fresh from school and still finding her way in the world. With the number of commitments that Wham! would be facing in the succeeding months, her stamina would be tested to the limit and it was not at all certain whether she would stay the course. Like many young groups, Wham! had begun as a clique of friends whose professional prospects were scarcely relevant. Although the backing singers and musicians were always perceived as a fluid line-up, it was still important to ensure that the personnel were completely dedicated to furthering the career of Wham! Poor Amanda could not have chosen a worse time to resurrect doubts about her longevity in the line-up.

The final decision was swift and nonchalant. One evening, Shirlie Holliman informed her partner that the boys had found a new girl. The word "fired" was never even mentioned. As far as Wham! were concerned, Washbourn was just a friend who had played with them on a temporary basis at a few low-key gigs. Inevitable as it may have been, the departure of Washbourn might have been handled with a little more understanding and tact. To this day, the girl is a little nonplussed and disappointed that George could not have told her to her face that her services were no longer required. It was not an untypical reaction from a zealously professional,

and occasionally ruthless, performer whose distaste for personal confrontation would always ensure that he was conspicuously absent whenever the
axe fell.

Amanda Washbourn's replacement was a more experienced 20 year-old,
who had already sung backing vocals on a number of obscure demo tapes.
Diane Catherine Sealey, professionally known as D.C. Lee, had a
chequered history before entering the music game. As a teenager in Dept-
ford, her ambitions did not extend far beyond working at a local boutique.
Her prospects were further hampered by problems at school, where she
was severely reprimanded for involving herself in a fracas after somebody
had called her a "black bitch". Family problems didn't help matters, but
Diane somehow found the confidence to seek employment at a nearby
modelling agency. Surprisingly, they took her on in spite of her crooked
teeth and lopsided grin. However, Sealey soon found that modelling was
less than glamorous especially when the only parts of her body deemed fit
to display were her hands and feet.

In order to supplement her income, Sealey decided to have a stab at
singing and soon found she could earn steady money doing session work.
Although she dreamed of achieving the status of the powerhouse session
vocalist Carole Kenyon, it all seemed a long way off. When Wham! intervened with an offer of work she decided to take a chance. The money
wasn't that great, but they were a newly signed group who might just fluke
a hit and take the ambitious D.C. Lee out of obscurity and on to greater
things.

Young, Gunning And Rapping

Although George Panos had shown some discernment in advising the girls about their presentation, he was still having problems keeping his own wardrobe in order. The thorny question of "Wham's Image" was first posited when Mark Dean took the aspiring duo to a meeting at CBS. After being introduced to George, one concerned official took Dean aside and enquired: "What the hell are we going to do with *him*?" When Mark clocked his fledgling superstar from a safe distance he fully understood what prompted the impertinent request:

> George looked so bad. He had bum fluff all over his face. He was fat. He wasn't particularly attractive. Yet, there was something about him. If I've seen the caterpillar turn into the butterfly, it was George Michael.

If the inspiration behind George's transformation could be summed up in two words, they surely would be "Andrew Ridgeley". The elder member of the duo provided the all important visual appeal which ensured that even the most cynical record company observers returned to Wham's demos for a second listen. Mark Dean still maintains that Ridgeley was the catalyst that enabled George to graduate from a homely soul boy into a pin-up hunk:

> George would never have made it without Andrew. He had a much higher part to play then. That was a time when it was a real partnership. Andrew was the style, Andrew was the star. He was so confident about what he was as a person. He had flashiness, style, an amazing amount of confidence and a happy-go-lucky attitude. He showed George what he could become and helped him combine his talents with good looks and good dress sense, and that was his contribution. He turned George from the ugly duckling into the swan. That was *all* Andrew Ridgeley, and that's what George Michael owes him.

Panos' increasing awareness of his pop star role was demonstrated in a number of sartorial improvements and, even more significantly, in a second change of surname. Realizing that Panos was little better than Panayiotou to the xenophobic media, the unpronounceable one henceforth became known as George Michael.

Setting up Wham! with a reputable producer was taking more time than

Dean had expected. Initially, the group held high hopes of working with Bob Sergeant, but he turned them down. Eventually, they settled on Bob Carter whose work with Linx and Junior made him the perfect candidate for their black-sounding début single, "Wham! Rap".

The summer of 1982 seemed an opportune moment to record an oblique protest song on the subject of youth unemployment. Even while "Wham! Rap" was being pressed, official figures revealed that a staggering 3,293,000 people were out of work. Statisticians estimated that approximately 306,000 of these were in the 16-17 year-old age bracket and those figures were expected to increase markedly when holidaying school-leavers returned to sign on the dole. Normally, such news would have provoked a wave of hard-hitting anti-Toryism, but neither record unemployment nor a national rail strike managed to deflate the pomposity which gripped the British nation in the wake of the Falklands Conflict. Jingoism was rife throughout the 75 days of undeclared war and when Argentina surrendered on 15 June, the tabloids reacted as though England had just won the World Cup. One week later, this state of national euphoria was strengthened by the arrival of a royal baby and probable future king. The Tories had never had it so good, and the opinion polls rapidly confirmed what everybody already expected – an imminent landslide electoral victory.

The charts of the period provided no visible signs of a country cataloguing the horrors of war or contemplating mass unemployment. The occasionally acerbic Madness chose to celebrate the times with the inappropriately titled "House Of Fun" and Captain Sensible sustained the slapstick mood with a zany revival of "Happy Talk". Both discs went on to top the charts, while subtle protests such as Robert Wyatt's reflective reading of Elvis Costello's "Shipbuilding" initially remained largely unheard. As if to add insult to insensitivity, the hypocritical, war-mongering British public had the nerve to place Nicole's unwittingly ironic "A Little Peace" at number 1. In such an unpredictable political climate "Wham! Rap" was bound to meet a mixed response. After receiving some day time radio play, it was given the cold shoulder by the BBC and sales plummetted. To this day, Wham! maintain that the song was seriously misinterpreted by critics on both sides of the political fence.

Originally conceived as a parody of disco rapping, "Wham! Rap" eventually emerged as an exhilarating dance number in its own right. The lyrics, however, were ambiguous and provocative enough to kindle some fiery value judgements. The radical music press praised the song as an inspirational and rousing assault on the stigma of unemployment. The *NME* enthused: "Rather than moan about the miserly prospects facing the jobless school leaver, Wham! sing of soul on the dole; of having a good time in spite of the hard times".

Well, that was half the story. The BBC watchdogs took a more literal view of the lyrics and noted some quite disturbing sentiments. A glance at the word sheet was enough to confirm their misgivings. The song evidently celebrated the anti-work ethic and went as far as championing the dole queue reject over the stolid, but socially responsible, 9 to 5 slogger. Indeed, it positively recommended unemployment as a streetwise alternative to getting an unexciting job. The soaraway *Sun*, had they been on the case, would have damned "Wham! Rap" as "an anthem for the spongers". Even more irritating was the glee with which the rapper derided his flabbergasted antagonist, whose point of view remained unuttered. He was dismissed as a jerk without street credibility whose only saving grace was his emotional conversion to the idea of joining the "Benefit Gang" and allowing the DHSS to fund his leisure pursuits. It is easy to see why some critics found the polemic a bit hard to swallow but, over the years, George Michael has consistently put forward his own eloquent defence of the song. Witness this viscid explanation to his early champions at the *NME*:

> It's not a totally serious song. It's not a matter of us saying that this is what people should be doing. If people take the song too seriously, they'll wonder what we're on about because there are lots of contradictions in there . . . What we are saying in the song is that unemployment is *there*. And, for all the campaigning that everyone is doing, it's not going to go away. What we *should* be doing is educating people into how to deal with it, how to use their leisure time. If you're not going to be able to do anything about it, you might as well have a laugh about it. We managed to do that quite well when we were on the dole. It is possible to have a reasonable time without that much money. If a lot of your mates are on the dole too, you can have quite a good time.

In truth, "Wham! Rap" was neither a subversive swipe at the Tebbetian work ethic nor a rallying cry for downtrodden youth, as some foolish observers reckoned, but a naïve piece of nonsense written from the blinkered perspective of a privileged school leaver who should have had the brains to know better. On that innocent level, at least, it was acceptable and deserved to be a hit. The real problem with "Wham! Rap", and this became more evident in later years, was overcoming the prejudices associated with the creators of the song. At one point, George and Andrew rather foolishly defended their controversial composition by bragging that they had suffered life on the dole and endured demeaning jobs and therefore knew what they were talking about. Of course, all this did was draw attention to their ignorance of the real problems of unemployment. What "Wham! Rap" actually presented was an accurately insular observation of how nice unemployment *seems* when you live with reasonably supportive *nouveau riche* parents in an opulent middle class neighbourhood, where everyday offers new indulgences and frivolous fun, and every night can be spent dancing and wassailling until the early hours of the following morning when your tired and hungover body can revitalise itself with a long soothing sleep. And as the boys rightly noted, the Benefit Gang will foot the bill. Well, not all of it. Implicit in Wham's vision of a DHSS funded Utopia is the possibility of signing off briefly to take up a part-time job as a disc jockey or cinema usher when the going gets too tough. There is no evidence to suggest that the Wham! boys ever wanted for an expensive pair of trousers or an exotic summer holiday, let alone a cooked dinner. Ultimately, "Wham! Rap" is a well informed comment on how the young can enjoy living on the dole in Radlett. However, as a universal panacea for the unemployment blues, it is about as sensible and convincing as the Bangles' condescending cover of "Going Down To Liverpool". And at least they had the excuse of being ill-informed aliens. The ambiguities in "Wham! Rap", compounded by the boys' own later hedonistic lifestyles, finally caught up with George Michael in 1986 when he explained that the song was never intended as an anthem for the unemployed but a satire which was misunderstood and probably lacking in political coherence.

One of the first people outside the Wham! camp to hear their début single was manager Jazz Summers. A week before the disc was released he listened to a demo playing at Island Music's offices and excitedly enquired "Who are they?" His host replied "Oh, they're Wham!" The name elicited a glimmer of recognition from Summers and the following week he purchased the single. Soon, he wanted to hear more.

The initial chart failure of "Wham! Rap" taught Mark Dean the important lesson that Innervision had to break the group themselves. In spite of peak sales of 200 a day, CBS was not convinced that Wham! was a hit act and declined to give their début strike force priority. Dean now realizes that his extreme youth and inexperience as a record company director probably alienated the sensitive middle management at CBS:

> If you're 21-22 and earning far more money than a 40 year-old marketing guy, that is a major problem. Those were the barriers we were trying to break through. Lo and behold, at the end of the day I liked CBS. They weren't bad at all, they were a very good company. It was just getting them into action. Once there, they were fantastic. But at the initial stage, we had to take a lot on our own shoulders and break the act. We did promotion, plugging, everything. We *had* to take it away from CBS because they didn't think it was going to happen.

During the summer of 1982, Dean was being hit from all sides. His argu-. ments with CBS had spilled over into a series of petty disagreements with the temperamental George Michael. Part of the problem was Wham's reluctance to appoint a personal manager and their increasing reliance on Dean to fulfil many administrative duties on a non-remunerative basis. His dual role as "quasi-manager" and record company mogul was an unsatisfactory arrangement guaranteed to create tension and false expectations. Events reached a head during an evening at the nightclub Xenon where Dean and Michael exchanged insults in a bitter argument. With a broken arm, encased in plaster, the Innervision director looked acutely vulnerable to verbal attack but turned his disadvantage to explosive effect by ferociously smashing down the offending limb on a nearby table and abruptly storming out of the club with a visage that betrayed barely disguised feelings of contempt and indignation. Looking back, he still marvels at the intensity of the moment, and its unhappy aftermath.

The boat was really rocking before they even made it! George and I actually didn't speak to each other for about six weeks. I can't remember why I smashed my arm down. It was the first time I'd had a real emotional outburst with him. It was just one of those things. I don't know what we were arguing about. I think Xenon were playing the 12″ instead of the 7″ or vice versa. I walked into the dressing room and he was screaming at the top of his lungs "Why don't you sort it out with Club Promotion?" I then walked out. It was the most unfortunate part of our relationship.

After successfully avoiding each other for several weeks, Dean and Michael resolved their differences and Innervision worked even harder attempting to break the second single "Young Guns". The indefatigable Shamsi Ahmed filed away the company accounts each afternoon and hotfooted along to Northern clubs, promoting the disc as though it was his own. Meanwhile, Dean overruled the gods at CBS and employed an independent record plugger, the aptly named Bullet, whose sharp-shooting promotion was soon rewarded with a chart entry at number 72. One week later, the record climbed to 48 and CBS were on the telephone enthusing about an appearance on *Top Of The Pops*. Further television plugs were still being negotiated the following week when the shock news came through that "Young Guns" had slipped out of the Top 50. Dean had to work like a maniac to salvage a hurriedly cancelled *Saturday Superstore* appearance, following which he turned his attention to Bullet. Fortunately, they were inspired by his screaming demands, and the record returned to chart glory, eventually peaking at number 3. Dean breathed a sigh of relief and, to this day, maintains that the boys' success stemmed from the hiring of an independent plugger: "If it wasn't for Bullet that week, I don't know whether Wham! would still have existed".

On the strength of "Young Guns", Wham! received considerable press coverage and were initially bracketed alongside the Kids From *Fame* and Musical Youth as harbingers of a new youth consciousness in pop. With their uncompromising angle on social problems affecting the modern teenager, Wham's early singles recalled the better lyrics of Madness and The Specials. Unlike those groups, however, they found themselves consistently fending off criticisms from word-conscious interrogators. The problem with "Young Guns" was unintentional sexism. In presenting a simplistic battle of the sexes, complete with a nagging fiancée and henpecked suitor, their ingenuity had stopped at the level of the average television situation comedy. Far from being a cautionary tale, tailored for the emancipated 80s, "Young Guns" added little to the celebratory misogynism of such songs as Dion's "The Wanderer" twenty years before. George Michael once again pleaded innocence, stressing that the song was intended as a satire and impatiently regretting that he had not incorporated a more affected macho vocal in the rapping section, though, in retrospect, that too would probably have been misinterpreted.

The success of "Young Guns" was followed three months later by a Top 10 hit remix of "Wham! Rap", proof positive that the boys were an extremely viable commodity. Throughout this period, a number of managers attempted to woo them into surrendering their independence, but, amazingly, the duo insisted that they could conduct their own business affairs. Their chief pursuer, an ex-radiographer turned entrepreneur, refused to take no for an answer and eventually his patience was to be rewarded.

Jazz Summers entered the pop scene at the relatively late age of 28. His youth had been sacrificed to the British Army at a time when 15 year-olds could still be legally cajoled into signing away the best nine years of their lives. Summers re-emerged in civvy street as a bitter 24 year-old, determined to erase the errors of his past. As a competent drummer, he flirted with the music business, before finding security as a superintendent radiographer in the X-Ray department of North Middlesex Hospital. It was not until 1972 that Jazz began his part-time management career, looking after folk singer Richard Digance and forming makeshift groups to play on the London pub circuit. During his three years with Digance, Summers visited the States and learned how to negotiate recording and publishing contracts. However, inexperience eventually weighed against him when Digance elected to appoint a professional agent. Disillusioned, Jazz abandoned the music game for a year, but in 1977 his interest was revitalized by the punk explosion. Four years of hard graft followed, with Summers picking his way through a veritable flotilla of doomed groups including The Stookers, The Crooks, The Autographs and The Late Show. It was not until 1981 that the energetic radiographer found the reckless courage to surrender his day job and devote all his energies to breaking Danse Society and Blue Zoo. The former achieved considerable success on the independent circuit and the latter hit the Top 20 with "Cry Boy Cry" during the same month as Wham's "Young Guns". Suddenly, struggling Summers was a happening manager with a promising future.

Even with chart success, the campaign to infiltrate the Wham! camp was proving remarkably difficult for the persistent Summers. A visit to Innervision ended in a fruitless meeting with Mark Dean, and Morrison/Leahy seemed equally unimpressed:

> They were all a bit cagey. It was a case of two young guys being signed to a small record company. I couldn't get to the boys or even get their telephone number.

Eventually, Summers was taken aside by Bryan Morrison and tactfully informed: "To be frank, Jazz, Wham! are going to be huge and you're not big enough to manage them". Although mildly indignant at the time, Summers now concedes that Morrison's summation was absolutely correct:

> What he meant was "You haven't proved yourself in managing a band of that magnitude". And he was right. I hadn't. They already had a huge hit with "Young Guns" and it was taking off in Australia. It was like A-Ha today, only not quite as advanced. But you could see the potential. You've only got to meet George Michael, who was 18 then, to know that the guy is a genius. I may not have known it then, but I know it now. And they were more familiar with him than I was. So Morrison was right.

What Summers needed was the financial and entrepreneurial expertise of a figure the equal of Morrison and Leahy. Several backers had attempted to invest in his future but Jazz was reluctant to finalize a deal. Unsure about which direction to take, he consulted a good friend, agent Neil Warnock, who warned him against surrendering his independence. Coincidentally, Warnock had recently lunched with another highly motivated manager who seemed uncharacteristically listless and in urgent need of a new challenge. Playing the boardroom matchmaker, Neil suggested that they might combine forces on some future project. It was an unlikely coupling, for the other party turned out to be a seasoned sensationalist, presently engaged in publishing a scurrilously vainglorious journal, detailing his hedonistic exploits during the mid 60s.

Simon Napier-Bell had become used to such epithets as "notorious" and "legendary". Indeed, he positively cultivated an image of Dionysian excess that pandered to the lowest forms of tabloid journalese. If we are to believe his scanty memoir of 60s pop, his life was spent eating, drinking and sexual buccaneering, with only occasional breaks for dreary managerial duties and scarcely believable financial coups. His tireless self-promotion, often disguised in calculatingly modest asides and expertly timed understatement, had wide-eyed journalists rushing to their typewriters eagerly cataloguing his achievements and marvelling at his uproarious adventures. So loquacious had this entrepreneur become that he was quite capable of reciting a well structured narrative, laced with digressive anecdotes, plausible historical re-evaluations and a carefully disarming hint of self-criticism. A generation of lazy writers took him at his word and an entrepreneurial legend was born. Suddenly, Napier-Bell was a genius 60s Svengali, a sensationalist supreme, the man behind such rock giants as The Yardbirds, and Marc Bolan, and a multi-millionaire to boot. One much respected and normally sober-blooded chronicler even added that his "fearful reputation made Allen Klein look sheepish".

Stripping away the P.R. hyperbole, what emerges is a rather more prosaic picture of a successful, middle division 60s manager, whose reputation and achievements were meagre in comparison to such immemorial greats as Larry Parnes or Brian Epstein. Simon's wild exploits and legendary hypes may now seem extraordinary, but they were exceedingly commonplace in an age which included such masters of controversy as Andrew Oldham, Tony Secunda and Kit Lambert. Like Oldham and Lambert, Napier-Bell produced several artistes and went one step further by co-writing songs. Even here, however, he was far from unique. Gordon Mills and Larry Page also put pen to paper – and they were former pop stars as well! As for the claim that Napier-Bell masterminded the careers of The Yardbirds and Marc Bolan, this is a popular misconception. He inherited The Yardbirds from the eccentric Giorgio Gomelsky, under whose guidance they had recorded all their chart hits, bar the Simon Napier-Bell produced "Over Under Sideways Down". And Marc Bolan, who boasted more managers than Henry VIII had wives, did not achieve success until several years after leaving Simon, and, in any case, was always very much his own man. Finally, the Klein comparison is even more curious and ludicrous. Placing Napier-Bell in the same entrepreneurial pantheon as Allen Klein or Don Arden is akin to tossing a pussycat into a den of rapacious lions. In reality, Napier-Bell is far less hard than his image suggests. For all his self-professed cynicism, he is actually a rather endearing fellow who infrequently displays a warmth and sentimentality which distances him from his more aggressive rivals. His handling of Japan during the 70s, for example, showed a humanity totally uncharacteristic of a money-making automaton. For years, the group was a financial liability, with a spending power that threatened even Napier-Bell's well advertised resources, and made him appear rather gullible in the process. A cautious, level-headed manager would have dumped them years before, but Napier-Bell proved loyal to a fault. It was probably his finest moment as a pop manager, a rare example of noble solicitude overcoming the profit motive. Japan eventually broke through in the New Romantic era, but split before Napier-Bell could earn a cumulative profit. Recovering from his efforts, he vowed to come back stronger than ever by managing one of the biggest groups in the world. History had been kind to him but now was the time to put his years of experience to effect and establish his name as a managerial all-time great.

For several months, Napier-Bell had been searching for an already established group whom he could propel to greatness. Slumped in front of *Top Of The Pops* one evening, he discovered the ideal candidates. Here was a young group whose inventive choreography and cocky showmanship, perfected over months of personal club appearances, upstaged their elder rivals with ease. Simon was immediately convinced that this was no fluke:

They did a magnificent *Top Of The Pops*. I know how *Top Of The Pops* is done and no director would have had the time to set that up. They must have devised how to present themselves in a *Top Of The Pops* framework and it was as if the show was created for them.

Napier-Bell was stunned. Never in his years as a pop manager had he seen such a visually powerful relationship between two male performers. The macho camaraderie that Wham! oozed had an understated, indefinable element of eroticism that Napier-Bell found fascinating, potent and hugely saleable. While listening to "Young Guns" his fertile imagination conjured up a vision of two rugged, leather-clad, Hollywood cowboys, whose partnership survives bar room brawls, family feuds, women problems and range warfare. He had even scripted an imaginary plot that would fit the image: "They're the best of friends . . . one gets married, one goes to a brothel but by the end of the film they ditch the girls and ride off together into the sunset."

Simon's cinematographical fantasies were still working overtime when Jazz Summers arrived for their fateful meeting several days later. After exchanging pleasantries and talking generally about their experiences in the music business, Napier-Bell brusquely came to the point.

"Well, what do you want?" he asked, in a tone which invited a reply of Faustian expectation.

"I don't really want anything," exclaimed Jazz, with surprise.

"Well, what are you sitting here for?" retorted the fabled financier, who had funded more projects than he cared to remember.

It took Jazz several more minutes to convince his future partner that he was not in search of a large interest free loan, but was seeking the opportunity to work with Napier-Bell as an equal on some mutually beneficial long-term project. Napier-Bell nodded sagely, impressed by Summers' confident enthusiasm. Soon, they were exchanging theories about artiste management and discussing the corporate structures which had thrived in America during the 70s. They both agreed that England lacked an international management company of US proportions. Several business lunches later, they were finalizing plans for a major new organization which would represent a stable of acts, building gradually into the biggest management company Britain had ever seen. That, at least, was the ultimate dream.

Christening their venture proved a less taxing exercise. Jazz was amused by Napier-Bell's clever paronomasia Nomis (Simon spelt backwards) and modestly declined to add his moniker to the company letterhead. "Nomis Management," he argued, would sell on the strength of his partner's name alone.

Nomis began its rapacious acquisition of new talent by swallowing two of Summers' groups, Danse Society and Blue Zoo. What Napier-Bell desired, however, was the opportunity to exercise his unquestionable organizational acumen on a fresh act. Summers was eager to secure the recently formed Eurythmics, but Napier-Bell's aversion to boy/girl duos, a hangover from his days with Diane Ferraz and Nicky Scott, put paid to that proposition. At least the pair was united in one resolve: the immediate signing of Wham! to Nomis Management. It was to prove more difficult than they could ever have imagined.

Mark Dean was not an entirely happy man towards the end of 1982. After eight months of hard work, Wham! had broken through, but Innervision was receiving minimal remuneration from single sales. The higher royalty percentages would not be forthcoming until they completed their debut album, and contractually that was not due until 1983. In the meantime, Innervision placed their financial hopes on a spree of new signings including Space Monkey, Jimmy The Hoover and Steve Walsh. In spite of Dean's optimistic predictions, however, a one-off hit by Jimmy The Hoover was the company's only reward. As Dean now realizes: ". . . the worst thing that happened to us was that we didn't have some minor hits before Wham! That would have built a foundation". Instead, the Bushey duo became the focal point of everyone's attention. CBS showed scant interest in the likes of Space Monkey and urged Dean to concentrate on furthering the recording career of Wham! The would-be record mogul knew that a one act label spelt long term disaster, but there was no denying that Wham! was poised to be huge. Innervision had created a golden goose that was also an albatross.

Towards the end of 1982, Dean received a telephone call from Simon Napier-Bell enquiring about Wham's management. The middle-aged entrepreneur boasted that he had a computer business and could exploit the act worldwide with his recently formed corporate management company. Dean showed little enthusiasm for Napier-Bell's bluster, for he was well aware of Wham's ambivalent attitude towards pop managers, especially those of the old school. However, they had recently toyed with the idea of appointing a mentor and approached Andy Stevens at CBS International who, to his credit, turned them down. Since then, they had buried themselves in work, and Dean saw no reason to interrupt their schedule. Although still technically acting as "quasi-manager", he seemed remarkably aware of a possible conflict of interest in negotiating with Nomis and proceeded with admirable caution: "I couldn't be seen to influence management decisions or managers." Instead, he suggested Napier-Bell attempt to contact the boys through Morrison/Leahy.

Both Bryan Morrison and Dick Leahy were well versed in Simon Napier-Bell's illustrious history, mythical and otherwise. All three had come up together in the bustling mid 60s when the lively gossip around Tin Pan Alley ensured that few managerial secrets remained behind closed doors. Now, this formidable trio sat together in an expensive restaurant discussing the future of two teenage boys, young enough to be their children. As the assembled company swapped anecdotes, they were joined by the 38 year-old Summers, who rather resembled a stranger at an old boys' reunion dinner. Characteristically, his eagerness to conclude a deal spilled over into effusion and slight cockiness. His opening salvo was the memorable riposte to Bryan Morrison: "Well, we're big enough to manage Wham! now". That, however, remained to be seen.

Morrison/Leahy duly informed Wham! of Nomis' intentions and a meeting took place at Napier-Bell's house in Bryanston Square. It proved inconclusive. Even Summers' engaging logic had failed to convince the boys that they needed Nomis' expertise to enhance their career prospects. Wham's staunch independence and intelligent caution merely encouraged Jazz and Simon to redouble their efforts but another month passed before a second meeting was arranged. Legend has it that Simon Napier-Bell finally won over Andrew Ridgeley by presenting him with a copy of his sleazy 60s memoir *You Don't Have To Say You Love Me*, but Wham! were far from subject to such spontaneous decisions at this stage and kept Nomis at arm's length for several months more.

The boys distanced themselves from the tortuous world of management business by returning to school for one last time. In the wake of Wham's rise to chart fame, Bushey Meads had been inundated with fan mail which had been dutifully redirected to the boys. Headmaster, John Earnshaw, seemed unperturbed by the administrative burden and genuinely wished the boys well with the same enthusiastic voice usually reserved for Oxbridge entrants. He later sent Jenny Ridgeley a letter of congratulations when Wham! finally achieved their first number 1. Although neither member of Wham! has spoken particularly fondly of school days, their surprise visit after winning chart glory was greatly appreciated by the Bushey Meads staff and pupils. However, it might never have happened without the intercessionary pleas of 6th former Nicola Holliman (Shirlie's younger sister) who cut through all the red tape, approached the boys direct, and booked them to play at the school's annual Christmas charity concert. The staff once again took the entrepreneurial advice of Jack Panayiotou who directed them towards the most reasonably priced wine, via his restaurant business. It was a memorable end of term celebration. As Wham! treaded the school boards as of old, it seemed momentarily that nothing had changed, but the New Year was to provide little opportunity for further nostalgia.

The Capture Of
The Golden Goose

By February 1983, Nomis was no nearer signing Wham! who evidently seemed unimpressed by their boasts of corporate international structures. While visiting the States, the boys began negotiating with Freddy De Mann and Ron Weisner, the celebrated managerial duo who oversee the affairs of such megastars as Michael Jackson and Madonna. What looked like a mutually rewarding association petered out after Wham! returned home, still undecided. With commitments looming, and Dean having long grown weary of the tag "quasi-manager", it was agreed that Wham! would appoint their solicitor, Robert Allan, on a temporary three month basis.

In May, Wham's long awaited third single at last reached the shops and wasted no time zooming to number 2 in the charts, but finally failed to dislodge the Police's formidable "Every Breath You Take". The New Pop had yet to reach its zenith.

"Bad Boys" was the first example of extravagance and uncertainty from George Michael. The disc had been recorded in three different studios at no small cost, and the once spontaneous boy wonder had laboured over the lyrics for three months. The theme, a witty observation of the generation gap, completed Wham's trilogy of tunes focusing on the social problems of the urban teenager. Although the production was stronger than ever and their accompanying dance routine the best yet, some commentators felt that the macho, young rebel image was wearing thin. Surprisingly, George Michael agreed with them and later dismissed the song as a formula record, designed to cash in on an already dated public persona. For George, it suddenly seemed embarrassingly false to exaggerate his former domestic turbulence at a time when he was still living at home in perfect harmony with his parents. Consequently, he assured ingratiating journalists that the soul/dole boy routine had run its course and promised that future recordings would mark a radical departure, both in lyrical content and visual imagery.

Paradoxically, the success of "Bad Boys" worsened Wham's relationship with their record company. Six months earlier, they had spoken frankly about their Innervision contract, and in spite of cataloguing its crippling limitations their mood was admirably stoic. "We knew we were going to be massive, so we didn't want a big advance," they bleated unconvincingly. "It was the usual job of panicking and signing when you shouldn't, but it's got us to where we are now, so it's nothing really to complain about. Any mistakes that we may have made, we'd still do it again to be number 10 this week. Every company has its advantages and disadvantages, there's not much difference."

Having checked their bank balances, however, Wham's attitude gradually hardened. Suddenly, it dawned upon them that Innervision was not like every other company. Rates which had once looked workable in theory now appeared decidedly parsimonious in comparison to what rival stars were receiving. Fuelled by indignation, they marched into Mark Dean's South Molton Street office, but received a cold response. If they felt undervalued and exploited, what about the paltry 1% profit margin that Innervision was receiving for their product? Although Wham! were meant to feel like Oliver Twists demanding an extra bowl of gruel, Dean was sufficiently concerned to remonstrate with CBS on the matter. They, in turn, implied that his demands were impertinent and unrealistic. He had signed a standard contract and all monies had been paid promptly in good faith. What more did he expect? The contractual conundrum had reached a dangerous impasse, which could not be maintained for much longer. As Dean now acknowledges: "That's where the relationship with Wham! started to fall apart. That's when the trouble started because CBS wouldn't renegotiate. Even *after* we'd sold all those records."

The coveted pop star life that George and Andrew had once fantasized over had now curdled and even a compensatory number 2 hit seemed poor reward for their present plight. Suddenly, George Michael was experiencing pressure from completely unexpected sources. After being cooped up in a recording studio for weeks, he discovered that it was no longer possible to enjoy an evening out on the town. Old friends, obnoxious drinkers, intrusive photographers and pushy fans seemed united in a conspiracy to spoil his late night fun. Old haunts, including his favourite local nightclub, welcomed him with one hand and demanded an entrance fee with the other. The star felt insulted. Even when he went for a quiet drink, a podgy girl appeared from the crowd, claiming she had won a dream date with the singer. She even produced congratulatory correspondence from a national teenage magazine which was enough, in her eyes, to overrule George's certain knowledge that Wham! had never approved such a scheme. Predictably, she was aghast when the singer betrayed reluctance to fulfil his courtly obligations there and then. Back home, fan mail continued to mount and not all of it was pleasant reading. One woman, of Greek Cypriot origin, demanded a picture of every part of his body for unspecified purposes, the mystery of which was enough to cause an involuntary mild shudder. The world, it seemed, had gone mad.

The effort expended in completing Wham's début album left George feeling exhausted. Never a prodigious songwriter, he had all but dried up during the past few months, a fact reviewers had already commented upon when "Bad Boys" arrived with an instrumental re-mix on the flip side. His muse had not been assisted by the impatient demands of his record company to complete the work before potential export sales were damaged by the imminent summer retail slump. George vowed to take a holiday as soon as it was all over. It was not a happy period. His relationship with Andrew had hit an all time low and his consumption of beer and cigarettes suddenly rivalled that of a professional darts player. It was only during a recuperative vacation in Cyprus that he finally made sense of recent events:

> Before I went on holiday I was starting to forget what we were making music for. We started out because we loved performance but once we were successful, we didn't seem to be doing any performance. There was too much business pressure on us too. It was ridiculous. We couldn't handle it.

The Cyprus sojourn also convinced George that he had insidiously transformed from a social smoker into a nicotine addict. Shocked at his packet a day habit, he stopped immediately.

The continued recording success of Wham! pushed them closer and closer towards the outstretched arms of Nomis Management. Suddenly, the act was taking off all over the world and CBS was crying out for product, live shows, interviews and television specials. When the pressure reached boiling point, George simply took his telephone off the hook. The breakdown of communication and attendant confusion were enough to convince Morrison/Leahy that the recruitment of a high-powered professional management team could be forestalled no longer. Meanwhile, the unfortunate Robert Allan was spending his three month managership of Wham! suffering correspondence and calls from self-aggrandizing salesmen and small fry dance hall managers, all in the hunt for an easy killing. By the end of June, the combined pressure of his solicitor's practice and management duties proved too much, and he was more than willing to pass over the reins to the long patient Napier-Bell/Summers team.

Breaking down Wham's prejudice of traditional pop managers was still a difficult problem, as Jazz recalls: "The image of the manager with the cigar, sitting in an office surrounded by gold records and saying 'I'll dress them up in pink and put them on *Top Of The Pops*' – that's what managers *did*. People still think that's what managers do". The extent to which the over-cautious Wham! refused to delegate their power had been made painfully clear to Napier-Bell during the tentative stages of the management negotiations. Winning their signatures meant not only coming to terms with their desire for self-determination, but making them understand the limitations of their isolationist policy. It was no easy task as he frankly admitted:

> Wham! came along incredibly self-sufficient with a great understanding of the music business, its visual and theatrical side and some understanding of what might be behind the business side. They were bright enough and clever enough to get into rock'n'roll without a manager and

thought perhaps they could do without a manager. But of course they couldn't because to have such a depth of knowledge of the musical side, virtually precluded them from having the time to acquire knowledge of the business side. Their idea was to break into the music business and take hold of it and make it theirs. But they didn't understand the extraordinary difficulties of distributing records in America where you have almost a three month breaking time for a single, where to do a press mail out for a single costs $200,000 alone. They didn't understand the enormous problems in dealing with Japan where the social nature of the country is so different from any other capitalist country and where business can't be conducted in the same aggressive way. You've got to understand the local customs. They didn't.

Of course, with the expertise of Morrison/Leahy in the background, Wham! had access to some, if not all, of this esoteric information. All they required from Nomis was the dexterity of an additional tentacle to hasten their mining of gold vinyl. Would the majesterial Napier-Bell be capable of suppressing his self-interested Svengali instincts in order to serve Wham!? That was a question that his salacious 60s journal had failed to answer, but any lingering doubts about his suitability were crushed upon hearing his inexhaustible personal philosophy of 80s management. The rhetoric still sounds mellifluous and convincing enough to serve as a managerial manual for the children of the New Pop:

> The rock manager is the President of the United States in terms of his acts. The less he does physically, the better. He should have an expert in every field. He should act as chairman, analyse the information, and the group should make the decisions. Frequently, the manager has to act on their behalf against his advice. I offer my advice as an outsider with experience. I offer my work as a manager or an instigator on the basis of what they choose after they've had my advice in conjunction with everybody else's. The nearest analogy is to a lawyer, a man of total independence who works for you.
>
> With management, you attach yourself to people who have incredibly powerful aims and need objects. Kids come to me and say "I want to get *there*". And I say "Great" because I can tell you how to get there and it makes a perfect relationship because I never have my objective pulling away from theirs.
>
> In the 60s, I'd say "Put those clothes on, do this song, I'll produce the record". Now what I say is "You must learn to look at clothes, decide which are correct and *educate yourself*". That's the only way to do it.
>
> I've realized that a manager with experience has to find artistes who are self-contained artistically. What I can offer is tremendous experience and ultimately *power*.

With a world view like that, how could Wham! reasonably refuse?

After the many months of waiting, Nomis was predictably easy-going about the small print. They accepted a 15% management commission, a far cry from those lucrative 60s days when Napier-Bell alone creamed off 20%. For Jazz Summers, the prospect of receiving a mere $7\frac{1}{2}$% for his efforts was greeted with magnanimous enthusiasm:

> We take 15% on *everything!* On live gigs we take 15% of net, after they've paid for lights, p.a., trucking and accommodation. That means "Don't go drinking champagne in your dressing room unless the promoter's throwing it in". In the old days, a band would earn £5,000, the manager would take his £1,000 (20%), and the artiste paid for everything else. So the artiste supported the tour with his record company earnings and earned a packet of cigarettes or a cup of tea from the gig if he was lucky, while the manager made a fortune. Pretty unfair. So we say "You earn the money, we earn the money".

A far more important concession from Wham's point of view was the willingness of Nomis to accept a three month management contract, rather than the standard five year agreement. Far from quibbling over this matter, the chirpy Napier-Bell exclaimed: "We'll do it week by week if you like. I don't bother with contracts". His unusual reasoning seemed engagingly logical: "The courts never uphold a contract for services. They'll only say, 'Yes, you *had* a contract, this artiste is going somewhere else and you can sue for damages'. But I've never yet managed an artiste, even one who behaved objectionably, that I'd want to sue. I work efficiently and if they want to go, they go". It was a calculated gamble. If Wham! dispensed with Nomis' services at the height of their fame, the company would have no long-term claim for damages, but since the contract was so fair and they would be unlikely to obtain a better deal elsewhere, it would be illogical for them to leave. Or so Napier-Bell assumed.

Nomis celebrated their new signing with a Top 5 hit, "Club Tropicana", and a chart topping album modestly titled *Fantastic*. The single was a shock *volte face* from the former dole boys, who suddenly seemed more interested in sunny holidays, panama hats, cocktails and lightweight pop melodies. Although "Club Tropicana" was ostensibly a parody of the media's fascination with élitist London clubland, the thrust of its satiric attack was blunted by Wham's own enjoyment of the very scene they derided. For most listeners, the parodic elements were so understated that they became irrelevant. It was difficult to avoid the conclusion that the song was nothing more than a glorification of beach brain hedonism and *nouveau riche* vulgarity. Under pressure, the boys once again claimed that they had been misinterpreted and quite rightly pointed to the fact that the song had been written two years before, a time when neither of them could have been described as flaunting their wealth. Yet, their willingness to embrace the Club Tropicana ethos drowned the sound of protestation. They had the perfect opportunity to demonstrate the subtlety of their satire by filming a video in some garish London nightclub and sending up the patrons something rotten. Instead, they slit their own throats by boarding a plane to Ibiza, where the cameras captured them revelling idly beside a swimming pool, like sun tanned young businessmen. In that moment Wham! became the parody of their own imaginings.

Their début album confirmed the lack of control Wham! still had over their product. It was difficult to escape the conclusion that they had allowed themselves to be bullied into completing the recording prematurely. With only eight tracks, half of which were singles, it left some nagging questions about George Michael's ability to pen an album's worth of songs. Most big name groups astonish with their début, but Wham's *Fantastic* left the bitter taste of expediency overcoming enterprise. Stripped of the singles, a carbon copy of a Miracles' song and the already ancient "Come On", the album contained a mere two genuinely *new* compositions. And that was after months of apparently intense work. The big mystery which the album failed to answer was what the hell Wham! were doing during those lost hours in the studio?

Wham's desire to be accepted as a straightforward pop group, rather than a dance troupe or junior Bucks Fizz, encouraged them to diminish the contribution of the girls to a scarcely audible level. Being thrust into the background so frustrated D.C. Lee that she left to seek new employment in the Style Council. Although grateful to Wham! for providing her with television exposure she clearly felt that her vocal talents remained unrecognized and unexploited: "They didn't really want me for my voice. I was just there to look good on their videos . . . I was missing out on real singing work to be free for their television appearances making them look glam. There had to be more to life than acting as a glammed-up chick in the background". Fortunately, there was more to life, as Lee found when she charted alongside her ex-employes during 1985.

From Russells With Love

The first few weeks of Nomis' management of Wham! were fraught with difficulties. George Michael was so frustrated with the Innervision deal that Napier-Bell feared he might leave the music business or put himself in a breach of contract that might never be healed. There was enormous pressure on Nomis to seek an immediate legal remedy but they needed time to build Wham's economic resources. Although *Fantastic* was selling in large quantities, the royalties were not substantial enough to subsidize Wham's proposed winter tour, let alone finance a lengthy High Court action. Wham! needed big money fast.

Napier-Bell concentrated his attention on the one aspect of the contract beyond the influence of Innervision. Thanks to Robert Allan, Wham! retained full control over merchandising rights and stood to make substantial profits from various licensing deals. Simon quickly concluded a lucrative transaction with the sportswear company Fila and boosted Wham's coffers further by introducing their name to advertisers in Japan. Meanwhile, Jazz Summers was fighting a stirring battle against piracy by attempting to secure control of Wham's photographs. A deal was struck with photographer Chris Craymer which ensured that Wham! had exclusive rights to photographic sessions and gave Craymer free rein in Fleet Street. Although a detailed contract was drafted, the document remained unsigned by either party. Nevertheless, Craymer's agency, Scope, upheld the spirit of the agreement and resisted lucrative offers for badges, t-shirts and picture books.

Nomis proved equally stern and succeeded in frightening off several music book publishing companies by demanding the earth for permission to use authorized photographs. One hopeful editor, intent on producing an exploitative Wham! picture book, was dumbfounded on being told by Summers that, in addition to the standard photographers' fees, Nomis required an £8,000 advance and 10% of all book receipts. The book proposal was rapidly shredded.

Summers' prohibitive ploy proved extremely effective in controlling the first wave of bootleg merchandising, but stemming the surging tide of illegal commerce that followed was not so easy. Within months, street markets were flooded with unauthorized material in frightening quantities. Craymer witnessed the big cash-in with a bemused shake of the head: "I'd walk through Carnaby Street and see Wham! mirrors and postcards and I'm sure that neither Wham!, nor Nomis, nor me, nor Scope, nor CBS were paid a penny for these. In concert, there was the official and the unofficial programme and a lot of photos in the latter were mine. I asked Scope to trace them, but we couldn't. It was impossible".

The conflict with Innervision had yet to erupt in open warfare. According to Jazz Summers, both Wham! and Nomis were willing to sit at the negotiating table and settle any differences in an amicable manner: "We didn't know we were going to split with Innervision. When we first took on George and Andrew, they wanted to be the biggest group in the world, crack America and get their contract renegotiated because it was lousy. They'd had three hit records and little money. There was no intention of splitting from Innervision, not even from Simon's point of view".

This charitable attitude towards Innervision did not last very long. Within days of taking over Wham's administrative affairs, Summers found himself involved in a heated argument with Dean over the funding of a promotional video. When Napier-Bell learned the details of this dispute, he wrote Dean a consoling but provocative letter which would later be used to spectacular effect in the Chancery Division of the Royal Courts of Justice.

The relationship between Dean and Napier-Bell was always less than cordial. In fact, it was largely non-existent. Concern and suspicion engulfed the Innervision director when he learned that his adversary was dealing direct with CBS and attempting to undermine the validity of his contract with Wham! For all his confidence, Dean was not entirely certain that CBS would back his claim and feared that under pressure they might deem it politic to take over Wham! themselves. The personality clash with Napier-Bell merely reinforced his worst fears: "Simon didn't particularly want to deal with me and I had no experience of that kind of manager. Napier-Bell works well with a major corporation but he doesn't know how to work with an independent. More to the point, there was such an age difference between us and such a lack of experience on our part that the two could never get on".

Indeed, Napier-Bell tended to regard Dean as a troublesome kid and dismissed the entire Innervision structure as a mad indulgence on CBS' part. Contrary to what Summers initially assumed, Simon was more than willing to split with Innervision and certainly made his feelings known to both CBS and Wham! However, his negotiations with the parent company were not proving as fruitful as Dean had feared, for CBS refused to be bullied. Napier-Bell admits his frustration at the intransigence of the corporate: "CBS had been very difficult. We warned them of the situation. We warned them that this was going to happen unless they organized a meeting soon and came to a settlement. But our terms were something they wouldn't give away. We insisted that we would not remain with Innervision whatever settlement was made because the relationship was disastrous. So, from then on, it was a big fight".

One of the few peacemakers in this "big fight" was Jazz Summers who genuinely appreciated the efforts of Innervision in breaking Wham! and was less committed to leaving them out in the cold. While Napier-Bell had hoped to unite CBS and Nomis against Innervision, his partner felt that the key to peace lay in a Nomis/Innervision pact against the corporate. During the early stages of attempted renegotiation, he played the diplomat by urging the Innervision director to concede his contractual advantage:

> I took Mark Dean to lunch with Dick Leahy, and Simon and I stayed on afterwards and had a cup of coffee and a brandy with Mark Dean. I said, "Why don't you renegotiate? Don't start arguing with us because if you don't renegotiate we're going to fight. We're going to go to the solicitors, Russells, and there will be a heavy fight." He said, "Jazz, there's a contract there." I said, "You're a young guy, nobody wants to fight with you, you've done well so far. But, if you fight, we will win because we're right. There's a lot of very determined people here, like Simon, myself, the boys and Russells. And as soon as CBS see you're on the losing side, they'll dump you." And that's exactly what happened to Mark Dean.

Unfortunately, Dean has no memory of the precise conversation recited by Summers, though he denies acting unnecessarily stubbornly:

> I don't remember that conversation taking place. All I remember is going to lunch with Jazz Summers, Simon Napier-Bell and Leahy and talking about touring, tour support and the "Club Tropicana" video . . . We never discussed "renegotiation". We were willing to renegotiate.

Summers insists that there were at least two occasions on which Dean affirmed his unwillingness to renegotiate. Apart from the alleged restaurant conversation, Dean attended a meeting at Napier-Bell's house in Bryanston Square and upon being asked to compromise his position retorted: "There's a contract there, and that's it!"

Dean now maintains that the whole question of a renegotiation was so complicated by the presence of CBS in the equation that Nomis and Innervision could never be united on mutually agreeable terms:

> A renegotiation would only have given them a couple of points more at the most. What they needed to do and the way the battle plan worked was to bring CBS into the firing line. While leaving me there, CBS could always stay out of it. They had to come out with a full frontal attack on me so that CBS would come down on me. That's the only way that situation could have worked out. They needed to get a lot more things sorted out than points and money.

Dean's analysis seems fairly close to the campaign mapped out by Napier-Bell, whose policy was to divide and conquer. The Innervision/

CBS pact was an irresistible power structure that had to be fragmented. But how was this to be achieved? The Wham! camp was unwilling to declare the Innervision contract void for fear of incurring the wrath of CBS. The boys were, after all, still a relatively minor league group whom CBS might destroy remorselessly in legal battle. Napier-Bell had little doubt that the parent company would support its infant Innervision, rather than set a dangerous precedent by compromising a standard CBS contract for a disgruntled group:

> CBS are a ruthless corporation. All corporations are ruthless. There are no personalities involved. There may be nice people working there, but the corporation is a total abstraction, with shareholders and shares. The purpose of the corporation is to make money and, in the long run, the corporation will do what it must to protect itself.

For Wham!, the psychological timing of their assault against Innervision was all important. They had to prove to the parent company that they were worth saving. If they struck at the peak of their commercial powers, with strong record sales and a high media profile, the financially-minded CBS might consider their talents too profitable to waste and force Innervision into making a settlement whereby the mother company inherited the golden goose. For this reason, Napier-Bell argued that legal action should be forestalled until the winter tour had completely sold out and the P.R. machine was in overdrive. It was a calculated gamble and not without some danger. For, every day that passed without taking legal action was another potential nail in Wham's coffin since they could be seen as continuing to accept and thereby affirm the terms of the Innervision contract. The fact that they now had the additional advice of a highly professional team made the need for action even more urgent. In the eyes of a judge, a late repudiation frequently confirms the validity of an otherwise unfair contract. In short, Wham! had to act without delay or find themselves forever trapped between the corporate hammer and the judicial anvil.

Napier-Bell spent considerable time discussing tactics with the ubiquitous Dick Leahy. One outcome of those sessions was the delivery of Wham! into the hands of Leahy's solicitors, Russells. The Mayfair based law firm, headed by Anthony David Russell, was already well known in music business circles for their colourful clients, who ranged from punk star Hazel O'Connor to the moody singer/songwriter Van Morrison. Russells' brief was to collate information in preparation for projected legal action on the first day of Wham's winter tour. Accordingly, Russells wrote to Halliwell Rodwell on 19 August announcing that they had replaced Robert Allan as Wham's solicitors. During the succeeding month, correspondence continued on a perfectly amicable basis and Rodwell's firm supplied a number of documents without hesitation. On 21 September, Rodwell requested a small variation in Wham's Innervision contract to deal with a "new technical form of record". Days passed, but the request remained unanswered. Dean claims that at this point he intervened with a telephone call to Napier-Bell in which he spoke vaguely about the prospect of a renegotiation. Simon declined an invitation to lunch but suggested that Dean clarify his proposals on paper and despatch them through his solicitor. The time for cosy theoretical chats was clearly over.

On 7 October, Mark Dean was sitting in his South Molton Street office when a messenger arrived bearing a large envelope. Upon breaking the seal, the Innervision director was immediately struck by the mysteriously provocative words "Strictly private and confidential: for the attention of Mr. Mark Dean and for his eyes only". His curiosity rapidly turned to consternation when he was greeted by the logo "RUSSELLS" at the head of the page. The letter was an unwieldy document, twenty-four A4 pages in length, but what was it doing in his hands? His solicitor, Paul Rodwell, was presently in mid-correspondence with Russells, and protocol dictated that legal communication be channelled through their respective offices. Intrigued by this odd departure from tradition, Dean read on, and before reaching the end of the first page, his eyes widened in astonishment. The letter was a fascinatingly detailed examination of Wham's early history which rapidly transmuted into a blistering catalogue of transgressions alleging, *inter alia*, that Wham's recording contract was obtained by fraudulent misrepresentations, contained unreasonable restrictions, unduly unfair terms and was made in circumstances of inequality of bargaining power. The extraordinarily lengthy epistle ended with a declaration that Wham! was now free to enter into a new recording agreement with whomever they chose and were also entitled to recover the rights to all master recordings delivered to Innervision. A final cautionary reminder of overdue royalties served almost as an irrelevant postscript in the context of what had gone before.

Dean was stunned by the weight of the cumulative allegations and had to sit down in order to quell the rapid beating of his overworked heart. Even now, he remembers that October day with a grimacing chill: "I nearly died. I couldn't believe it, especially when I read it. I thought, 'God, what is this? I don't believe this'. It was a bloody nightmare."

Precisely why young Dean had been forced to suffer such anguish rather than have the blow softened by correspondence from his own solicitor was supposedly due to Russells' concern about the contents of their extraordinary letter. In sending the document to Halliwell Rodwell, they would technically be publishing the work to a third party and Dean could conceivably contest their words as allegedly defamatory. The fact that such revelations would have been broadcast to one person only, himself a legally appointed adviser to Dean, underlines the extreme caution with which Russells were proceeding. The learned Mr. Justice Harman was himself surprised about the method of correspondence chosen by Russells and wryly commented on the matter: "I was told that this apparent gross discourtesy was due to fears of libel. I confess to having found the explanation glib and unconvincing." Unfortunately, the good Justice failed to enlighten us with any alternate theories which might exculpate Russells' "apparent gross discourtesy."

Dean recovered his poise sufficiently to inform Halliwell/Rodwell that Wham! had flown the nest. A reply was mercilessly swift. Innervision sought an injunction restraining Wham! from taking their services elsewhere and a hearing was set to commence on Thursday 3 November.

Wham's thoughts were distracted from legal matters by their 31 date nationwide "Club Fantastic" tour. Commencing in Aberdeen, with Andrew assuring the world that Wham! were not splitting, the tour was generally well received, although several dates were postponed when George fell victim to laryngitis. Having invested heavily in preparatory P.R., Wham! was guaranteed national press coverage and their show was different enough to warrant some sizeable features.

Instead of the customary support act, Wham! opened their shows with a disco courtesy of Capital Radio's cheerful cockney disc jockey Gary Crowley, who always introduced them, amid a barrage of screeches, as "those bad boys from Bushey". With the emphasis on dance, rather than listening pleasure, his roadshow proved particularly effective in unseated venues. As expected, Wham! employed a heavy duty backing group, Dream Merchant, led by bassist Deon Estes and including their inevitable special guest, David Mortimer. Their musicianship was supplemented by the choreography of Shirlie Holliman and new girl Pepsi De Manque. Recruited by Napier-Bell, De Manque was a former session singer, black and busty in striking visual contrast to her blonde flat-chested partner. Amazingly, she had learned the dance routines less than 24 hours before the tour began. With five costume changes, from shimmering white dresses to black studded leather, the girls were featured extensively in the press photographs of the show. Nothing was left to chance.

In order to offset the glam, Wham! introduced a 15 minute video of snapshots from their childhood days onwards, which provoked both screams and howls of laughter. As George remarked: "The idea of the home movies is to get away from the image of us being untouchable . . . a lot of kids will go home feeling they know us a little better." The fans would have learned a lot more about the boys' family life had they ventured backstage where George's sisters, Melanie and Yioda, were busy styling hair and advising on make-up. Even the duo's parents appeared at several shows in a grand display of family loyalty.

In spite of the cosy, family image, the concerts were not without their moments of controversy. Dressed in Fila sportswear, the boys played a game of badminton onstage and part of the routine involved them thrusting shuttlecocks down their shorts and then serving the offending items into the audience. Some newspapers feigned outrage at their sexy antics and, in Nottingham, angry parents attacked their getaway car after the gig.

By the time the show reached London, several music critics were sharpening their knives in stern reaction against the press hyperbole. One review concluded: "Wham! are a clever façade whose dearth of talent takes a back seat to their inexcusably manipulative techniques. It's difficult to tell if they themselves had the brains to orchestrate such a monstrous scam or if they're merely the gullible puppets of some far more scheming mind." It didn't need a crystal ball to work out which scheming mind the reviewer was referring to. Old reputations die hard and Simon Napier-Bell was back in the firing line. When I spoke to him shortly after those concerts, he accepted my favourite adage that a role assumed is not easily discarded:

> Suddenly I'm now the manager who manufactures groups. It's a repu-tation I had before and lost. This time it's because Wham! suddenly turned up in shorts. People were saying I'd pulled a scam to get them in the papers. Absolute rubbish. George came to me and said "We're going to do the tour in shorts." I said, "Maybe you should start in shorts and revert to jeans later." But he said, "No. It's none of your business. We'll do it our way." That's how it should be. He was right because you don't make the front pages or centre spreads of the nationals and have every show sold out if you've got it wrong. What you do lose is credibility with all the groups who haven't happened yet, who are jealous of what you're doing. Loss of credibility in this business is often the same as success.

Of course, at this stage, few people knew of the astute bargain that Wham! had negotiated with Nomis, nor the extent to which George Michael would continue to dominate the songwriting and production credits without a sign of his new mentor's creative involvement.

There was, however, one clue to George Michael's future musical direc-tion. During the "Club Fantastic" tour, the familiar Wham! hits were sup-plemented by a solo rendition of "Careless Whisper". Recorded in America, with legendary producer Jerry Wexler, the disc was originally scheduled for release to coincide with the tour, but Michael had a sudden change of heart. Dissatisfied with Wexler's treatment and his own vocal performance, he consulted Dick Leahy, who supported his decision to re-record the song at a later date and produce the final product himself. It was a brave decision, and the first indication of Wham's refusal to record further material until their dispute with Innervision had been resolved.

Disputes were multiplying at an alarming rate during that troubled winter of 1983. In the States, Wham! found themselves in the unenviable position of fighting an American disco group over the rights to their name. Originally, it was hoped that the disagreement would be settled amicably and the boys even agreed to issue their American releases under the name "Wham UK". By November, however, the American Wham! were still pursuing their lawsuit and claiming the absurdly astronomical damages of $19.6 million dollars in the process. Yet, for all its press coverage, the dis-pute was relatively inconsequential in comparison to the battle royal presently unfolding in the Royal Courts of Justice.

The Perspicacious Pronouncements Of Mr Justice Harman

Innervision Limited v George Panayiotou and Andrew Ridgeley was a gripping power struggle and an immensely entertaining spectacle of rhetoric, ingenious argument and awe-inspiring judicial wisdom. On 3 November, the combatants presented their arguments most forcibly and several interesting facts emerged. Dean's Q.C., Andrew Bateson, claimed that Innervision had taken considerable risk in signing Wham! and spent £127,000 on advance publicity, money which would have been irrecoverable if the group had proven unsuccessful. As it was, their royalties stood at £282,000 and, after costs, the duo was due to be paid £154,000. The defendants' solicitor replied that with the right contract Wham! could earn £1 million in the next two years. It was an intriguing proposition.

Over the next few days, the evidence was unhappily given in a formidable exchange of sworn statements. The principle evidence on behalf of Wham! lay in an enormously lengthy affidavit presented by their solicitor, Tony Russell. However, his interpretation of events failed to impress the sagacious Mr. Justice Harman who concluded sternly:

> As must be apparent from the history I have set out, Mr. Russell knows nothing of the facts about the making of the recording agreement. He only came into the matter about August 1983. His affidavit is almost entirely argumentative and contains very few allegations of fact. At the hearing of the motion Mr. Grabiner (Wham's QC) appeared for the Defendants and argued the matter persistently, lucidly and courteously. I was greatly assisted by his argument. Mr. Russell's affidavit was far less well expressed, not the proper way to present argument for the court and wasted a good deal of time.

Round one to Innervision, it seemed.

Wham's ingenious attempts to prevent the interlocutory injunction being granted ultimately rested on a handful of legal arguments. During the early stages of the motion, their QC, the much praised Mr. Grabiner, attempted to make a case for "undue influence", but the point remained undeveloped and was later dropped. Next came a suggestion that the recording contract was in "restraint of trade". Simply put, the imperious Grabiner was arguing that, if the injunction was granted, Wham! would be

prevented from exercising their talents effectively in the pop world.
Andrew Bateson, on behalf of Innervision, replied that the contract did not
prevent Wham! from writing songs and licensing them to Morrison/Leahy
for commercial gain. Nor were Wham! being prevented from performing
their work live. Indeed, they were touring Britain at the time of the hearing
and were expected to earn between £5,000 to £10,000 from these gigs.
They were also free to venture into films and exploit merchandising rights
which were, of course, entirely in their control. After listening to this
declaration of contractual independence, Mr. Justice Harman concluded
that, on motion, he could not support the argument for restraint of trade.

Moving on, the indefatigable Grabiner next brought up the old personal
services ruling. This was the judgement that thwarted Larry Page's
campaign to restrain The Troggs from leaving his Page One record
company back in 1968. Since becoming case law, it had put the fear of God
into every mogul-minded manager and was the main reason why Napier-
Bell meekly accepted a three month contract from Wham! Mr. Grabiner
was now suggesting, quite rightly, that the Innervision contract was
concerned specifically with the making of master recordings and therefore
involved some co-operation between the record company and Wham! He
argued further that there would have to be personal contact between Dean
and the boys, but Mr. Justice Harman remained unconvinced. He retorted
that Wham! now had the managerial services of the great Napier-Bell, who
was quite capable of negotiating with Innervision on their behalf. For once,
the old personal services argument was being overruled, and as Harman
delicately pointed out:

> Contracts for personal services, it has been said, are to be thought of as
> contracts analogous to the contracts between master and servant. A very
> obvious one is of course the familiar one of a contract between a manager
> and a pop group where plainly intimate personal contact and personal
> services are involved, but that is not this case, although it was of course
> the case in *Page One Records v Britton*.

With their defensive walls crumbling, Wham! still voiced the conviction
that the confidence between the parties had irrevocably broken down.
Perusing the affidavits, however, Mr. Justice Harman could find nothing to
suggest that the recording sessions had been badly handled or the promotion inadequately executed. Indeed, the group's very success suggested the
opposite. Looking at Wham's history more critically, Mr. Justice Harman
betrayed his own suspicions about their unfortunate breakdown of
confidence:

> It may be that the confidence between the parties has failed, but then
> there arises the question as to what caused the failure. I cannot help
> observing that until Mr. Napier-Bell in July and Messrs Russells in
> August came on the scene there was never a word or a hint of a failure of
> all confidence . . . There seems to me to be the strongest possible

indication that the dissatisfaction which is alleged now by the Defendants with the Plaintiff are due to the fact that it has now been pointed out to them that, having got into the charts as a result of their own talent and the promotional efforts of the Plaintiff combined, there are now open to them fresh fields and pastures new and they long to get into them. In my judgement that is not the same thing as a breakdown of confidence due to internecine strife over the matter which is the subject of the contract itself.

It was at this point in the judgement that one of the most controversial and strenuously contested arguments came under the Justice's hammer. For this, we must thank Simon Napier-Bell, whose love of drama added a much needed spice to the proceedings. He claims that several days after taking over Wham's management, an argument took place over the telephone between his partner, Jazz Summers, and Mark Dean. Jazz confirms this allegation, adding that his anger stemmed from Innervision's intransigence over the funding of a Wham! promotional video. In the heat of the moment, Dean allegedly lost his patience and uttered some disparaging remarks which Jazz reported back to his partner. Simon was delighted by this turn of events and now claims: "I knew we had to get something to wave in court", a clear admission that legal action was anticipated almost from the outset of his taking over the management of Wham! Of course, you cannot "wave" unrecorded telephone conversations in court, but the vulpine Napier-Bell felt that Dean's agitation could be exploited to Nomis's and Wham's advantage. With Machiavellian cunning, he wrote Dean an ingratiatingly polite letter indicating his desire for a friendly working relationship before adding, in mock indignation, his regret that the Innervision director should speak so discourteously to his Nomis partner. Needless to say, Napier-Bell took great pains to quote everything Dean had allegedly uttered. The letter was subtly, but deliberately, provocative. What Napier-Bell wanted was a written reply, so vituperate that it could be used against Dean at a later date. Twenty-four hours later, a document, overflowing with vitriol, found its way into the hands of the wily 60s entrepreneur: "A letter was delivered by hand. It was threatening, illiterate and rude, unsigned, on Innervision paper. So I put it in the safe."

At a suitable moment in the hearing, the anonymous letter was removed from Simon's safe, attached to an affidavit and placed before Mr. Justice Harman. According to Napier-Bell, the sober-blooded Justice was so taken aback by the content of the letter that his body visibly tensed. From that point onwards, conflicting affidavits came thick and fast. Some remarkably clever theories were presented to explain how the document might have come into Napier-Bell's possession, many of them worthy of a Sherlock Holmes mystery writer.

Both parties still stick by their original statements, so the controversy will probably never be resolved. Although Napier-Bell's testimony was supported by a former Innervision secretary, Dean remains curiously mystified by the entire episode:

> We'll never know to this day where that letter came from. I think I asked for forensic tests to be done just to prove that it didn't come from my typewriter, but Harman wouldn't do it. My memory is that it didn't come from me. Whether it came from my office, I don't know. There was always a big question about that letter. It surprised me as well. All I know is I never sent that letter. There was no proof that I lied.

In spite of Napier-Bell's burning conviction about the "letter", even he knew that it would not be sufficient in itself to influence the outcome of the hearing. Even the supporting statement from Dean's secretary was not enough to swing the issue. Without the benefit of cross-examination, Mr. Justice Harman was forced to throw water on the entire debate:

> The allegations of unattractive conduct, the letter which was produced (and which was a matter of extremely contradictory evidence) alleged to have been received by Mr. Napier-Bell as a letter from Mr. Dean, but which is said by Mr. Dean never to have been a letter at all, an issue which I cannot resolve at this time on paper evidence, is obviously unattractive. But that is a row between Mr. Napier-Bell and the Plaintiff, and he has, after all, on his own account, a record of, I think he calls it, needling record companies for the benefit of course of his client and thus indirectly of himself, but primarily of his client, and that matter does not seem to me to show a breakdown of confidence between the Defendants and the Plaintiff in respect of the matters which are the subject of this particular recording contract.

Although Wham! had made a concerted attempt to break free from their record company without suffering the expense of a trial, Mr. Justice Harman felt obliged to consider the incalculable damage that might be done to Innervision if the injunction was refused. His final words must have been a cruel, if not entirely unexpected blow to Wham's beleaguered morale:

> In my judgement there being really a very difficult weighing up, heavy weights on both sides of the balance of convenience, the court is entitled to and will turn to preserving the *status quo ante*, that is to keep the recording contract intact and on foot until trial. It seems to me plainly a case where a speedy trial should be had. If these allegations of misrepresentation which are made by Mr. Panos and Mr. Ridgeley were true and if such misrepresentations were made in circumstances in which they may have been made, it would be a matter of the utmost seriousness for both sides and would warrant an immediate dissolution of the contract. Such a point can only be resolved on cross-examination and that should take place as soon as possible and before memories are blurred.

Sadly, this most fascinating and entertaining of motions was not destined to go the full distance to trial. As a result, the biggest issue emerging from the injunction, the question of fraudulent misrepresentation, was never put to the test under cross-examination. It remains an intriguing puzzler, stretching back to the earliest association between Wham! and Innervision. The crucial point arose from what Mark Dean may or may not have said to the boys during the course of their negotiations in that Holloway cafe back in 1982. Did he make a statement to Wham! indicating that the contract which they were about to sign contained revisions proposed by the solicitors advising them? As we now know, the contract contained some, but not all, of the revisions suggested by Robert Allan. Therefore, if Dean claimed the revisions had been included, such a representation would not have been strictly true. Indeed, we would be dealing here with a serious misrepresentation along one of the following lines: "innocent" (Dean genuinely and rationally believed that the substance of Allan's amendments were contained in the contract); "negligent" (Dean did not know and failed to inquire of his own solicitor whether Allan's amendments were incorporated) or "fraudulent" (Dean knew perfectly well that some alterations had been excluded in which case his alleged statement to Wham! would have been a lie). This entire question was crucially important because the Chancery Courts have never granted specific performance of a contract where said contract has been a result of misrepresentation whether (in ascending order) innocent, negligent or fraudulent.

In the interlocutory hearing, Mr. Justice Harman addressed this issue at some length but, since there was no cross-examination, misrepresentation could not be proved or disproved. As he lucidly put it,

> Of course, no court case would order specific performances of a contract obtained by misrepresentation. But at the moment I cannot decide that this contract was in fact obtained by misrepresentation . . . There is now plainly on the record (Mr. Bateson submits there always was) a denial of any misrepresentation. On motion, with merely paper evidence before him (and no application to cross-examine was made to me although time to consider it was given) no judge can, in my opinion, properly make findings of fact.
>
> Accordingly, I hold that where an allegation of misrepresentation, fraudulent or not, is made on motion and that allegation is positively denied so that the conflicting stories must be tested to find the truth, the judge must proceed on the basis that there *may* have been no misrepresentation at all. On that basis no lack of clean hands is shown. They may or may not be dirty.

When I questioned Dean about the signing of Wham!, he claimed that, after consulting his solicitor and picking up the revised contracts, he went to the Holloway rehearsal studio in all innocence, assuming that the documents had been fully amended. I then asked, "But did you *tell* Wham! it had the amendments in?" "Yes," Dean replied, emphatically. Here, Dean was effectively saying that he had, after all, innocently misrepresented the boys. When I put this to him, he paused for a second, then conceded "Yes, I probably did at the end of the day." If there had been a cross-examination of Dean at the interlocutory stage, and if he had then admitted telling the boys the amendments were in, and misrepresentation thereby proven, Innervision's motion would have been defeated. But, unfortunately for Wham!, that did not occur.

Rather than celebrating a glorious victory, Wham's champions found themselves under new and unexpected pressures. On the final day of the injunction hearing, Innervision had gone on the counter-offensive by issuing a writ against Napier-Bell, Tony Russell and Jazz Summers (representing Nomis) alleging conspiracy and inducement to break contract. That action was soon dropped and Dean now regards the matter with a mixture of embarrassment and regret:

> It was a bad mistake. We should never have done that . . . It was a stupid idea. It was pathetic. It was childish. We'd already won the injunction. We should have been satisfied with that . . . It made the whole thing into a personal war. It was a bad move. We'd got enough. We had a good point to negotiate from. It wasn't important that you start killing the women and children as well after you've won the war.

In spite of Dean's retrospective distaste for the action, Jazz Summers maintains that it was tactically effective: "It was very heavy . . . it definitely worked because it put a strain on Russells. It put a strain on everybody! You start getting writs for conspiracy, and you've got to fight." For a time, one of Nomis's greatest worries was that in contesting a conspiracy action involving Wham!, Russells might be prevented from continuing to represent the boys in the contractual dispute with Innervision. It was a chilling consideration. Appointing a new solicitor from scratch would not only prove disheartening, but enormously expensive. Fortunately, that nightmare remained unrealized.

The Cost Of Freedom

The Innervision dispute effectively forced Wham! into a long period of inactivity, which was to drag on until the spring of 1984. During the interim, relations between the parties continued to deteriorate. With no product forthcoming from Wham!, Innervision issued the appalling "Club Fantastic Megamix", cobbling together "A Ray Of Sunshine", "Come On" and "Love Machine" from the already well-milked début album. The group reacted angrily by issuing a scathing press release, dissociating themselves from the product and imploring fans to resist purchasing the factitious item. Their efforts proved only marginally successful. The disc reached number 15 in the charts.

CBS continued to watch from the sidelines with a grim, corporate countenance. Unwilling to intervene, they could not ignore the enormous press coverage that Wham! had received in 1983 nor the continued sales of *Fantastic*, which soon passed the million mark. Napier-Bell was convinced that CBS would force a settlement, but, as time passed, frustration grew in the Wham! camp. At one point, Simon threw up his hands and exclaimed: "Let's go to trial – to hell with it". But it wasn't that easy. Everybody knew that another year in the wilderness would virtually destroy Wham's chances of making a successful comeback, and no legal victory, however emphatic, could compensate for that. As Jazz Summers ruefully acknowledged: "We wanted to settle out of court. We didn't want to proceed to trial. It'd cost a fortune. Look at the Elton John case. I'd never advise an artiste to get involved in litigation unless they had to".

While Wham! were stuck in limbo, awaiting a trial that was still an age away, Innervision slowly slipped into deep financial waters. Dean had already invested £80,000 in the court case and with no more hit acts, and much of the Wham! money tied up, he needed the powerful assistance of CBS. However, the parent company was already growing weary of the struggle and began to feel that a settlement should be enforced. Having played most of his cards in winning the interlocutory hearing, Dean suddenly found that his patron was threatening to raise the stakes and force him out of the game: "They were going to put in the receivers unless I agreed the deal . . . and as the backers they had every right to do so. It would have destroyed the whole situation. I would have been liquidated overnight".

As the drama unfolded, Wham! found security in the distraction of an imaginary schedule. It was already agreed that, in the event of a settlement, the group would blitz the charts with a calculated series of singles, culminating in a Christmas tour. In the meantime, George Michael was re-assuring Morrison/Leahy of his commercial worth by penning several potential hits. While visiting Andrew's house, he glanced at a note that the star had left his early rising mother. It read: "Wake me up before you go". Sometime later, the boys were driving home after an evening in town, when George hummed the chorus of an extremely catchy tune. After only a few minutes, they unanimously agreed that the song would make the perfect "comeback" single. It was titled "Wake Me Up Before You Go-Go".

The Ridgeley residence once again played unconscious host to Michael's muse during one cold Saturday evening in February. While watching *Match Of The Day* with Andrew, George's mind began to stray to the ghosts of Christmas past. Recalling classic yuletide singles, he voiced the opinion that Wham! should pen their own festive tribute. Encouraged by Ridgeley, the over-imaginative songsmith found himself staying up half the night until "Last Christmas" was completed.

The joyous news that Wham! would be free to release their backlog of material came towards the end of March. CBS had deemed it meet that the battle should end with the parent company inheriting the litigious superstars. The boys were relieved that it was all over and eagerly rejoined the industry of human happiness by signing to CBS' sister company, Epic. Characteristically, Simon Napier-Bell interpreted this turn of events as a spectacular and unprecedented moral, political and economic victory for his side:

> I think we're the only people in the history of CBS to take them on and win. Of course, CBS would say that we didn't win at all, that we'd taken on Innervision and the gentlemen that they were, they settled out of court. But, effectively, we *beat* them. And they know that. And they're respectful for it.
>
> The new contract with CBS was effectively the same as if we'd never had a contract. It wasn't a restricted settlement, not the kind you'd do out of court. It was what we'd have got if we'd just gone to sign as Wham!, give or take one per cent. That's why I say we won. They knew they would lose at the trial. The problem was it could have been extended for a year. That's the only point they had to bring us to settlement. Wham! would have faded away a year from now, so we couldn't really afford it.

The loss of Wham! precipitated the decline of Innervision as a profitable company and by 1985 it had ceased trading. Mark Dean was cast in the role of the vanquished, a fate made bearable only by his absolute conviction that Wham! could never have been saved:

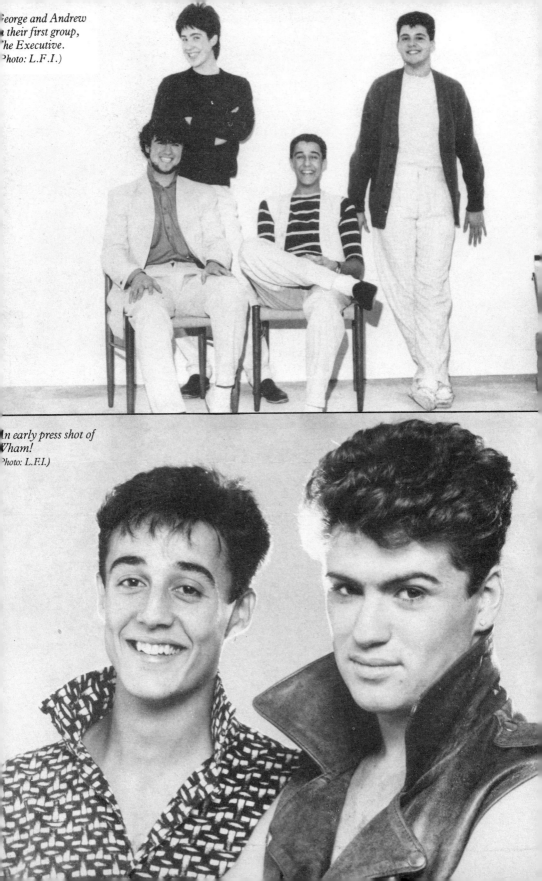

*George and Andrew
in their first group,
The Executive.
(Photo: L.F.I.)*

*An early press shot of
Wham!
(Photo: L.F.I.)*

Amanda Washbourne.
(Photo: Rex Features Ltd.)

Simon Napier-Bell

Mark Dean, founder of
Innervision Records.
(Photo: Julian
Simmonds/Select.)

Jazz Summers
(Photo: Rex Features Ltd.)

psi and Shirley
hoto: Rex Features Ltd.)

Photo: Chris Craymer.

oto: Allan Ballard.

In China.
(Photo: L.F.I.)

Photo: Chris Craymer.

Andrew, with girlfriend
Donna Fiorentico
(Photo: L.F.I)

orge with American
ress Brooke Shields.
o: L.F.I.)

Andrew, with his parents, in China.
(Photo: L.F.I.)

George and Andrew with Tory Party Chairman Norman Tebbit at the BPI Awards, 1985.
(Photo: L.F.I.)

It was the way circumstance lent itself. There was no other way for it to go than the way it went. There was too much power play going on, too many egos, too many reputations to be scored, and not enough peace-makers. And CBS had to save their arse. Were CBS wrong? In twenty years time, in their position, would I do the same with a 21 year-old kid? The answer is "I don't know" . . . I could have stayed with CBS through all this. One day we'll work together again, but I know them better and they know me better.

Dean was not entirely destroyed by the peripeteia which had robbed him of Wham! He received an undisclosed settlement which included future royalties on Wham! recordings, but it was all small beer in comparison to what might have been. At one point in our conversation, he turned logic on its head by insisting, "I earned more out of losing Wham! than I'd ever have earned out of keeping them." However, further questioning confirmed that the fallen mogul was speaking philosophically, rather than financially:

Why? Because I learned one of the best lessons in life: experience. It also made me grow up a lot and look at life in a different way. It changed me as a person. Monetary-wise, I came out with almost nothing. I'll tell you that. But, as a person, today, I can sit here with no fear, no worry. I'm happy with myself and I'm going to go on and do great things. But I'll do it with experience behind me. It was a nasty period in my life, but millions of pounds could never have bought me that experience. I'm glad that I can look back and see that I was on the receiving end with no bitterness, knowing that it was just something that happens. I wasn't the greatest brain in the world. I needed to learn those valuable lessons in life and that's what it gave me. I *swear* to you, I don't have any regrets.

There's an old saying in the music business that following protracted litigation "the only real winners are the lawyers". On this occasion, however, Russells won much more than they bargained for. After representing Dick Leahy and the superstar Wham! boys, they received an unexpected letter from another prospective client. Yes, Russells now look after Mark Dean too. It was an extraordinarily ironic conclusion to a hard fought and enthralling High Court extravaganza.

With Innervision an already fading bad memory, Wham! bounced back in exuberant style with an aggressive PR push. Their rivalry with other groups, sexual conquests, drinking habits, clothes and political attitudes all featured heavily in the tabloids and in the midst of the media overkill came the big comeback single. It was greeted with almost universal disdain by a hostile pop press sick of Wham's blatant calculation. The *New Musical Express* consigned the disc to their postscript column "The Rest" and the reviewer spent several lines expressing regret for once having written a favourable piece on the boys. The apologetic tone was reiterated in an even more trenchant *Melody Maker* review. Under the heading "Single Of The

Week", the poor reviewer was forced to swallow his prejudice ("I hate Wham! and all they stand for") and come to terms with the realization that "Wake Me Up Before You Go-Go" was actually a damn good pop record. ("I've either had a mental breakdown or someone's spiked my cocoa, but I think this is terrific"). The reluctant praise was typical of the 1984 music press, which resented Wham! pandering to the lowest common denominator of public taste. But after six months' exile, the duo was in no mood for arcane adventurousness. Uncomplicated, catchy pop melodies would continue to define their appeal hereafter.

The chart topping "Wake Me Up Before You Go-Go" was followed by a much publicized trip to France, where Wham! set about recording their second album. During a taxi ride to the airport, the Michael muse once more came to life with an ear-pricking melody. Within a few days a lyric was added, all about a devoted boy attempting to come to terms with his girlfriend's promiscuity. The song was titled "Freedom". Three months later, it was number 1.

Between "Wake Me Up . . ." and "Freedom", George released the long overdue 'Careless Whisper", one of the most profitable songs in the Morrison/Leahy catalogue. A couple of months before its release, I scuttled across to Bryanston Square to spend another long afternoon debating managerial strategies with Simon Napier-Bell. By the end of that meeting, I had a bookful of Wham! facts and theories. I learned that George Michael was supposedly capable of writing an album full of songs for Andy Williams; that "Wake Me Up . . ." was intended to appeal to 40 year-old mums, as well as screaming teenagers; and, no, the recent rumours about an impending Wham! split were complete rubbish. Simon skilfully dodged the "political" questions by offering some unconvincing comments on Wham's "classlessness" before providing his well-worn comparisons between George and Andrew and Butch Cassidy and the Sundance Kid. Wham's across the board appeal had not been seen in pop music since the heyday of The Beatles, he enthused confidently. Forget Duran Duran and Culture Club – Boy George was guilty of overexposing his image and the fickle British public are easily bored. In a year's time he'd be one of yesterday's men . . . All this was standard SNB proselytizing, but what followed was different. After a few hours, Napier-Bell exhausted his P.R. hyperbole and, for the first time, spoke frankly about the long term aims of Wham! Suddenly, it seemed that they had not merely mapped out the whole of 1984, but the remainder of their performing lives. The old Svengali had it all down pat:

> They have the potential to be what they want to be and they always said they wanted to be the biggest group in the world. One recognizes it doesn't last long . . . America is the crucial question, and I would have thought Wham! have the potential to be the biggest group in America. They'll get there in the next two years, and stay there for two years,

mainly because of George's incredible songwriting.

We are aware of the English market and what will happen is the group will hit here, capture the public imagination and fade within 1-2 years. Inevitably. In America, it will take 1-2 years so, as they fade here, their reputation there will grow and that may bring them back to a constant level.

It should be borne in mind that the above statement was made *before* Wham! had their first number 1. "Wake Me Up . . ." was poised to top the charts and their future looked bright, yet here was Napier-Bell predicting their *inevitable* downfall in 1986. He was proved largely correct, of course, and his comments now have an eerily fatidical ring. Exactly two years and 27 days after our discussion, they ceased to exist.

The imminent commercial decline of Culture Club, already predicted by Napier-Bell, was confirmed when Wham! beat them to the top of the charts in October. Chart statistics among the pop élite suddenly appeared to have more relevance than at any time since 1964. The clock had magically been turned back to an era when petty rivalries and well publicized feuds governed the lives of the pop aristocracy and dominated the pages of the sensationalist pop press. There was a certain playfulness in all this, rather like grammar school boys competing for *Top of the Form*. Fleet Street remained the great adjudicator, championing Duran Duran one week, Culture Club the next, and pitting them both against Wham! in some imaginary pop Colosseum. The images spilling forth from the media were consistent and beyond parody. Duran Duran and Wham! were portrayed as pop star hedonists whose exotic lives consisted of wild parties, ephemeral love affairs, all-night dancing, luxurious holidays and, of course, the occasional pop record and tour. Neither act did much to dispel such rumours. On the contrary, they positively welcomed journalists and reinforced their steadfast images as vacuous tin gods of teen. At least everybody knew where they stood . . . until Wham! complicated matters.

One afternoon, Jazz Summers received a telephone call from a representative of the National Union of Mineworkers. The NUM, spearheaded by Arthur Scargill, was striking against the closure of pits and the loss of 21,000 jobs. A benefit had been planned at the Royal Festival Hall to relieve the suffering of the beleaguered miners' families and several pop stars agreed to appear. Would Wham! be interested? Summers, a professed socialist, was sympathetic towards the strike and engaged the boys' support with little effort. Their appearance on the bill, alongside the politically-minded Style Council, caused a few raised eyebrows. Many felt, with considerable justification, that Wham's lifestyle and general outlook epitomised everything that socialism opposed. Their politics had always been, at best, confused and, apart from an admission to voting Labour in the 1983 election, they had little to recommend them to the hard Left. It was difficult to imagine anything further removed from the harsh realities of Northern mining life than the sight of rich pop stars flaunting their wealth in garish nightclubs and downing cocktails on sun-kissed beaches. Yet, here were Wham! betraying a social conscience. For some, it seemed not merely incongruous but insincere and patronizing. Not content to be applauded as affluent flash Harry stars, Wham! wanted philanthropic credibility as well.

The cynics were given the perfect opportunity to put the knife in when Wham! appeared without a backing group and mimed their entire set. At one point, their backing tape malfunctioned and George announced the wrong song. Inevitably, this provoked an outburst of jeering from the partisan Style Council supporters and, the following week, the music press had a field day. It was even suggested that the NUM should have billed the concert as a "mimers' benefit".

George Michael was deflated by the criticism which he felt was unnecessarily vindictive. He later pleaded "What are we supposed to do? Go on in grey overcoats and say, 'This is our single *Wake Me Up Before You Go-Go* we're really sorry it's been number 1 but listen to it anyway'." Denying that Wham! had any ulterior motives for offering their services, he pointed out how easily they could have transformed the event into a PR exercise with front page headlines in every tabloid paper. Instead, they kept an uncharacteristically low profile throughout the affair. Nevertheless, images speak louder than actions or words in the music world, and Wham! could hardly have expected to reverse long held prejudices overnight. What neither the group nor their management realized was the degree to which media stereotyping now defined Wham! in the public consciousness. Jazz Summers' eloquent defence of the boys underlines the gap between private motives and public expectations:

> It may *seem contradictory* but they wanted to do the Miners' gig. They went on stage there because they wanted to raise money to give those miners' kids some food to eat . . . There was no hypocrisy. The people at the Festival Hall were middle-class civil servants who saw things from their political armchairs. That place was full of pseudo-socialists who were probably members of the S.W.P. or college students who felt trendy to be Left. They failed to see that, irrespective of what these people stood for, they were raising money, and Wham!, especially, filled that place and made more money than anybody else. And the audience failed to see that they were doing some good. They were blinded by their own propaganda. They were the contradiction, not Wham! Scargill was aware and took time out to come backstage and thank them for doing it.

Not even Mr. Scargill's courtesy could heal the ego blow which Wham! suffered that evening. Indeed, George Michael later denounced the NUM leader as a "meglomaniac" who was secretly enjoying the drama of the miners' plight. It was an astonishing accusation, which Summers can only explain away as a misunderstanding:

> I could understand Scargill. He'd been fighting and fighting so rather than saying "It's been great, you're helping a lot of people", he went into a real political tirade about the police and this and that and the boys went "Ah!" They'd never seen anything like that before. It was very strange. George went "Cor, maybe we shouldn't have done this" because Scargill came over so badly. But look at the pressure he was under. That's why it happened.

Wham's jump into the political pool proved a sobering experience which they chose not to repeat. In later interviews, the chastened Michael hardened against his radical peers and refused to support such movements as Red Wedge, which he derided as unimaginative and impotent. One cannot help wondering what might have happened if the Festival Hall hecklers had taken Wham! to their socialist hearts rather than laughing at their pomposity.

For the remainder of the year, Wham! reinforced the worst aspects of their hedonic lifestyle with regular splashes in the Sunday papers. The PR machine ground out further gossip and smiling photographs in preparation for the all important Christmas album and tour. Feeding miners' families was put in a new perspective when the boys threw a launch party for the *Make It Big* album. The tab was liberally estimated at £10,000. The setting for this champagne guzzling gala was Xenon, the nightclub where George Michael and Mark Dean had their memorable first argument. Now, it was the scene of gratuitous celebration. Stars came and went in droves, among them various members of Spandau Ballet and Duran Duran, not to mention Bob Geldof, Nick Heyward, Captain Sensible, Lulu, Sandie Shaw, Koo Stark and an endless list of models and comedians. Wham's Italian publicist, Connie Fillippello, purred with satisfaction when the boys reaped acres of space in both the tabloids and the music press.

Make It Big zoomed to number 1 in its first week of release and sold in vast quantities, just as everyone had expected. In terms of musical influence, it was a more varied album than its predecessor with strong echoes of 60s/70s Tamla Motown. George modestly claimed that his music was largely derivative and confessed to an inordinate love of clichéd chord patterns. What he failed to observe was the extent to which *Make It Big* shared the faults of the anti-climactic *Fantastic*. Once again, the record buyer was short changed with an eight track album comprising three singles, an Isley Brothers cover, a lightweight throwaway ("Heartbeat") and the monumentally banal "Credit Card Baby". Only the inspired "Everything She Wants", which revealed what Michael could produce if more care was taken, brought a vestige of dignity to the enterprise, and that was hardly sufficient to rid the taste of another anti-climax.

If nothing else, *Make It Big* confirmed that Ridgeley was no longer in the running as a co-composer. During the early sessions for the album, when George Michael was under pressure to complete a set of songs, Jazz Summers approached Andrew about the possibility of penning some material. Ridgeley shrugged his shoulders and said: "The guy's a brilliant songwriter. If I write a song, he'll come up with a better one, so why bother?" The schoolmasterly Summers wagged his finger and instructed the boy to try and stimulate his partner. Andrew laughingly retorted: "I don't think he needs stimulating." As Jazz concluded, "I couldn't argue with that." From that point onwards, Andrew's creative inertia was never mentioned.

As Christmas 1984 approached, public attention was focused on the appalling famine in Ethiopia. Over three thousand people a day were dying of starvation and television pictures captured the grotesque enormity of the catastrophe. Drought, coupled with the failure of a development pro- gramme in West and North East Africa, had caused the disaster, but the suffering was worsened by political inhumanity. Ethiopia was receiving a paltry $6 per head per year in overseas aid, while the pro-Western areas, such as Somalia, were granted over three times that amount. The scale of the tragedy had a profound effect on public opinion, but it took the indig- nation of a nondescript pop star to transform that pity into hard cash.

The indomitable Bob Geldof implored, cajoled and herded the top British pop stars of the day – including George Michael – into a London recording studio where they rapidly completed the eleemosynary "Do They Know It's Christmas?" The single went on to top the charts, selling a staggering 3 million copies along the way. Thanks to Geldof's foresight in gaining financial control of every aspect of the record's production, manu- facture and distribution, famine relief received over 96p of the £1.35 retail price.

The tremendous success of Band Aid prevented Wham's "Last Christmas" from reaching number 1, but George Michael could feel proud at having sung on two of the all time seasonal best sellers. Wham's festive philanthropy was topped off with an extravagant and much publicized donation of million selling record royalties to the Ethiopian Appeal. This charitable gesture may have saved the boys from another of those intermit- tent High Court flurries. For, several months later, Dick James Music took proceedings against George Michael, alleging that his composition, "Last Christmas", infringed their copyright of "Can't Smile Without You", a 1978 Barry Manilow hit. As a result, artiste royalties from the Wham! million seller, all of which were destined for famine relief, had to be frozen until the legal dispute was resolved. Morrison/Leahy and CBS expected a lengthy action, but, fortunately, Dick James had second thoughts and dropped his mean-spirited action, withdrew the allegations of infringe- ment, agreed to pay costs and requested the royalty collecting agencies to release all monies forthwith. For once, George Michael provided a sarcastic comment which was pointedly apposite: "If they had won, would they have asked the starving to give back the food?"

Wham! In China!
A Cultural Revolution?

Nomis' masterplan for 1984 had proved remarkably successful. Wham! had notched up two number 1 singles, a Christmas number 2 and an even bigger hit for soloist George Michael. As Napier-Bell predicted, Culture Club finally fell from critical and commercial grace with the much maligned "War Song" and suddenly seemed set for bleaker times in the future. The Duran Duran contingent had cautiously resisted the temptation to tackle Wham! head-on at the height of their restorative powers and wisely lay low for most of the year. Yet, for all of their hit parade domination and well conceived plans, Wham! were far from the undisputed chart champions of 1984. The dramatic emergence of Frankie Goes To Hollywood had stolen much of their thunder and made them look tame in the process. It was bad enough that Frankie released better records and broke virtually every chart statistic in the book, but what really irked Napier-Bell was the way they outmanoeuvred his boys as media manipulators. The controversy provoked by the irreverent video of "The Power Of Love", the anti-Reaganite sentiments of "Two Tribes" and the sexual playfulness of "Relax", ensured blanket rebukes from moral crusaders, politicians and the clergy. The attendant "shock" revelations concerning the sexuality of Holly Johnson and Paul Rutherford virtually guaranteed Frankie tabloid exposure of near Beatles proportions.

Behind the Frankie image was the sharp marketing of their record label ZTT, with former *New Musical Express* journalist Paul Morley playing Andrew Oldham to Trevor Horn's Phil Spector. The slick promotion and epic production for Frankie was refreshingly original, delightfully daring and contrasted markedly with Wham's carefully calculated careerist campaigns. Even Napier-Bell's well-rehearsed manipulative tactics momentarily seemed passe by comparison. In short, the old Svengali and his two teenage charges had been outplayed and outhyped by a modern and more imaginative outfit.

The clash between Frankie and Wham! left both groups exhausted and neither seemed in strong shape for an all action replay in 1985. Amid the New Year celebrations, news filtered through from both camps that no further product would be forthcoming for at least four months. Nobody, it seemed was willing to risk a fatal fall into Culture Club's gaping death trap of premature overkill. In any case, with Duran Duran still licking their wounds, it was safe enough to leave the charts to lesser mortals.

Frankie's avowed intention during early 1985 was to invade the States in the same dramatic style as they had conquered their home country. Twenty one years before, their Liverpudlian ancestors, The Beatles, had set forth on a far tougher campaign and against the odds captured the hearts and minds of teenage America. Their efforts had been tragically aided by the recent assassination of President John F. Kennedy whose funeral had plunged the nation into a protracted period of mourning and moribund lethargy. The dejected American public clearly needed some form of cathartic release and the Fab Four provided a distraction which rapidly grew into a phenomenon. Frankie did not have the events of world history on their side, but at least they arrived at a time when British groups were in the ascendant. It was intended that the boys would excel the achievements of the MTV aided Culture Club and Duran Duran by not merely breaking into the charts, but creating a wave of sensationalist press that would establish them as the undisputed kings of the New Pop. Unfortunately, the mock-subversive tactics that had worked so spectacularly in Britain the previous year left the Americans unimpressed. Like The Sex Pistols seven years before, Frankie were reduced to the level of side-show curios. They struggled through a series of gigs which the American media failed to publicize as extensively as ZTT had hoped. Their records fared almost as badly which was hardly surprising in view of the reactionary atmosphere. Contrary to expectation, the kids were not impressed by Frankie's unflattering depiction of Ronald Reagan, whose popularity among the young was greater than ever. Unlike The Beatles, Frankie discovered a political and moral climate in which their much touted image was deemed not only undesirable, but irrelevant.

Napier-Bell watched disinterestedly from afar knowing that the war for America had already been won. Unlike Frankie, Wham! were not alien to the American Dream, but positively oozed a consumerist ethos perfectly suited to the yuppie mentality and equally ideal for MTV kids in search of fresh blow-waved, sun-tanned demi-gods. It was no surprise when "Wake Me Up Before You Go-Go" hit number 1, and by February 1985, "Careless Whisper" had followed suit. The aggressive late challenge from Frankie had been rendered redundant.

The American invasion was largely plotted by Jazz Summers whose enthusiasm for the "big breakthrough" would reach grandiose proportions later in the year. Given Napier-Bell's experience of the American music business, it may seem strange that he chose to play such a relatively minor role in administering the U.S. campaign. However, it soon transpired that his expansionist passion lay elsewhere. While Jazz dutifully attended meetings with American business moguls, Simon undertook a more difficult mission on the other side of the globe.

The unlikely idea of unleashing Wham! upon the pop starved Chinese had been germinating in Napier-Bell's mind for over a year. Bigger acts,

such as The Rolling Stones and Elton John, had frequently voiced their
willingness to assail the mysterious Orient, but their efforts invariably met
with a cold response from China's Ministry of Culture. Record companies
had also despaired of China as a possible market and appeared powerless in
the face of a blanket ban on the sale of foreign product. Napier-Bell,
however, was more optimistic and, spurred on by his successes in Japan,
decided to investigate the Chinese market for possible outlets. He had
heard all the old stories about China's unyielding resistance to Western
pop music: the bans on dancing, the unavailability of L.P. records, the
limited appeal of radio and the numbing conformity of a culturally impo-
verished populace. When he arrived in Canton, however, the city was in
the grip of a disco craze. A Cantonese record company had taken advantage
of the insidious new liberalism by releasing sub-standard disco albums
which were selling in excess of 40,000 copies. While considering the implications of this unusual trend, Napier-Bell's eyes feasted on an article in the
China Youth Daily which read: "Play is also a form of production. Only
with an adequate amount of wining and dining and fun and games will the
productive power of the workers be restored." The hedonic tone sounded
like vintage Napier-Bell. If the Cantonese were intent on wining and dining then they were about to meet an unrepentant ambassador of culinary
indulgence.

In order to satisfy his curiosity, Napier-Bell consulted recent demographic surveys of Chinese youth. The figures revealed over 200 million
people aged between 18 and 32, most of whom would marry late. Records
and cassettes were still perceived as luxuries, though recent sales suggested
that a vast number of youngsters were more than willing to squander their
yuan. The potential for Western infiltration was self-evident, so Napier-
Bell steeled himself for a diplomatic exchange with the Cultural Attaché.
The problems he faced were seemingly insurmountable: Western pop
groups had never played China and foreign recordings were vetoed as a
matter of course. This double-edged sword effectively precluded any
opportunity to introduce Wham! to China, let alone make some sly money.

Undeterred by officialdom, Simon sought a loophole in the government's strict policy and armed himself with a weighty dossier of regional
bye-laws. Eventually, he discovered that the Cultural Exchange Depart-
ments of local provincial governments had been granted the freedom to
release recordings by foreign artistes on condition that the receipts were
donated to a local charity. Exploring this avenue further, Napier-Bell met
with characteristic Chinese caution, but eventually the Cultural Attache
agreed to consider his proposals and despatched a delegation of embassy
officials to scrutinize Wham's 1984 Hong Kong performance.

Napier-Bell's brush with Chinese officialdom proved enlightening and
he was pleasantly surprised to discover a coterie of urbane, sophisticated
left-wing intellectuals far removed from the stereotyped working-class
revolutionaries of media mythology. Many of them had studied at foreign

universities and evidently approved of the new fangled Western trends, including pop music. The more liberal Cantonese representatives agreed in principle to Napier-Bell's request to release a Wham! record, but insisted on setting the ambitious entrepreneur several additional hurdles. In return for a nominal royalty on the recording, Wham! was required to play concerts in Canton and Peking. This presented Napier-Bell with the further headache of securing an invitation from the far more traditionally-minded bureaucrats of the capital city. After several months of fruitless negotiation, the weary Westerner finally found a sympathetic ear at the All China Youth Federation, an association representing that all important 200 million age group.

Napier-Bell employed all his rhetoric and salesmanship patter in an attempt to win over the Federation, but they were not easily assuaged. First, they demanded translations of Wham's lyrics and insisted on a private viewing of their promotional videos. Napier-Bell mulled over the possible consequences with apprehension. As he sifted through Wham's video catalogue, his concern intensified. The footage for "Wake Me Up Before You Go-Go" featured the boys in shorts exultantly parading their pop star sexuality before hordes of screaming teenagers; "Careless Whisper" presented George Michael as a promiscuous two-timer and even included a steamy bedroom scene with semi-naked lovers in the preparatory stages of copulation; finally, "Club Tropicana" seemed nothing less than a socially irresponsible celebration of unbridled hedonic indulgence. Simon switched off the video recorder with muted resignation. His attempt to perceive Wham! through Chinese eyes had led to a single inescapable conclusion – they were the epitome of Western decadence. Recovering his spirits sufficiently to seek further footage, Simon sat through a low key video of "Freedom", set amidst the sedate surroundings of a *Top Of The Pops* studio. It seemed the best of an unacceptable bunch and was duly despatched to Peking. Fortunately for Wham!, the sensitive Chinese censors did not interpret "Freedom" as some form of oblique political commentary. However, they were quick to spot objectionable lyrics in "Love Machine" and censured the group for their sexually provocative gyrations and unacceptable volume. Napier-Bell intervened with some appeasing words and promised to reduce the decibel level, modify the choreography and edit the video material used during the shows.

Following a further period of prevarication, the Youth Federation eventually agreed to accept Napier-Bell's modifications, but still managed to drive a mercilessly hard bargain. The middle-aged 60s Svengali gulped as they reiterated their demand for 100 per cent of the gate receipts. And that was just the beginning. Wham! was contracted to pay for everything, including the renting of the auditorium, the construction of the stage and even the printing of a *free* programme. In strictly financial terms, it was the worst deal of Napier-Bell's entrepreneurial career, but the temptation to infiltrate the Chinese market remained irresistible. The Wham! boys were finally converted to the idea, fully aware that the world-wide publicity accompanying the concerts would increase their record sales substantially and introduce their name to many uncharted territories. Beyond these economic considerations there lurked the unquenchable ambition and rampant egos of two pop stars and a publicity-mad manager. Ultimately, the lust to earn a small place in history was sufficient motivation to overcome the inscrutable pedantry of oriental bureaucracy.

In an attempt to offset a fraction of the inevitable losses resulting from the China visit, Napier-Bell and Summers arranged a couple of lucrative warm-up gigs in Hong Kong. With the press already biting at Wham's heels it was not too difficult to persuade the tabloids to invest in the trip. Four newspapers, *The Sun, Daily Express, Daily Mirror* and *The Star* reputedly paid £10,000 in order to join the entourage and provide the boys with free publicity back home. Implausible as this sounds, offset against aeroplane fares and hotel expenses, it was probably a reasonable deal. The subsidiary killing that Napier-Bell gambled on was the much touted film of the tour, tentatively titled *Wham! In China! A Cultural Revolution.* The renowned director, Lindsay Anderson, whose past credits included the public school satire *If* and the surreal futurist black comedy *O Lucky Man,* had committed himself to the project, joining forces with pop video specialist Martin Lewis. Although the film promised the possibility of a hefty return, the running costs, estimated in the ludicrous region of one and a half million pounds, easily exceeded the cumulative losses envisaged for the entire tour. Wham! were clearly playing for high stakes with the ever present possibility of doubling their deficit.

Upon arriving in Hong Kong, the jetlagged duo was confronted by a gang of local journalists and soon found themselves fending off aggressive questions about exorbitant ticket prices. While the charity concert in China had been standardized at approximately £1.50, the residents of Hong Kong found themselves shelling out up to £22 for an opportunity to study the Wham! phenomenon. Only students of ancient history would remember that the populace had suffered the same shock when The Beatles played there in 1964.

After glimpsing the teeth of the Hong Kong press, Wham! next fell into the jaws of scoop-hungry English tabloid journalists at their greedy zenith. The chief offender at this early stage was *The Mirror's* celebrated John Blake who provided his readers with the memorable, but hugely exaggerated, headline "Wham! Star Cracks Up And Cries". In a highly conjectural psychological profile of George Michael, Blake catalogued the dramatic change in the star's personality from the happy-go-lucky joker of the previous year to the present moody misanthrope, subject to tempestuous outbursts at the drop of a hat. The sombre Blake concluded with the italicized warning ". . . Now a large question mark hangs over Wham's historic dater (sic) in China". Minus the melodramatic hyperbole, it seems that the understandably tense singer had ejected an overly intrusive television crew prior to his all important performance at the Coliseum. Like most pop stars at the height of their fame, Michael was merely fighting the losing battle for some body space and a few private moments away from a world seemingly obsessed with his every utterance. The inference about question marks hanging over the China visit even upset the normally implacable Napier-Bell who retorted: "Anyone who tries to embarrass the visit before it has begun is harming a lot more than Wham! and its management."

In fairness to Blake, his "exclusive" was no mere fabrication but the unhappy climax of a small scale newspaper war. Having established himself as Britain's top pop columnist in *The Sun*, this blond haired *wunderkind* had been wooed away by a highly competitive offer from the rival *Daily Mirror*. *Sun* proprietor, Rupert Murdoch, was determined to win back Blake at any cost, and when his bid failed, the two papers embroiled themselves in regular cut throat skirmishes for pop news. Cheque book journalism momentarily ran rampant and "exclusive" was heaped upon "exclusive" as *The Sun* desperately attempted to maintain credibility in the face of *The Mirror's* new found ambition to achieve a long sought supremacy. In different circumstances, Hong Kong might have seemed a reasonably neutral ground with each paper receiving similar stories at identical times, but this was no ordinary tour. There was no love lost between the rival tabloids and, as Blake reveals, the temperament of the Wham! boys served only to increase the tension:

> That was when things were really heavy. It was out and out war. George Michael actually did throw a wobbler . . . and there was a bit of a fracas. Everybody was a little hysterical. That particular trip was the worst pop trip I've been on in my life. Wham! had been on holiday having finished their hard work and then Simon set up all these concerts. It was like being called back from a school holiday and told to go to China. They hated it so consequently they were very hostile and unpleasant and the whole trip wasn't much fun.

When Blake decided to investigate the rumours concerning George's alleged upset, he was told by a stage hand that the star was in tears backstage. But the real misinformation came from one of Blake's rivals who graciously provided him with some unusually candid words from Jazz Summers. It was not until after he filed the story that the scoop-hungry Blake learned that his innocent informant had deliberately fabricated the entire quote. Blake had been set up and temporarily discredited. As he ruefully reflects: "It was unprofessional really, just one of those things."

For their part, Wham! gave the lie to any lingering suspicions about George Michael's professionalism. After bounding off stage at the Coliseum, the sweat drenched singer confronted the *paparazzi* with a surly plea: "Do I look as if I'm cracking up? It's just a bunch of lies." His chirpy indignation was rewarded with a big spread in the *Daily Mail* defending the reputation of the slighted star from the fury of their ill-informed tabloid rivals.

The concern over fair publicity in Britain was not merely some fatuous desire for pop star hagiography. Even as the Wham! entourage flew into Peking, Napier-Bell knew that certain political knives were being sharpened in anticipation of an ideological killing. Since completing arrangements for the tour, the pro-Western Chinese hierarchy had found themselves under fire from their left wing opponents in the Communist Party. Criticism over foreign investments, private enterprise and other Western economic practices had extended to hard questioning on the impact of bourgeois decadent culture. Although the pre-eminent minister Deng Liquin had already permitted a latitude in cultural affairs that would have been unthinkable in the heyday of Chairman Mao, he had recently voiced considerable concern over the "spiritual pollution" seeping through from the West. His ambivalent attitude clearly underlined the caution with which China intended to greet Wham!, and pop music in general. Not surprisingly, the pro-Western lobby had gone overboard in their attempts to whitewash Wham's public image for communist consumption. *The Peking Evening News* politely ignored the Club Tropicana high jinks, preferring the gray image of dole queue rejects bravely fighting a personal crusade for high quality pop music. They concluded with a sombre tribute to the socialist Bushey boys: "Their poor and miserable life gave them impetus and courage to strive for art". Even the less serious reports painted Wham! as clean-cut virgins renowned for "popular and fluent tunes, full of youth, vitality and with it rhythms". The prose revealed all the hallmarks of partisanship with an added dash of purblind Chinese politeness.

For their part, Wham! played up to the image of impeccably behaved young tourists, leaning elegantly on the Great Wall of China and sipping tea in the British Ambassador's back garden. George Michael's well-rehearsed speech at the Chinese Youth Federation banquet was a characteristically careful mingling of demulcent diplomacy and socio-cultural awareness:

> I'd like to start by saying my partner Andrew and I are extremely flattered and honoured to be here today. We just hope our performance will represent a cultural introduction between young people here and in the West and help them see what goes on in the rest of the world. And I think I speak for everyone when I say this may be a small step for Wham! but a great step for the youth of the world!

In keeping with the stress on "culture", the Chinese ensured that a Peking opera star was in attendance for a recital. Beneath this veneer of formal politeness, however, lay the uncertainty and scepticism of cautious politicians. Even Zhou Nan, the foreign aide who was China's chief negotiator in arranging the historic concerts, declined to attend the banquet at the eleventh hour.

Whatever reservations the hard Left may have had about Wham!, were not shared by the Chinese public. Although the group was still virtually unknown in Peking, news of the forthcoming concerts had provoked an astonishing appetite for tickets. More than one thousand expectant fans queued overnight outside the Peking Workers' Gymnasium box office. The patient vigil was overseen by a solid block of one hundred green-uniformed and plain clothes police who continually barked out orders over a loudspeaker. At one point, it seemed that the traditionally urbane Chinese youth were on the verge of losing their cool but the monotonous drone "Ticket buying comrades, please stay in line" served its anaesthetic purpose.

Unlike their Western counterparts, the Chinese impresarios had at least taken strong and effective measures against ticket-touting. All customers were personally vetted and required to produce a letter of introduction from their respective work units. Even that document guaranteed only a small block of tickets thereby ensuring that the black market was badly served. In spite of these commendable precautions, the stink of corruption hung heavy in the air. Prior to the concert, excited fans enthused about the free cassettes of *Make It Big*, which were intended for distribution with the tickets. Yet, of the ten thousand cassettes available, just over half reached the general public, the remainder being held back by anonymous officials. One week later, thousands of counterfeit copies flooded the black market ensuring a financial killing for the nameless faces behind this piratical operation. The only consolation for Wham! was knowing that their name had probably become synonymous with pop music in China.

On the historic evening of Sunday 7 April 1985, the unfamiliar strains of Western disco music enveloped the Workers' Gymnasium as 10,000 perplexed fans waited in hungry but patient anticipation for the arrival of two former unemployed Watford youths, lately transformed into arguably the most powerful demi-gods housed within the pullulating pantheon of 80s pop. The audience, dressed uniformly in standard Mao blue and brown suits, seemed nothing less than a perverse inversion of the peacock costumed throng that habitually congregated in the bars and foyers of similarly sized British and American concert halls. Not even in the pre-rock'n' roll days of the early 50s had there been such an eerily muted response at the beginning of a major concert. The p.a. system, already cut to half volume, issued forth a selection of barely audible European hit records, the vitality of which seldom rose above the somnabulistic.

With the unerring punctuality of a West End theatrical performance, the lights dimmed and a solitary figure emerged from the wings to take his place at centre stage. His attentive choreography immediately identified the mystery man as Trevor, the British dancer promised as support act in the Wham! programme. Clearly, the Bushey superstars were taking no chances. Having learned of the Chinese unfamiliarity with rock'n'roll, they had sagely despatched a professional young choreographer to instruct the audience in the ignoble art of jiving, breakdancing and bodypopping. Spurred on by Trevor's eager admonitions, several members of the audience rose spontaneously to their feet and attempted to ape his elaborate gyrations. Their immodest enthusiasm was short-lived. Suddenly, the background music was drowned by the urgent authoritarian tone of a Chinese official requesting calm. While the irrepressible Trevor continued throwing his elastic body across the stage, the disembodied voice repeated a plea which began to sound more and more like an ominous warning: "Dancing is not allowed. All those standing sit down, *now!*"

Backstage, the Wham! duo was unaware of this turn of events, still hoping that their choreographer had provided the spark which they would now effortlessly ignite. While the Wham! backing band took their places onstage and the house lights dimmed, George and Andrew separated backstage and strode towards their twin posts, poised nervously for a well-rehearsed dramatic entry. At the sound of a vaguely recognizable series of opening chords, two brightly coloured pop stars emerged from their respective wings and ran down congruently opposite staircases like dancers from a 40s Hollywood musical. The repeated phrase "jitterbug", sung in a negroid baritone, identified the familiar number 1 hit "Wake Me Up Before You Go-Go". The sound was polished, yet strangely distant, as though the group was playing in a hall twice the size of the Workers' Gymnasium. The carefully controlled volume and lack of audience participation robbed this crucial opening number of the bite and vitality which the group had not unreasonably expected. Suddenly, the boys looked terribly vulnerable.

The realization that this was indeed the toughest performing assignment of their lives was reinforced by the lack of teenage female fans, who were considerably outnumbered by older males. Unlike the usual screaming hordes, this mature discerning audience seemed intent on dissecting every note of Wham's unique performance. After months of unrelenting and unbridled fan hysteria, this was a novel but chilling experience for George Michael. As a young, dynamic performer, he had grown accustomed to intense displays of female adulation and noisy partisanship from his audience. Although he was aware of the cultural chasm between China and the West, it was still difficult not to misinterpret the audience's apparently cool response for genuine disapproval. To make matters worse, the first few rows of seats consisted of privileged middle aged Chinese officials who, from a distance, resembled waxwork mannequins. When the myopic George scrutinized the front row, he met the piercing eyes of Xiao Hua, probably the only 70 year-old ever to attend a Wham! concert. For one terrible moment, it seemed that the generative conflict dramatized in "Young Guns" was about to be realized on a Peking stage. The boys' fears about their communicative performing powers might have been assuaged had they known of the public warnings and large police presence which effectively lulled their audience into a state of safe serenity. Instead,

Wham! moved rapidly through another five songs, masking their nerves with a performance that was competent but decidedly wooden.

While Wham! consoled themselves with a relaxing ten minute break, George's sexy "Careless Whisper" video was screened amid much uncomfortable shuffling of seats. Backstage, the boys psyched themselves up for a more enthusiastic second half during which they determined to demolish the wall of obdurate Chinese apathy. Although the Peking audience had been largely confused and mesmerized by strobe lights, scantily dressed backing singers and pulsating beat music, there were small pockets of Western college students whose cheers gradually grew more vociferous. Wham! seemed to draw inspiration and energy from their response and during the second half they appeared revitalized, confident and relaxed. After overcoming some minor lighting problems, the group visibly loosened up and Andrew sauntered across the stage to utter a brief "xia xia" (thank you, thank you) before introducing "Freedom" with a cheekily worded plug for Western capitalism: "This is a number 1 hit in our country, and I hope that one day it will be number 1 in China with your help. It is called 'Freedom'." The boys might not have seemed so assured had they considered that the ageing Chinese officials were the only members of the audience blessed with on the spot interpreters.

Although the majority of the audience obeyed tradition and remained firmly seated and stony silent, the pro-Wham! lobby managed to encourage nearly one hundred youths to stand up and voice their appreciation. From the stage apron, George and Andrew could clearly distinguish the pleasing spectacle of grinning fans with arms raised aloft to display their full colour Wham! programmes. Unfortunately, the security officers took a dimmer view of this unexpected display of adulation and proceeded to pacify several of their countrymen, though their efforts were greeted with loud jeers. One teenager who ignored police requests to extinguish a cigarette soon found himself in a scuffle and was eventually placed under arrest. For Xiao Hua and his colleagues, this must have seemed like an unprecedented act of defiance.

The historic concert ended as punctually as it had begun and in keeping with Chinese tradition, there was no encore. As the masses headed for the exit doors, a linguistically talented journalist from *The Times* succeeded in interviewing several recalcitrant young fans, including Chien Jingling, a 28 year-old cook who had successfully defied the police throughout the show. His views and public behaviour, though anathema to the ears of Chinese officials, must have warmed the entrepreneurial heart of Simon Napier-Bell:

> I feel very good and very free. The cost of the ticket was nothing in view of the experience. We should have more such performances.

That spirit of rock'n'roll rebellion apparently extended to Xiao Hua, the elderly Vice Chairman of the Chinese People's Consultative Conference, who was credited with the dubious words: "It is the best political step since the signing of the treaty in Hong Kong." His apocryphal praise bore the distinctive tongue-in-cheek flippancy of a wily Fleet Street tabloid caption writer. More sober observers came closer to the truth in pointing out that Xiao Hua had sat stone faced throughout the proceedings. Indeed, it was only the deputy foreign minister, Zhou Nan, who showed some enthusiasm during the show, smiling occasionally and exchanging pleasantries with the British Ambassador, Sir David Evans. Other Chinese officials were more curt, and as one astutely noted: "I think shows like this contain certain aspects which do not suit our present condition." It was not too difficult to locate these pejorative "certain elements" which had caused the officials such consternation. The provocative dress of Wham! certainly raised a few eyebrows, particularly when Michael appeared barechested beneath his jacket and the girls took the stage clad in black leather skirts, slit to the thigh. Even the censured "Careless Whisper" video had elicited murmers of disapproval, but it was the audience response which caused greatest concern. It was always clear that anything less than exemplary behaviour would weigh heavily against any possible future tours, and the Chinese fans were officially deemed "over enthusiastic". The scuffles with police and the single unfortunate arrest proved embarrassing enough to jam the doors which Wham! had boasted of opening in China.

Although Wham! had been made to feel like major stars in Peking, the media response to their historic concert was ominously quiet. The only newspaper to mention the performance was the English language *China Daily* which carried a heavily censored Reuters report, omitting all references to police intervention during the show. Rather more amusing was the New China News Agency which briefly mentioned 10,000 people attending a concert given by the "well known British Wham electronic orchestra". It was left to George Michael to sum up the Peking concert in a philosophical but disillusioned tone:

> There is a huge cultural difference which there is no way you are going to cross in an hour and a half . . . I turned my microphone down. I didn't do anything particularly sexy which is not my usual angle . . . We noticed the police were very nervous about the possibility of everyone joining in. But I wonder what they could have expected. They know we're a dance band.

As the Wham! entourage prepared to leave Peking, the management spoke candidly about their financial losses. With pocket calculators to hand, British news reporters reckoned the deficit at between £1-1.4 million. Several claimed that these liberal figures were exclusive of the filming fees which were equally astronomical. In reality, the complete tour, *including* filming and related expenses did not exceed a million pounds, as Napier-Bell now admits. Nevertheless, there were a number of service charges, hidden extras and backhanders which caused considerable annoyance. Prior to the Peking concert, for example, Wham's management were approached by an official demanding an additional £1,700 fee with the attendant threat: "If you don't pay, your equipment won't be allowed to be moved off stage". Even the projected documentary filming hit a few unforeseen snags when the authorities demanded an additional $100,000 on the grounds that 35mm film was being used. Reluctantly, the film crew switched to 16mm, in order to avoid the charge while continuing their work. The cumulative hidden charges provoked many witty comments from members of the Wham! entourage who generally agreed that the Chinese could teach the West a few tricks about mercenary capitalism. Jazz Summers' wry rejoinder to sympathetic newsmen was quickly translated into a cheeky headline: "The Chinese have taken us to the cleaners."

Although there was still one big concert to play in Canton, the general mood of the party suggested that the Wham! boys were slowly winding down from their protracted period on the road. Only a couple of Fleet Street reporters remained for the final leg of the tour which seemed destined to end in anti-climax. The entourage had a haggard look and several bore the scars of a punishingly long campaign. Keyboard player, Mark Fisher, had collapsed from exhaustion while taking a shower in Hong Kong and famed director Lindsay Anderson had fallen from the Great Wall of China and was now confined to a wheelchair. Only George, Andrew and their managers retained the stamina to stomach more interviews and personal appearances in Peking, so the attendant retinue booked themselves on an earlier flight to the refuge of Canton. Ironically, it was not the publicity-seeking Napier-Bell nor his over exposed young proteges who captured the following day's headlines but those weary, sepulchral backing musicians, ferociously attentive security officers and perpetually harassed road managers who even now, trooped towards the departure lounge of Peking Airport unaware that one of their number was about to reveal the hidden talents of a media pyrotechnist.

The strange and dramatic episode that was played out aboard CAA Flight 1301 on the afternoon of 8 April 1985 effectively transformed the tail end of the tour into the most spectacular display of tabloid mass hysteria since the invasion of the Falklands. Even that master of hype Simon Napier-Bell could not have devised such an unintentionally ingenious publicity grabbing exercise nor anticipated the sensationalist response from *every* Fleet Street paper. For once, fact and fiction, the serious and the salacious, were indistinguishable amid the twin hyperbole of *Sun* speak and *Times* highbrow.

The drama began innocently enough with the Wham! entourage settling down for a pleasant, uneventful flight to Canton. At the rear of the flight cabin, Wham! backing singers Shirlie Holliman and Pepsi De Manque, were seated next to their Portuguese trumpeter, Raul De Oliviera. He had been acting rather moodily during the previous couple of days but such behaviour was by no means unexpected on such a long and arduous tour.

As the plane ascended, Raul appeared to be muttering something to himself. Ten minutes later, he was screaming his lungs out and writhing in agony in his seat. As his screeching sobs grew louder, adjacent passengers noticed a pen-knife in his hand poised precariously close to his stomach. Fearing that the man was about to plunge the weapon into himself, Wham's security officers, Dave Moulder and Benny Collins, burst into action. As stewards vainly attempted to console startled passengers, the burly duo overpowered the bemused trumpeter and released the knife from his grip. His manic strength proved so overwhelming that they could barely restrain him from breaking loose and were eventually forced to pin him down by his arms and neck. Throughout the struggle, his eerie-sounding sobs grew more demonic, like a man possessed. Even the calmer passengers now shifted nervously in their seats, fearing for their own safety. Meanwhile, Shirlie and Pepsi found their exit blocked by the fracas and cowered in a corner like terrified children. Suddenly, without warning, the plane rapidly plunged downwards, while the screaming continued incessantly.

Within minutes, the relieved passengers found themselves back on the Peking Airport runway, shaken but safe. When the plane doors finally opened, a doctor was hurried through to administer an anaesthetic to the overwrought trumpeter. In one final moment of black comedy, the demented Oliviera grasped his precious trumpet and attempted to play "The Legion's Last Patrol" as he was quickly led away. Seconds later, he was carted off in an ambulance to the psychiatric ward of a local hospital. It was difficult to believe that the entire scenario was not some ingeniously bizarre Simon Napier-Bell publicity stunt, but the condition of Raul De Oliviera left no doubt about the chilling reality of his sudden breakdown.

From a crude publicity angle, De Oliviera's outburst could not have happened at a more fortuitous moment. Public interest in Wham's Chinese escapades had waned considerably in the wake of saturation media coverage. The reports that filtered through to the offices of tired editors seemed passe and pedestrian, and it was generally agreed that the "revolutionary" aspects of the tour had been done to death. Weary journalists, unable to gain exclusive interviews with the pop star duo, found themselves being spoon-fed exaggerated stories about the costs and logistics of the tour. After a stormy start with George's dubious "crack-up" revelations, the Wham! management now had Fleet Street firmly under its thumb. Having milked the media dry, Napier-Bell could even afford to dismiss those tabloids that had paid good money to accompany the Wham! entourage. Their services were no longer needed and in their hearts they knew that there was little more to be said.

The De Oliviera debacle altered that perspective and suddenly transformed the docile puppies of Fleet Street into a rout of ravenous, razor-toothed wolves. Free from their uncomfortable role as public relations fodder, this pack of press hounds turned on their erstwhile masters and gleefully despatched front page bulletins which threatened to embarrass Wham! and transform their mission of diplomacy into a catalogue of disaster. The quality of the coverage notwithstanding, one fact was certain – Wham! were back in the news and would remain there for the duration of the tour.

The ever sensationalist *Sun* summed up the hysterical reaction of Fleet Street editors with a bold and arresting headline: "Wham! Man In Hara-Kiri Terror". Like most of their competitors, they transformed the De Oliviera episode into a gothic horror tale, guaranteed to enliven the breakfast tables of their multitudinous readership. Significantly, the Wham! scam replaced what would have been another provocative headline detailing the recent exploits of Culture Club's fallen hero: "Boy George Gives £14,000 To Aids Probe". Even in the realm of undesirable publicity, the recalcitrant Boy could no longer compete effectively with the self-generating publicity machine surrounding Wham!

In the fiercely competitive rush for an exclusive account of the De Oliviera incident, it was the *Star's* Rick Sky who reached the hero of the hour. Dave Moulder, the Wham! minder who had successfully restrained the manic trumpeter, provided Sky's readers with a scintillating on the spot report:

> Raul went off his rocker. He was screaming and foaming at the mouth. No one was sure what was going on, and we were very frightened. He was hallucinating and seemed to be in a trance. He thought he was possessed by the devil and was dying.

The Star's rivals replied with more tales of *hara-kiri*, stabbing and diabolism, all of which were ridiculously exaggerated. It soon transpired that Raul's self-inflicted stab wound was nothing more than a superficial graze. Other reports, filed by desperate journalists urgently seeking a new angle, alleged that De Oliviera had broken into the pilots' cockpit, hijacked the plane and caused the aircraft to plunge a thousand feet before being overpowered by Wham's personal bodyguard. Reading some of the reports, the impression conveyed was that the Wham! entourage barely escaped a major air disaster. While such sensationalist journalism was to be expected from the cutthroat tabloids, it is interesting to note that *The Daily Telegraph*, *The Guardian* and *The Times* were almost equally inventive in their approaches. *The Daily Telegraph* with its tabloid style headline "Wham! Man Goes Berserk" speculated at some length on the "stabbing" incident, but ultimately emerged as the most accurate and credible of the many reports. Interestingly, it was the only paper that immediately concerned itself with the after effects of Raul's breakdown and correspondent Hugh Davies abandoned the sensationalist style of his rivals in favour of a frank and prosaic appraisal from no less a dignitary than the Portuguese Ambassador Antonio Leal De Costa Lobo, who opined: "He seemed to have recovered from the incident. His injury was not serious. He explained to me that he had not had much sleep for four nights and was under tremendous stress."

Surprisingly, Britain's two other "highbrow" papers merely seemed to follow the tabloids' lead. In a report titled "Trumpeter Whams Himself", *The Guardian* informed its readers "He wanted to commit *hara-kiri*." The oft-repeated *hara-kiri* quote, originally used by *The Sun*, was allegedly elicited from a particularly suspect source – "a diplomat who declined to be named". Finally, the traditionally least sensationalist of all the Fleet Street papers, *The Times*, entered the fray with a questionable headline ("Plane scare as Wham! man stabs himself") followed by some highly dubious assertions which implied that the hapless trumpeter had almost unwittingly caused an air calamity: "He went bananas. He went in the cockpit. The plane dived."

Although Wham! had encountered problems with the Street of Shame in recent times, the reporting of the De Oliviera affair was unique. For once, both the tabloid and highbrow press were virtually indistinguishable in their respective approaches, and left several conflicting accounts unanswered. Ironically, it was the soaraway *Sun*, arguably the newspaper least renowned for mundane accuracy, which elected to elicit some response from the one genuinely unfortunate victim of the media ballyhoo. Their exclusive interview with Raul De Oliviera contained the obligatory sensationalist trappings but allowed the maligned musician to place the incident in a much clearer perspective. In the article, humorously titled "I Am Not Off My Rocker Says Wham! Star", the embarrassed trumpeter explained his dismay about the episode and countered previous reports with a scathing dismissal: "It's untrue I went off my rocker". And I never thought I was possessed by the Devil. It's a joke". However, Raul admitted that he had no memory of what occurred during the flight, so it was impossible to discredit Dave Moulder's vivid and highly entertaining account printed earlier. What emerged most clearly from the piece, however, was the intense pressure that the backing musicians had felt during the long tour and the insidious way in which constant travelling and lack of sleep can undermine the stability of even the most professional players. Fortunately, De Oliviera recovered quickly and has since demonstrated his durability by backing a number of pop stars, most notably, Elton John.

By the time the Wham! entourage reached Canton, their morale was at a low ebb. De Oliviera's breakdown had undermined their confidence and prompted misgivings about the political nature of the tour. What had begun as an exciting trip into unchartered territories suddenly seemed void of fun and relevance. Although the media had rekindled flickering public interest in spectacular fashion, few readers were aware of the omnipresent lethargy that had enveloped the entourage. In a rare moment of public introspection, a crestfallen Shirlie Holliman poured out her heart to a writer from the teenzine *Smash Hits*:

I just think what we're doing here is bad. I don't want to sound funny or anything but I just don't think it's right that we're playing here. People here are sad, they want freedom but they're not allowed to have it, and, in a way, we're giving them a taste of something they can't really have. I just think it was awful the way that boy was taken out of last night's concert and beaten. That wouldn't have happened if we hadn't come here. It was just so sad. I just want to go home.

Even the resilient George Michael, whose lust for pop star fame had once seemed insatiable, reiterated much of Holliman's world weariness in an uncharacteristically revealing aside:

We've been on the road for 15 months. It's enough. It's all very well being told we can't rest up because we're the world's number 1 band. This is a dangerous period. We have to get out of the headlines – have a low profile. Then it's going to be a long rest.

Although their intense schedule theoretically allowed Wham! two free days in Canton, the presence of film cameras, press photographers and prying journalists ensured that there was little chance of any much needed privacy. Intrigued by the prospect of observing everyday life in Canton, the Wham! entourage toured the market-places but soon became nauseated by the sight of headless cats, skinned dogs and other local delicacies. With their Western sensibilities grossly offended by the unexpected poverty of the working-class Cantonese, the Wham! retinue returned to their hotel and blotted out recent memories by indulging themselves in an all night party. Their forced revelry merely served to increase their lethargy and remind them of the numbing mindlessness frequently produced by over-extensive touring.

The following day provided a much needed therapeutic release in the form of a soccer match between the musicians and road crew. Even with the cameras rolling, the boys took full advantage of the opportunity to relinquish the mantle of pop star fame and pretend that they were still care-free kids kicking a football across the playground of Bushey Meads School. The delusion proved frustratingly ephemeral for within hours Wham! were attending another official welcoming banquet, making brief obsequious speeches and suffering the bland entertainment of a Cantonese cabaret star. The next morning they had a well deserved lie-in.

While Wham! slept soundly in their beds, Simon Napier-Bell and Jazz Summers were conducting a press conference, the subject of which added a fresh dimension to the Chinese tour. It was revealed that a selection of Wham! recordings were to be rush released in China, and even more amazingly, the group had been placed on a full scale royalty. The historic deal involved a contractual tie-up between Nomis, CBS Records, the Chinese Cultural Exchange Centre and a Hong Kong company, International Yamagen. The recording package consisted of two tape releases, the first comprising selections from *Fantastic* and *Make It Big*. This was to be followed a fortnight later by an intriguing compendium cassette containing five Wham! recordings and five cover versions by China's leading female pop singer, Cheng Fang Yuen. With an initial tape run of 600,000, it was expected that the recordings would rapidly sell out and repeat orders exceed the million mark within a matter of months. Seemingly, the only loser in this capitalist conglomerate was the chirpy Miss Yuen whose contribution to the Chinese economy netted her a paltry £15 a week standard wage. The Wham! boys were reportedly so embarrassed by this financial anomaly that they magnanimously offered the girl an unsolicited one per cent commission. It still sounded like peanuts, but compared to her £15 a week salary represented a sizeable increase in income. At the end of the press conference, Napier-Bell proudly proclaimed: "We have set a fantastic precedent."

Suddenly, all the long term plans concerning oriental cultural enrichment were placed in an apparently clearer economic perspective. For the first time during the tour, Wham's management were effectively admitting that the concerts were primarily a promotional device to secure this all important deal. However, it would later transpire that this was yet further obfuscation, designed to distract journalistic attention from a more remote and important geographical goldmine.

The remainder of the tour was surprisingly relaxed and free from the uncomfortable glare of Chinese officials. Film cameras still dogged the pop duo's every move, following them into saunas and stage managing a *tete a tete* with Cheng Fang Yuen, but George and Andrew appeared oblivious to their presence. The knowledge that the concert at Canton's Zhongshan Memorial Hall signalled the end of their visit revitalized their spirits and pumped fresh adrenalin into weary limbs. The fear of a lackadaisical audience response was considerably alleviated by the knowledge that Canton was far more susceptible to Western cultural influence than China's capital city. Any lingering doubts about the conquest of Canton were put to rest as early as the opening number of the show when hordes of screaming fans stood up in unison. Although police activity was once more in evidence, it was clear that the Cantonese fans could not be restrained from expressing their feelings. By the second half of the concert, a contingent of wailing female fans controlled the centre of the hall, encouraging others to join them in a mass celebration of Wham! hysteria. Seizing the moment, George Michael concentrated all his efforts on maintaining their frenzy and in a spectacular finale of hit songs ended Wham's Eastern mission on a note of unexpected triumph.

The hyperbole that had followed Wham! across the world continued upon their return to the U.K., but the myths of cultural conquest and victorious Western marketing gradually grew more threadbare and unconvincing. Wham! themselves had sown the seeds of doubt in a series of scathing references to China's backwardness and hypocrisy. George Michael, in an interview with *The Face*, launched into a long tirade about

the mealy-mouthed materialism of Chinese political leaders, the ineffec-
tuality of the government in caring for the environment and the unholy
stink of corruption and greed in almost every conceivable sphere of
influence. His self-righteous condemnation culminated in a bitter acceptance of China's own fallibility in mistaking the exploited for the exploiter:

> The basic reason for going to China was to introduce our wonderful
> culture. It was to *do* something . . . Just for once it was nice that you
> were the first and quite possibly the last. There is a certain privilege
> attached to that. But once we got there I just thought the whole thing
> was a shambles. What was basically going on was that the Chinese
> government was trying to encourage the Western world to accept
> Chinese product. They were saying "Look we have our arms open, we
> are going to accept Western music." That was total bollocks. They used
> us. We were a propaganda item.

In case any Chinese officials happened to be reading his comments,
Michael ended with a clench-toothed promise: "I'd never go there again".
Wham! colleague, Andrew Ridgeley, was equally undiplomatic, dismissing
the entire tour as "a pain in the arse". His forceful attack on Chinese
communism, reported in *Smash Hits*, was sufficiently insulting to preclude
the likelihood of an imminent return visit:

> We were so controlled in what we did and what we saw, it was difficult
> to see what the place was really like. It just seemed really oppressive.
> And the people seemed really lazy. Chinese people outside China always
> do really well for themselves and work really hard. But there . . . there
> just isn't any incentive. All the joys of life we take for granted, they've
> simply been taken from them. And the Chinese authorities, for all this
> talk of socialism, were the biggest bunch of capitalists and mercenaries
> we've ever come across.

The scornful disillusionment of Ridgeley and Michael contrasted
sharply with the final splutterings of the publicity machine which auto-
matically reiterated Wham's triumph in China. Beyond the tabloid hysteria
and obsequious profiles of the serious press, however, there lurked the
growing suspicion that Wham's cultural mission had been in vain. A per-
ceptive article in *Music Week* transcended the hype to ask a pointed
question about the relevance of the tour: "Is China Ready For Pop?" A
hard look at the results of the expedition suggests that it was not.

The pipe dream of a nationwide Western pop infiltration ignored the
stark reality of Chinese geography. Covering an area two thousand miles
north to south and four thousand miles east to west would likely result in
such enormous overheads that the populace could not afford the product
on offer, even assuming a foreign company would finance the operation.
That problem was in itself compounded by the fact that large numbers of
the Chinese population live in rural areas, often several hundred miles

from a big city. Napier-Bell's promising lightning demographic survey had highlighted the potential number of record buyers but ignored the crucial consideration of where they actually lived. Even assuming that transportational headaches could be overcome, the conversion of the Chinese to pop remained an improbable proposition. Western marketing strategies seemed virtually non-applicable, for even the record shops were so tiny that it was impossible to erect posters or advertisements. The virulent apathy shown towards television and the press also suggested that a larger financial outlay in those areas would be economically suicidal. Behind all these important considerations lay a further stumbling block in the inscrutable politics of the Chinese government which continued to vacillate between anti-bourgeois Left wing morality and pro-Western liberalist reforms. The attitude displayed towards Wham! and their product was at best lukewarm with mild criticisms voiced alongside cautiously approving whispers.

Within weeks of Wham's departure, the general consensus appeared to be that China would have a long wait before the next Western pop group arrived. Remarkably, the most sober commentator on the implications of the tour was Jonathan Morrish, head of Epic's press department, who, in a voice void of public relations partisanship, exposed the absurdity of equating Wham! with a "cultural revolution":

> Just because Wham! have performed there does not necessarily mean that the country in a year's time will be full of English groups releasing product there. You cannot expect a country that has distanced itself from the rest of the world for years to become Westernized overnight. The country is like a giant awakening from a sleep and nobody really knows which way it's going to turn.

For Wham!, it must have seemed that the giant had slumped into a state of permanent somnolism. As the months passed, there was no further media feedback on Wham's recorded output in China nor any news of their much touted film originally mooted for "imminent" transmission on Channel 4 to be followed by commercial availability in selected retail outlets. In fact, the video was held back until the summer of 1986, by which time Napier-Bell was sceptical about its profitability. There will no doubt be a much longer wait before Wham! or any other group capitalize on the Eastern visit, though Napier-Bell still insists that China has not turned a deaf ear to pop:

> The record industry saw that China was a viable territory to move into. There were a lot of repercussions. We now have records released in China. I've just set up a deal where CBS will be the first American company to have their own record company in China. I admit they won't have any rock groups playing there in the foreseeable future, but they don't object to the music. They object to the "dangerous" rapport a large group will have with an audience. As long as it doesn't offend their morals and there aren't videos of naked girls, they're perfectly

happy for pop music to come into China. I've been back thirteen times since we played there and a lot of records are beginning to get released.

Napier-Bell's prognosis sounds characteristically over-optimistic and begs the awkward question: "Was it all worthwhile?" The media has waxed lyrical about cultural breakthroughs and potentially vast record sales but the entire rationale behind the tour still sounds extremely odd. Given that Wham's avowed intention was to establish themselves as an internationally successful and extremely wealthy pop group their ludicrously expensive China mission seems like an inexplicably indulgent aberration. Pop group managers are not noted for their altruism and even though Wham! themselves have contributed towards starving Ethiopians and downtrodden miners, it strains my credulity to the utmost that they would willingly finance a tour primarily to assist the ailing capitalist British pop industry. It is all very well extolling the virtues of cultural enrichment and revolutionizing the British music industry by prising open obscure foreign territories, but such marketing exercises should surely be the prerogative of music business corporations and speculators with heavy organizational interests rather than an aspiring young pop group.

Even if Wham! singlehandedly had paved the way for rapacious Western record companies, their rewards were likely to be minimal. At best, it would have taken several years to mastermind a "cultural/marketing revolution" and by that time Wham! would have split or found themselves playing second fiddle to new, younger pop heroes. So why spend valuable time and huge sums of money opening up new markets for the benefit of record companies and future pop idols? That was a question that none of the hysterical tabloids even bothered to consider.

My own theory was that Napier-Bell and Wham! were pursuing the China trail largely for publicity, ego gratification and the hope of establishing their name in remote foreign territories. From the latter they might at least accrue some revenue via record sales and publishing, though even these sums hardly merited such a costly campaign. All things considered, the trip seemed an extremely worthwhile venture, but somewhat out of character for a group and manager intent on achieving an easy profit alongside international success. However, it now transpires that there *was* an unexpected sting in the tail, for the tour apparently had relatively little to do with cultural enrichment or foreign sales. Napier-Bell presently argues that, contrary to spoonfed newspaper reports, the tour was a red-herring employed to exploit Wham! product in a far bigger market on the opposite side of the planet:

You don't go around saying *why* you really did it! When people asked me what I thought of it all I told them it was marvellous, it was a challenge, it was great to help the music industry into new territories. But, actually, to tell you the truth, it was a publicity stunt. What the hell do you think it was?! It was a rather classier one than getting on page three

of *The Sun* with a nude standing beside you. It was a classy way to get
Wham! attention and get them known. Of course, in the course of setting it up one does get taken in by one's own publicity. But it was
designed as a major image-building stunt to shove Wham! into the
American consciousness. In the process of doing that I realized I was
opening up a territory to the world and doing something commercially
for the music industry which was important. But I don't want to get all
pious about it. That wasn't why I thought it up or why I did it.

In retrospect, Napier-Bell argues that Wham's silent invasion of
America was the culmination of an elaborately orchestrated campaign
engineered several years before its subtle execution:

The whole point of the China trip was how to break yourself in America
without three years of touring, press and photographers. How, in one
fell swoop, you could dodge three years' hard work. That's how it was
devised. When we sat down and planned Wham's three year trip to the
top of the music business we realized the problem with America.
There's no national press and therefore they're not susceptible to image-
building in the English sense. A Top 10 hit depends on music and
endless touring. At least three 60 day tours is the quickest anybody's
done it, whether you're talking about Madonna, Billy Idol or anyone
else going back to the Beatles. In fact, only the Beatles did it nationally
without touring. Nowadays, touring requires doing interviews every
single day, having photographs taken and talking to local radio stations.
And George wouldn't do it. He wanted to be top, but not as much as he
didn't want to do all that. Which is fair enough. It's his decision and I
can understand. With that kind of schedule you have to have a personality that likes promotion, or at least doesn't mind. It's probably worse
to do it if your personality isn't like that otherwise you'll end up being
rude to people. So we had to sit down and decide how to dodge that
three years of slogging around America.

The plan, of course, required a stunt which would guarantee Wham!
worldwide newspaper headlines for a relatively long period of time. Simon
maintains that the China hype fulfilled all those aims and broke America in
a fashion beyond the imagination of Frankie Goes To Hollywood, Culture
Club and their ilk:

In America, people will know the song and maybe the name but they
won't really be aware of the face. So I had the idea of making Wham! the
first pop group to play in China. It took a year to set up and it was pretty
miraculous that I pulled it off. But we got press all over the world. In the
U.S., we were on ABC, CBS and NBC national news every day for a
week. After that week only Reagan was better known in America. In one
week we achieved what should have taken three years.

Simon Napier-Bell is so deliberately obfuscating at times that it is difficult to decide whether his retrospective comments are not merely another smart attempt to re-write history to his own advantage. Whether the Wham! scam in China was quite as intricately planned as he now argues, there is no denying the success of the campaign in magnifying their profile in the States. However, it is by no means unlikely that Wham! would have achieved spectacular success in America regardless of the China tour. With two number ones behind them and a particularly ambitious plan already germinating in Jazz Summers' brain, the three year trip to international fame would probably have been foreshortened in any case. Nevertheless, Napier-Bell's oblique strategy, whether wholly genuine or partly exaggerated, consumately achieved its stated aim. Wham! are, without doubt, the only group in pop history to set forth on an expedition to China in order to conquer the United States.

From One Stadium To Another

With the triumph and misery of China still reverberating around the Nomis office, Wham! announced their inclusion in the epoch-making *Live Aid* extravaganza. The "global jukebox" brought together the most commercially successful acts in the world in a combined effort to relieve famine-plagued Ethiopia. Wham's contribution was brief, but memorable. They were ushered on to the stage by their old friend, Elton John, and George repaid that compliment by singing a surprisingly effective version of the piano player's 1974 hit "Don't Let The Sun Go Down On Me", with Ridgeley and Kiki Dee on backing vocals. For some time, Elton John had been taking an almost fatherly interest in George Michael, complimenting his songwriting prowess at the Ivor Novello awards and later appearing backstage at his U.S. concerts. Several months after "Live Aid", Michael took time off to sing on John's hit "Wrap Her Up" and the press hinted that further collaborations were likely in the future.

With China and Live Aid behind them, Wham! were psychologically equipped to deal with the pressures of performing before vast stadium audiences in the States. Although the U.S. invasion seemed like a logical development in Wham's bid for world domination, it came about more from accident than design. Originally conceived by Napier-Bell and Summers as an easy way of exploiting the duo's MTV popularity, the idea received a cool response from American promoters and agents. When Jazz pleaded the case Stateside, he was dismissed as naive, inexperienced and, frankly, quite crazy. Overweight impresarios took great pleasure in lecturing him on how to break a group: "You've got to do the club circuit twice, the concert halls three times, the small halls four times and then you can do stadiums, like Springsteen." When Summers protested that those days were gone, and argued that Wham! could easily pull regular crowds of 40,000 plus, jaded promoters raised their eyes skyward and deadpanned: "Who do you think you are – The Beatles?"

Summers' ambitious plans took a further blow upon returning to England. The previously enthusiastic Napier-Bell suddenly seemed less certain about the practicality of a stadium tour and the boys themselves showed scant interest. On a number of occasions, Jazz took George Michael aside and told him "For your future, whether you're with Wham! or whether you're not, you must go out onstage and play to as many people as possible. If you don't make your presence felt, Wham! will only be regarded as a radio or MTV pop band." Michael listened, but remained largely unmoved by the persuasive nagging. Eventually, a general meeting was held at Napier-Bell's house in Bryanston Square. There, for an entire evening, the powerful "Wham! Committee" sat to discuss Summers' proposals.

Looking back at Wham's history, it is clear that most commentators completely misunderstood, or neglected to consider, the way in which the group ran their business affairs. The press, fed on a regular diet of breast-beating PR, generally assumed that Napier-Bell was the Svengali brain behind Wham!, with George Michael fighting an impressive rearguard action to maintain the group's integrity and independence. In reality, the Wham! committee was a six man quorum, comprising the boys, Simon and Jazz, and Morrison/Leahy. The music publishers were actively involved in every managerial decision and their influence in swaying a proposal was powerful indeed. Unfortunately for Summers, neither Leahy nor Morrison was convinced by his arguments and the motion seemed doomed to defeat. The former radiographer was still insisting he was right, and refusing to compromise on the issue, when his partner joined the anti-stadium lobby. Jazz recalls the complex group dynamics in a revelatory comment about his Nomis partner:

> Simon looked around that room, saw George and Andrew, Dick and Bryan, and me and himself. Four people said they didn't want to do it. I said I did. So he went with the majority. That's his personality. That's the way he runs his life. And it can work very well that way because if you keep going like that you're always there when opinions and decisions are being made and it'll work. If you go my way, it's brick walls all the time, but when it comes through, it comes through big.

With a majority of five to one against, Summers needed a miracle to break down this particular brick wall of resistance. His prayers were answered later that evening when news filtered through from the States of an unusual story concerning Wham!

In Miami, a radio station had announced that Wham! would be appearing at a local venue and the box office was besieged with requests for tickets. Tentative arrangements were made and the venue sold 30,000 tickets in a weekend, without advertising. The overwhelming public response convinced Jazz that his stadium dream could be realized, and even the redoubtable Dick Leahy relented when the full implications of those statistics sank in. From the verge of defeat, Summers' US stadium extravaganza had become a reality.

Wham! commenced their American tour with the confidence and security of three *Billboard* number 1 hits behind them. They played before a total of 310,000 people, in eight shows, spread across a gruelling twelve days. The itinerary took in Chicago, Philadelphia, Miami, San Francisco and Los Angeles, and along the way Wham! enjoyed the support of a number of famous acts including The Pointer Sisters, Sister Sledge, Chaka Khan and Katrina and The Waves. Ironically, it was Miami, source of that miraculous ticket stampede, which almost played host to a Wham! disaster. The show itself had proven extremely successful and the entire entourage retired to a nearby nightclub to celebrate their latest triumph. There, dreadlocked bassist, Deon Estes, began "chatting up" a girl at the bar, who inexplicably turned nasty and produced a revolver from her handbag. Conversations stopped and expressions froze as the mysterious girl began waving the weapon in the general direction of the seated entourage. The Wham! duo stared helplessly, no doubt feeling that a sensational pop assassination was a distinct possibility. Fortunately, the over excitable young lady was eventually relieved of her weapon by a tactful Wham! minder, but the incident was not forgotten and security was tightened up following future shows.

Back in Britain, tabloid headlines proclaimed "Wham! Flop In America", a view based solely on the evidence of one cancelled performance. The real trouble in the States was not the size of the crowds, but the attitude of the performers. George Michael was disillusioned by the falseness and sycophancy thrust upon the group, and following a round of social and business engagements, he quipped: "If you want to get to the top in America, you have to compromise to the very end".

One area of compromise strenuously resisted was the continual requests for more money from the backing crew. Musical director Tommy Eyre quit in disgust three days before the end of the tour complaining: "We had to fight for every penny". Eyre evidently resented the boys travelling first class and staying in palatial hotels while the backing musicians suffered economy travel and two-bit hostelries. Vocalist Pepsi De Manque had made similar criticisms of the accommodation in Los Angeles, but blamed bad organization rather than the boys. For Eyre, a much respected session player who began his career as a member of Joe Cocker's Grease Band in the 60s, high expectations outweighed rewards and he wryly observed that the only thank-you gifts Wham! foisted upon their loyal backing crew were a £5 t-shirt and a souvenir programme. Yet, his hurt seemed as much emotional as financial. "They didn't even bother to say goodbye" was his surprisingly poignant cry at the end of the tour. In retrospect, part of this indignation stemmed from the excessive publicity given to Wham's extravagance and generosity. Their charitable donations, nightclubbing exploits and willingness to scrap horrendously expensive video sessions, simply because George's hair was out of place, suggested that they had money to burn. In truth, the Wham! boys kept a firm hold on the purse strings and although this was far from unusual among children of the New Pop, older musicians clearly expected a more luxurious passage. Once more, it seemed, Wham's ostentatious media image had unexpectedly backfired.

One of the songs George Michael composed on an internal flight across the States was rush released in November. Lyrically, "I'm Your Man" was probably his most banal composition to date, but it was a reasonable pop melody and showed Wham! back on the upbeat. As it soared to the top a few angry American parents claimed that the accompanying black and white promotional video contained a subliminal message flashed across the screen. And the message was "sex".

Sex, and the problems of fame, loomed large in George Michael's life towards the end of 1985. For the past two years, the popular press had done Wham! to death and at last the effects were beginning to show. Although the boys initially had encouraged media scrutiny and attempted to beat the press at their own game, they were gradually worn down by the sheer weight of unwelcome column inches. Ridgeley somehow thrived on all this pressure and took an almost perverse delight in continuing to "crash" racing cars and drink the night away in fashionable clubs, while photographers clicked merrily away and journalists concocted ever more unlikely tales of debauchery and grossly offensive behaviour. George Michael had been spared such bad press, though the *paparazzi* kept a keen eye on his movements in the vain hope of unearthing some steamy, surreptitious love affair. It was now virtually impossible to go anywhere without being recognized or followed, so Michael became more withdrawn and tended to stay at home in his Knightsbridge flat working on his music.

By November 1985, even Nomis was showing concern over George's unhappiness with his public image. Since his critical castigation at the Miners' Benefit, Michael had vowed never to deal with the serious music press again. Initially, this policy worked to his advantage, for the tabloids were content with trivial PR fodder and the glossy weeklies took a sympathetic and occasionally sycophantic view of his life and works. All that was missing was "serious" criticism and respect. By his own choosing, George Michael had been reduced to the level of a vacuous teen idol, whose much vaunted songwriting and musical talent had been overshadowed completely by the image mongering of Wham! What he needed was a sympathetic hearing from one of the most serious and influential music papers in the country. Jazz decided to ignore circulation figures and risk a confrontation with the politically-minded *New Musical Express*:

We selected the *NME* interview because we knew of George's frustration in that he's only regarded as some pop star who won't last two months before he's gone like Kajagoogoo.

George Michael wasted little time in voicing his gripes and re-writing his image specifically for the *New Musical Express* readership:

Wham! don't need music press publicity any more but I need something where I'm written about intelligently, even if it's a slag off. I'm sick of people treating me like I've only got one brain cell and only three lines of conversation. I'm sick of being presented in one line quotes, and I'm sick of walking into rooms filled with complete strangers who have a totally wrong idea about me.

Reading between the lines, it sounded very much like George Michael was sick of being Wham!

The *New Musical Express* interviewer showed the expected tolerance and sympathy, training all his guns on the absent Andrew Ridgeley, who was dismissed as a "mobile vomit fountain" and an "ass". Summers had hoped that Ridgeley might also consider some serious press, for several journalists had agreed to talk frankly with him about his future plans as a racing driver and film star. But Andrew turned down all requests, seemingly content to continue getting stick from the tabloids. His supporters at the less serious glossies did manage a quick question and answer session and one of his comments proved particularly revelatory. When quizzed about his partner's personality, he suggested, "The nature of his work has dulled his sense of humour. Well not so much *dulled*, but he's not so carefree anymore. He's very singleminded these days. A lot of the things he used to like doing have been whittled away until all he does is music."

Clearly, one of the things that had been "whittled away" was his buccaneering exploits with Ridgeley. Whereas once they had been photographed almost exclusively together, it was now Andrew's sole exploits that provoked that familiar and unimaginative headline "Wham! Bam!" Whatever Wham! meant in the tabloid consciousness had been virtually inherited by the less musically talented of the duo.

Throughout 1985, there had been strong rumours that Wham! were splitting. Yet, there were also indications of new material forthcoming from the group. In the States, they had previewed another obvious hit single, "The Edge Of Heaven", plus an impressive cover of Was (Not Was)' "Where Did Your Heart Go?", which Michael was also threatening to release as a 45. A third number, "The Colour Of My Love", suggested that the group had about 40% of an album in reserve. The trouble was that George Michael also intended to record a solo album. He had been tinkering with a song called "Stephen" and had already cut a demo of "A Different Corner". A worried Jazz confided that his boy was finding it difficult writing two sets of songs simultaneously.

Although Summers dared not reveal the truth, a decision had already been made. George and Andrew confided that they were ending Wham! in 1986. They wanted to bury the group in spectacular fashion with a big show and a multi-million selling album. And if the songwriting commitments proved too much for George Michael, then the final record would be a double E.P.

The Great South African Disaster... And Its Aftermath

Wham's decision to disband came as no great shock to Napier-Bell and Summers. Since early 1985, George Michael had been complaining publicly about the pressures of superstardom and seemed sick of the intrusive presence of an unrestrained media circus. Napier-Bell had already confessed to *The Daily Mail* that a Wham! split would probably occur within two years, and, not surprisingly, Nomis was already making contingency plans. Chief amongst these was a delicate negotiation which promised to fulfil the company's original dream of establishing itself as the most powerful international management structure in British pop music history.

The ever approachable Napier-Bell regularly entertained plausible grey-suited businessmen from the City, whose ice-cool bonhomie was animated by the rhetoric of boardroom brinksmanship and boastful takeover offers which threatened to reduce Nomis' rivals to the stature of back street novices. Simon indulged these munificent Lucifers in endless exploratory discussions, but nothing was ever finalized. Summers, an infrequent visitor at these strangely urbane, but high powered, meetings, listened intently, but took an intuitive dislike to this unctuous band of gold-diggers, who spoke so nonchalantly of turning over millions of pounds at the touch of an intercom button. "It sounded crazy. All they were going to do was go in, make a fast buck at the Stock Exchange, go away, buy another box of cigars, and leave us carrying the baby."

In spite of his reservations, Summers conceded that the selling of Nomis to a public company would be the speediest and safest way of ensuring their ultimate goal. During a subsequent lunch date with Wham! promoter Harvey Goldsmith, Summers confided his dilemma and met with an alert and sympathetic response. With an air of rustic hospitality, Goldsmith abruptly suggested: "We'd be interested in acquiring you. We've just been taken over. We've got £15 million in the bank and we're expanding". Summers was immediately attracted by this unexpected and intriguing proposition, not least because of his admiration for the stocky, bearded promoter whose unaffected forthrightness had already won him the grudging respect of the music business community.

Harvey Goldsmith had worked his way up through the 70s to become one of the most successful concert promoters in the country. Along the way, he had experienced the related problems and rewards of music management, overseeing the affairs of a select number of artistes including Van Morrison, Billy Connolly and After The Fire. An indefatigable advocate of the entrepreneurial work ethic, Goldsmith also had a soft spot for charities. He had been heavily involved in the Kampuchian relief campaign, accompanying the saintly Joan Baez on her fund raising efforts and providing free administrative assistance. More recently, he had been made a trustee of Band Aid and played a crucial role in organizing the Live Aid spectacular. In every respect, he seemed a far more suitable partner than the anonymous men from the City.

Summers informed Napier-Bell of Goldsmith's interest in their company and a fruitful meeting soon followed. Perusing the promoter's recent track record, it was clear that his organization was developing along a similarly ambitious route to Nomis. In 1984, Harvey Goldsmith Enterprises had merged with Hotel Television Network Ltd. to form Allied Entertainments. Early the following year, Allied went public and in August was swallowed up by Kunick Leisure, owners of the London Dungeon. Goldsmith had agreed to Kunick's £6.7 million takeover, largely because he required their expertise and financial clout to fulfil his latest dream – the creation of a £100 million leisure complex in London's Dockland. Such a gargantuan project would have consumed the imagination of a less expansionist entrepreneur, but Goldsmith was prepared to entertain the equally appealing dreams of Napier-Bell and Summers.

Transfixed by the financial wonders of Kunick, Nomis penned plans for a broad-based company which, on paper, looked formidable indeed. The group was to be split into several divisions: Artiste Management (headed by Napier-Bell and Summers), Concert Promotion (headed by Goldsmith) and Film/Television Distribution, Marketing and Sponsorship (headed by Goldsmith's partner, Ed Simons). The latter section was a new departure for both companies, reflecting Nomis' desire to bridge the gap between pop, rock, theatre and celluloid. Napier-Bell was already involved in the much-publicized aristocratic soap opera *The Legacy*, a project which could be greatly enhanced by this new deal. Summers, meanwhile, was enjoying hitherto undiscovered talents as a film producer busily attempting to salvage "Wham! In China" footage from the cutting room floor. He had also taken on a new role as a theatrical agent, signing the highly praised actor Tim Roth. Future plans included the scripting of a film *Get Me Out Of Here*, based on Summers' nightmarish nine year stint in the army. Roth had even agreed to play the part of his new manager! Nomis, it seemed, was threatening a creative explosion powerful enough to offset the imminent demise of Wham!

Having mapped out their grand scheme, Napier-Bell and Summers were ushered into the presence of Kunick chairman, David Hudd. The meeting progressed smoothly until the punctilious executive casually enquired:

"Does the South African connection bother you?" Immediately, there was an embarrassed silence. Summers, a bitter opponent of South African policies, understandably sought clarification. In the ensuing discussion, Hudd explained that one of Kunick's largest shareholders was Sol Kerzner, owner of Sun Hotels International, a British registered subsidiary of the South African company Kersef Investments. Kerzner was presently in the process of building up his interests outside South Africa and had a number of hotels and casinos littered across the globe. Several exotic resorts were mentioned including Mauritius, Mozambique and a place called Bophuthatswana. As Jazz recalls: "That's as much as I knew. Nobody said he was involved in Sun City. *Nobody*." David Hudd, of course, had held nothing back. What Nomis failed to do was make a logical deduction based on the information presented to them. The mention of Bophuthatswana and the give away name "Sun" Hotels failed to sound any warning bells and, remarkably, the Sun City link remained undetected. It sounds incredible, but Summers' testimony is independently supported, point for point, by his partner. And as Jazz rightly retorts: "You're sitting there now and you *know* the answers."

Summers and Napier-Bell considered the implications of the South African connexion, but ultimately dismissed the issue as irrelevant. Napier-Bell's rationale was disarmingly plausible:

> I'm not very fond of South Africa or South Africans, but we considered it and felt it really didn't make any difference. So 30% of a public company is held by South Africans. In a public company, what they have today may be sold tomorrow, or they may increase it. These were shares that were on the stockmarket and if currently 30% are held by South Africans, then they are. But that's the nature of public company share dealings. We were well aware that there was a South African shareholding, but we *weren't* aware that the people who owned the shares were Sun City. We genuinely *didn't* know that and I think we might have cared more if we'd known, but maybe not, because my attitude was very much, supposing South Africans didn't own these shares when we did the deal and then bought them the next week. We would be in no different position really.

Such retrospective logic makes mellifluous reading, but merely papers over Nomis' fundamental error. They had failed to do their homework by checking up on the mysterious Sol Kerzner. Their prospective boardroom partner was blithely dismissed as just another white South African, building his interests abroad like a number of prominent figures in the British music business. His involvement with an entrepreneur of Harvey Goldsmith's prestigious standing placed his reputation beyond question.

Once Summers convinced himself that Nomis weren't being funded by "boss" the deal proceeded and preliminary contracts were signed. The proposed Kunick takeover provided Nomis with £5 million in cash, loan stock and facilities, representing nothing less than the entrepreneurial enshrinement of a dream. For the former radiographer turned pop manager, it was a historic moment to be treasured: "I walked out of that door thinking 'Well, I've just made a million quid, I'm getting a nice salary, I can travel wherever I want and get involved with whomever I want'." Of course, the complete deal still had to be ratified at Kunick's Annual General Meeting on 10 March, but that was just a formality. Or so everyone assumed.

Kunick was taking a remarkable gamble in assimilating Nomis, for it later transpired that their primary interest was in a single asset – Wham! Placing £5 million on the longevity of a group, already rumoured to be splitting, was a crazy long shot, made plausible only by Kunick's belief that George Michael would continue to achieve solo success under Nomis' tutelage.* Even here, however, there should have been cause for concern, for Kunick was acquiring an act bound only by a flimsy three month contract. Several days before Summers signed the Kunick agreement, I reminded him of the dangers of Nomis's management contract with Wham!, and impolitely suggested that he and Napier-Bell were incautiously trustworthy. Hadn't they unwittingly created a charter for poaching? What was to prevent Wham! unceremoniously dumping them whenever they chose? Weren't they concerned about their 15% commission? Wasn't it suicidal to put themselves in a position where they were unable to threaten Wham! with long term putative damages in the event of a calculated breach of contract? But Jazz would have none of such cynicism and expressed an endearingly naive faith in the loyalty of his charges:

> If George and Andrew were to find somebody better to manage them, then I'd say "Fine. If you think they're better than us *go*". But I don't think they will because we do a bloody good job and we're not greedy. So, *I don't think we'll lose anybody*. With a contract like this, you can build up a relationship with the artiste, especially if they know they can go if they want to. That contract goes for every artiste throughout our

---

*Both Napier-Bell and Summers insist that Kunick was blissfully unaware that Wham! was on the brink of disbanding, though it strains my credulity. Given George Michael's statements of disillusionment in the popular press and Napier-Bell's cavalier comment about a probable split within two years, it was hardly the world's best kept secret. Even before signing the Kunick deal, the normally cautious Summers was indiscreet enough to conjecture "I *think* they'll record *one* more album" and when I mentioned a split he agreed that it was "inevitable". I left his office convinced that their demise was at hand. Admittedly, the Kunick directors may not have been cogniscent with music industry gossip but with £5 million on the table they *surely* had their ears to the ground.

company. And a lot of people like you have said, "Don't do that! Someone will poach you".

Four weeks later, many of those words were to have a sadly ironic resonance.

Summers concedes that Nomis' biggest blunder was failing to investigate Kerzner's properties, but they compounded that error by neglecting to inform Wham! of the already tangible South African link, which was deemed "irrelevant" and "unimportant". As Summers myopically noted, "We felt we were going into partnership with Harvey and Ed." Upon being informed of the proposed £5 million deal, George Michael's only memorable comment was a tersely re-assuring, "Yeah, I like Harvey." His words were also blessed with a retrospective irony.

The story almost ended there, happily and lucratively for both Nomis and Allied. The Kunick takeover was reported as a major coup in the financial pages of the serious press and although the tabloids tried to stir up a controversy in a teacup with "Wham! Sold" headlines, the boys were unagitated by the arrangement. Shortly afterwards, Andrew disappeared to France to concentrate on his motor racing, and George flew to California to complete some recording. Two weeks later, Michael was staring at a news item in the *Hollywood Reporter* and *Variety* which resembled a parachronistic April Fool's Day spoof. He could barely bring himself to articulate the words: "WHAM! SOLD TO SUN CITY".

"Sun City" was already a taboo name in rock circles. A $90 million Las Vegas styled gambling paradise smack in the middle of the independent black homeland of Bophuthatswana, the resort attracted a number of prominent pop stars due to its professed non-apartheid policy. Many artistes glibly accepted their fat fees with a clear conscience through the simple expedient of half-closing their eyes and neglecting to ask awkward questions. A brisk walkabout would have revealed how few blacks danced at the Sun City disco or gambled in the plush casino or attended the highly priced Superbowl concerts. Where were the dark-skinned settlers who had been forcibly relocated to this idyllic homeland? An exploratory tourist could find them living in ghettos and shanty towns whose primitiveness documented a social and economic polarization of chilling proportions. These banthustan blacks evidently enjoyed equality in law, a privilege which separated them from the unfortunates still living under the apartheid system. The independent homeland of Bophuthatswana magnanimously offered them a personal freedom, which could be gauged in poverty, barrenness, and a perpetually tantalizing white affluence. Sun City was a grotesque and obscene joke, a diamond crusted Afrikaner fantasy world erected in the midst of a distopian niggerdom.

The political and moral ramifications of apartheid weighed heavily on George Michael's artistic shoulders during 1986. But it had not always been so. Two years before, the anti-apartheid superstar could be heard

uttering views indistinguishable from those of Queen, Elton John, Rod
Stewart, Ray Charles or the other artistes who had chosen to play in that
trouble-torn country. When questioned about his success in South Africa,
Michael betrayed a moral evasiveness which Pontius Pilate would have
envied:

> I don't care where I sell records. I don't want to get involved in their
> political issues. I actually think it's pathetic the way people are sanc-
> tioned for going there . . . All we think is that we're far too selfish and
> ambitious to want to do something political and risk our careers. That's
> why we wouldn't go there. But if I really thought it wouldn't affect my
> future then I'd go.

The calculation and cynicism voiced here sound extraordinary, particularly in the light of Michael's subsequent actions and pontifications, but, as
Summers charitably observed, "George was young then."

The greatest underlying irony in the Nomis/Wham/Sun City saga was
that the maligned Summers had previously criticized Michael for his apoli-
tical stance on South Africa. Exactly two years before, Summers auto-
matically turned down a lucrative offer for Wham! to appear in the
country. Michael, however, displayed mixed feelings about the decision,
suggesting "Perhaps I should go out there and play, and then when I come
back I might have a better idea of it." It was the old argument that so many
stars had used to convince themselves they were open-minded and morally
sound. Jazz interrupted his protege's train of thought with a warning,
"Purely by going there you're supporting that regime and they'll use that.
So you really shouldn't go there." Michael agreed that it wasn't worth the
trouble, so they changed the subject and talked about the next Wham!
single.

In the months following that South African dialogue, Michael's blasé
attitude had altered beyond recognition. The anti-apartheid lobby, heavily
backed by the Musicians' Union and the ever hip, caring, socialist music
press, had evidently captured the heart of the capricious Wham! superstar.
By November 1985, he could even be heard complaining to *The Guardian*
about not being invited to participate in the recording of the protest song
"Sun City": "We're one of the biggest groups in the world and would've
helped to sell it, but we were never contacted."

Michael's indignation might have been less acute if he had recollected
some of his unsupportive comments the previous year. Far from warrant-
ing an invitation, he was rather fortunate not to receive a bitchy sideswipe
condemning his tacit support for musicians who had defied their unions'
wishes by playing there.

Although snubbed by the already overmanned Sun City protesters,
Michael seized another chance to voice his new found radicalism by
recording an anti-apartheid song with Stevie Wonder. This fraternization
with black musicians evidently increased his antipathy towards racial

segregation. He had just reached a pitch of righteous criticism against South African policies when the news broke that his management had sold Wham! into the hands of Sun City. The timing was unbelievable.

While radio transistors blasted out the rock elite's message that they were definitely *not* playing Sun City, Michael was left to ponder the embarrassment of his own position. At first, he had difficulty coming to terms with the enormity of Nomis' transgression. As he later remarked, "I found it amazing that they could take such a risk on something that they knew if I had any idea about they wouldn't see me for dust." What Michael apparently failed to consider was that his managers were actually *innocent*. Back in London, Summers was only beginning to discover the full implications of the deal he had recently signed. It was Ralph Simon, the South African director of Zomba Productions, who, still reeling from the news of the Kerzner connection, telephoned Jazz to ask incredulously: "Do you know who your new partner actually *is*?" Summers wasted no time in finding out. Within hours, he was attending a meeting at Harvey Goldsmith's Oxford Street office, where all his worst fears were confirmed. Ed Simons effectively destroyed their empire-building dreams in five solemn words: "Sol Kerzner owns Sun City." An uncharacteristically bemused and embarrassed Harvey Goldsmith chimed in with a re-assuring "I didn't know he *owned* it. I just thought he developed it!" Summers already had his head in his hands and was crying in exasperation: "Jesus Christ, what is going on here?" Shortly afterwards, the former radiographer left Goldsmith's office vowing to pull Nomis out of Kunick at the earliest opportunity.

The millions had already vanished, but now a greater crisis loomed which threatened the very existence of Nomis. Summers had to act swiftly before the wrath of Michael ravaged their managerial realm. Napier-Bell was less upset about the Sun City shareholding than his ideological partner, but agreed that it was a stupid error which had to be rectified. The major problem lay in extricating themselves from the deal before Michael's disillusionment turned to anger. With documents already signed, it was virtually impossible to obtain a release until Kunick's annual shareholders' meeting on 10 March. Until then, Nomis had to plead and sweat. As Jazz reveals, "Millions of pounds were flying about, as well as offices and staff. Everybody was in complete turmoil."

Upon Michael's return from the States, a lunch date was hastily arranged at which he confronted his management with the Sun City rumours. The situation was explained and Nomis requested an amnesty during which they intended to move heaven and earth to nullify the deal. George seemed surprisingly amicable throughout the meeting and though some signs of exasperation were evident, he departed in reasonable spirits. Summers was quietly confident that a crisis could be averted, though his psychological reading of Michael's reactions may have been faulty. Napier-Bell suggests that, like himself, the superstar singer intensely dislikes confrontation, preferring to manipulate situations to his own advantage. It is quite conceivable that he reached a decision even before leaving America, but could not stomach an imagined scenario of apologies, excuses and straw-clutching recriminations.

Summers refused to believe that the axe was nigh and placed his faith in a reconciliation. Already, though, events had taken an ominous turn. Nomis's sole means of communication with Michael was through his solicitor, Tony Russell. The superstar was once more avoiding a personal confrontation. Before relations deteriorated further, Nomis attempted to arrange another meeting and secure a moritorium from Michael. If his allegiance held until 10 March, all might yet be well. But George's patience was already being eroded by the strain of intense press speculation concerning the Sun City link. One way or the other, some announcement had to be made soon. On Sunday 16 February, he visited his favourite mentor, Dick Leahy, and, two days later, they attended a meeting with CBS Managing Director Paul Russell. Neither Summers nor Napier-Bell was invited. Jazz was disturbed by this latest turn of events, fearing that his influence over Michael had waned irrevocably. He could not escape the feeling that his and Nomis' fate now lay in other hands.

Even as George Michael was lifting the axe, Summers dolefully looked to Dick Leahy as his one forlorn hope for a stay of execution. Leahy alone now had Michael's ear, and his influence over the star was inestimable. If he chose to champion Nomis and convince the troubled boy that it had all been some terrible mistake, then the loss of Wham! might miraculously be averted. But Summers could find few plausible reasons why Leahy should endanger his own position by interceding on behalf of the doomed.

Leahy was of the living; Nomis of the living dead. Summers could almost feel the blade of the axe cutting through the air as he remembered the times he had crossed Leahy . . . Morbidly, he looked to boardroom confrontations past, as if seeking to confirm his imminent execution.

Relations between Morrison/Leahy and Nomis had been exemplary during the peak period of Wham's career, but recent meetings had proven less fruitful. Since the US stadium tour, Summers had been working industriously on the long overdue China film. The project had eaten up several directors, producers and editors, leaving Jazz as the sole survivor. Eventually, he had emerged with a package which at last seemed destined for worldwide cinema release. Neither Morrison nor Leahy was convinced, however, and had insisted that the proposed movie was a big mistake. Leahy was emphatic in his disapproval and had greeted Summers' euphoria with icy curtness: "I don't want this film to come out." That was his final comment. Summers had gamely resisted the publishers' steely resolve and in a dextrous display of boardroom politics won the guarded approval of Michael and Ridgeley. With a confidence reinforced by the passion of creative endeavour, Summers seemed set for a historic political victory over the imperious Leahy: "He knew that for the first time in the three years that we'd worked together with Wham!, that Dick Leahy wasn't going to get his own way because I wanted that film out."

Even that small victory now seemed destined to be undone by the Sun City scandal. If Michael axed Nomis, the dream of the Wham! film would doubtless be reduced to the level of a home video or forgotten entirely. Leahy logic would surely prevail.

As Summers sat awaiting his destiny, he conjured up another recent meeting. His unlikely saviour Dick Leahy once again featured heavily. They were arguing over plans for The Final. Leahy had urged, "Let's finish it now!" He wanted Wham! to split there and then so that George Michael could complete an album for release at the end of 1986. He seemed convinced that was what Michael *really* wanted. Napier-Bell and Summers had countered the motion, arguing that George desired Wham! to end with a bang, after which he intended to renegotiate his contract with CBS and then take a long sabbatical. Leahy digested the information, but he didn't seem too pleased.

Summers felt he had already done enough to convince Leahy that he was deliberately driving a wedge between the publisher and his superstar asset. Although he felt guiltless of such intrigue, Summers feared that his board-room virility might have been misinterpreted. Looking ahead, he saw a time when he might enjoy some of the exclusive power that Leahy now wielded. George Michael's publishing contract with Morrison/Leahy was due to expire in 1987, and, in his capacity as manager, Summers would feel called upon to advise his superstar client. What he had in mind was the equivalent of placing Morrison/Leahy on the same executioner's block that he and Napier-Bell now unhappily occupied:

> I would have sat down with George and said, "You should form George Michael Music, go out and get as much money as you need. The most important thing is to get the biggest percentage and ownership of your copyright."

Summers' ultimate plan was to take Michael to a corporate publisher, and pull off a 90 per cent deal, plus copyright ownership. He even felt confident about winning a 100 per cent deal whereby the publisher earned money solely from the interest logged during the royalty collecting process. In his mercy, he might even have offered Morrison/Leahy a similar arrangement, in respect of previous good services.

If Leahy suspected Summers' intentions, then it would have been ludicrous to dissuade Michael from proceeding with the execution. Jazz realized as much, and worse. For it was by no means clear whether Leahy even believed Nomis was innocent of the Kunick/Sun City connexion. As days passed, Summers concluded that a spectacular diplomatic coup would not be forthcoming from the awesome Leahy. Tactically, Nomis was in an almost untenable position. The only hope lay in gaining an audience with the increasingly elusive Michael and convincing him of their innocence.

Napier-Bell had rushed back from Peking anticipating an all important confrontation with his disenchanted superstar, but it was not to be. Upon telephoning Michael's legal representative, Tony Russell, he was informed that the axe was falling. A statement confirming Michael's departure from his management was about to be circulated. On the afternoon of Friday 21 February 1986, Nomis suffered a decapitating blow which drained all life from the ailing company.

The decollation was so sudden and incisive that only one name appeared on the executioner's certificate. Ridgeley, conspicuous by his absence throughout the drama, was at a Monte Carlo hotel when Tony Russell telephoned Michael's decision. They wanted to add his name to the press release and confirm that Wham! was unified in its severance from Nomis. Ridgeley had no stomach for such business and demanded more time to consider the fate of his management. He received no more than four hours before the deed was done without his sanction or involvement.

The press converged on Nomis's Gosfield Street office within minutes of the announcement, but Summers had already disappeared. He sought refuge at Harvey Goldsmith's Oxford Street headquarters, where the mood was sombre, but stoical. Jazz concluded that the ruthless public disavowal of Nomis had been forced by circumstance. "By making it clear-cut and taking a strong stand it squashed immediately any doubts in anybody's mind that George Michael would be associated with apartheid."

For all the pressure Michael suffered, the decision still smacked of expediency and convenience. The Kunick AGM was less than a fortnight away and Nomis had already promised to forego their £5 million deal. Michael could easily have compromised *and* won over the voracious press. How noble it would have been to inform his media tormentors that, in his magnanimity, he was allowing Nomis a 10 day stay of execution to sever the Sun City link, while adding a stern warning that failure would immediately be punished by retribution on the eleventh day. That would have been the perfect speech, a splendid mixture of forceful rectitude and self-abnegation which Fleet Street would have translated into headlines such as "GEORGE'S ULTIMATUM".

The newshounds would have camped outside the Kunick building on 3 March, hungrily awaiting Nomis' decision before converging on Michael for his grand announcement. At that point, the axe could have fallen with a justifiably resounding bump or Michael could have offered a dramatic last minute parole. Either way, he would have emerged the media hero as a benevolent idealist forcing his management to surrender £5 million, or a principled humanitarian striking a blow against apartheid. Instead, he appeared tough, but unreasonable. The years of service that his management had provided were not even deemed worthy of ten measly days. His decision was so mercilessly obdurate that it left only two probable conclusions, either (a) Michael had been intending to leave Nomis in any case and exploited the Kunick disaster for his own political ends, or (b) his hurt over the matter was exacerbated, and finally transformed into righteous wrath, by the belief that he had been deliberately deceived by Napier-Bell and Summers.

Napier-Bell lends credence to theory (a) with an interesting insight into the Michael character:

> George *never*, even when it looks like it, does things impetuously. He's the most considered person. He doesn't make quick decisions. There-fore, it's perfectly obvious that this was an opportunity to do what he wanted to do, which would otherwise have been very awkward for him. After all, how does he come to Jazz and me and say, "I want to leave your management". We'd been fabulous managers and done everything he wanted. Yet, he knew, in three months' time that what he wanted more than anything else was to run his life, and not be managed. It is very difficult. It's a bit like leaving your wife when she's never been nasty to you. You definitely want to leave her. You've lived with her for years, and she's been a perfectly good wife. How do you tell her you're leaving? Then you come home one day and she's in bed with the milk-man. So you say, "That's it. I'm leaving".

Napier-Bell's theory is made more plausible by the revelation that Michael had previously confided a wish to run his own life after Wham! However, George never placed any date upon his probable departure from Nomis and it is quite possible that he would have remained with the company for several years more.

Napier-Bell's "milkman in bed with wife" analogy should not distract from the important fact that Michael was legally free to terminate the Nomis contract at any time, giving three months' notice. If the star felt humble enough to *need* an excuse for leaving, then the imminent dissolu-tion of Wham! surely would have been reason enough. Summers discounts the expedient theory, preferring to believe that George genuinely sus-pected subterfuge and lost faith in Nomis:

> I think he would have stuck with us. He sat down the week before and said, "Jazz, over the next ten years, I'm going to be in this business. I don't want to be associated with this." I think he was kind of indicating "Look, you've got 10 years with me. Why are you doing this?" It was tough on us, but we made a mistake. And, to be quite honest, it was a *big* mistake. Perhaps an artiste of that magnitude thinks, "Well, if they make a mistake like that, they could make another one." I can under-stand his sentiments. He was concerned and worried, and we had made a balls up. I don't think he was looking for an excuse to leave our manage-ment at all.

Two opinions, the cynical and the charitable, but what of Michael's perspective? As might be guessed from his ruthless action, he had little sympathy left for Nomis. He accused them of greed and laughed off the suggestion that they knew nothing of the Sun City connection. His favourite refrain was "You don't make a £5 million deal and not look at your shareholders". The crucial point, however, is that Nomis *did* know the identity of the shareholders. They knew Sol Kerzner had a 30% interest in Kunick and that his Sun Hotels International had a wealth of interests worldwide. But that was all they knew, and that was all they needed to know. It was enough that he was an extremely wealthy businessman with rock solid securities. Michael appears to have expected Nomis to look into the properties of each and every Kunick shareholder before concluding the deal. Unfortunately, neither Summers nor Napier-Bell was as perspicacious as the Sun City spotting journalists of the *Hollywood Reporter* and *Variety* and that was their most heinous flaw.

In spite of Michael's damning rationalization, there were a number of good reasons for his accepting Nomis' guilelessness. Firstly, there was Summers' previously voiced anti-apartheid views. Here was a manager who boasted a half-black girlfriend, and had once advised his star *never* to appear in South Africa. Would he really have abandoned his principles so readily to seek profit from a system he vehemently opposed? Ideology and good character aside, would he, or indeed Napier-Bell, be reckless enough to risk their most valuable asset by entering into such a contentious contract? Kunick was not alone in seeking Nomis' hand and there were plenty of other public companies without unwelcome Sun City relatives. Such doubts should have played on Michael's mind as he sharpened his axe, but his execution was clinical.

Michael's announcement, unsupported by Ridgeley, had the knock-on effect of alerting the press to a potentially far bigger story – the death of Wham! Napier-Bell claims that George was desperate to announce the group's impending dissolution, but it was Nomis' own carefully worded press statement which fanned the flames of speculation. Annoyed by Michael's "unreasonable" attitude in avoiding conciliatory talks, they issued a press release which pointedly indicated that he alone was leaving Nomis. The names Sol Kerzner and Sun City were conspicuously absent, for, as Jazz confesses, "That would be like crucifying yourself. We know how Fleet Street works." The sleuthhounds responded to the news by converging on a bemused Andrew Ridgeley in Monte Carlo. Upon being informed that Wham! had split, a fact confirmed in neither press release, Ridgeley lost patience with his interrogators and stormed, "Nobody told me anything. The whole business makes me 'effing sick." In a blatant paraphrasing of his retort for their own ends, the *Daily Mirror* headlined "Wham! Off! George Makes Me Sick".

While the public was spoonfed innuendoes of an imaginary Michael vs. Ridgeley feud, Nomis enjoyed a reasonably healthy settlement based on present Wham! earnings and roughly calculated future royalties. According to Summers, "We probably took a bit less than we would have received, but we got it up front and there were no court cases". On 3

March, Nomis was spared any further embarrassment over the Sun City link when Kunick declined to finalize the deal. Shorn of the lucrative Wham!/George Michael asset, Nomis no longer looked a £5 million investment.

While Napier-Bell and Summers felt buffeted throughout this period of turmoil, the unfortunate Harvey Goldsmith was dealt several more serious body blows. As a leading promoter of international acts, Goldsmith could ill afford the wrath of the Sun City protesters who counted among their number Bob Dylan, Bruce Springsteen, Keith Richard, Ronnie Wood, Peter Gabriel, Bob Geldof, Jackson Browne, Lou Reed, Hall and Oates, Bono and Pat Benatar. His dilemma was not made easier by his exalted position as a president of the Live Aid Foundation and a trustee of Band Aid. The music press, sensing the pop equivalent of a political scandal, bore down mercilessly on the beleagured promoter, who increasingly resembled a sinking entrepreneur flailing wildly to free himself from a quicksand. His muddled sophistry was captured most poignantly in *Sounds* where indignation and ignorance were mixed in almost equal measure:

We were aware of the Sun Hotel International's involvement in Kunick, but we didn't think it had any connection with our business. We still don't. When the "Sun City" single came out, we obviously felt uncom-fortable . . . I don't really understand what the "Sun City" single was trying to say. I'm not going to defend Sun City itself, but it's not part of the apartheid system. I don't believe politics and music mix and I wouldn't deal with segregated audiences anywhere in the world. I don't understand why all this attention has been focussed on me in this affair.

Goldsmith's astounding naivety about Sun City and the politics of his own position in the affair was almost endearing. He concluded with a broadside aimed against those pontificating artistes who enjoyed substantial South African royalties ("I've never heard of any artiste asking to have his records withdrawn from sale there"). Here again, however, Harvey betrayed an unawareness of the depth of anti-apartheid feeling. Several major artistes were already in the process of renegotiating their recording contracts in order to boycott South Africa, while others had successfully diverted their "apartheid royalties" into anti-apartheid organizations. Interestingly, George Michael ("I don't make empty gestures") was not among them.

Like Nomis, Goldsmith had vowed to extricate himself from the Kunick Organization, but he had much more to lose. At the end of March, with backing from Albion Trust Holdings, he finally succeeded in buying out Allied and formed a new company, capitalised at £6 million. The discovery of the Sun City link had cost him dearly, but he emerged with his repu-tation intact. His strenuous efforts were not enough to win back the support of George Michael who transferred the organization of The Final into the hands of rival promoter, Mel Bush.*

The reverberations of Michael's sensational departure continued to shake the foundations of Nomis. Wham! producer Chris Porter dissociated himself from the company and Nomis's much prized personal assistant Siobhan Bailey went independent. Freed from the shackles of Sun City, Summers and Goldsmith were still optimistic about re-uniting their companies and pursuing the immemorial corporate dream. Minus Kunick backing, however, the terms seemed less enticing and Napier-Bell soon dropped out. Without Wham!, Simon and Jazz suddenly lost their sense of common ground and Nomis literally crumbled overnight. Summers doggedly persisted with the Allied union, but with Harvey still stinging from the Kunick buy-out, a mutually acceptable financial package proved elusive. Jazz Summers summed up the catalogue of lost dreams in a few short sentences: "It was an accident. One minute we were managing the biggest act since The Beatles. Within 10 days we'd lost the biggest pop band in the world and the £5 million deal."

Recoiling from their self-destruction, Nomis attempted to fulfil the terms of their Wham! contract by managing the group until The Final. It was a stoical and affectionate gesture which Summers felt would end the relationship with Wham! on a positive note. Like everything else in this final phase, however, Summers' simple sentiments were reduced to the level of suspicion and petty pop politics. Three of the major figures behind Wham! convened for a final meeting which, according to Summers, was most memorable for its tone of mutual ill feeling:

> Dick Leahy came around asking why, what and how? Simon, who was in a bad mood, got a bit surly and then Dick Leahy said to me "I hear you've been saying things about me in the business." So I answered that bluntly and told him I hadn't, and I still don't say things about him. I just answer questions for you.

Leahy promised to consider their unusual proposal, but telephoned Napier-Bell several days later expressing the view that it was unworkable. Nomis was well and truly dead. Summers sighed resignedly: "We'd served our purpose."

Napier-Bell still hopes to inherit Ridgeley's management from Wham! but that would depend upon the former star abandoning motor racing in favour of film work. As for Michael, Simon predicts he will maintain a low profile, taking more time over songwriting and recording, and declining touring opportunities for at least three years. He also hints that Morrison/Leahy's power could be eroded:

---

*The vastly experienced Mel Bush was no stranger to Wembley Stadium. In 1974, he presented the Crosby, Stills, Nash & Young, Band and Joni Mitchell extravaganza, and the following year pitted Elton John alongside The Beach Boys and The Eagles.

There are three interests now that George is not going to tour: his interests, the publisher's interests and the record company's interests. Ultimately, he can ditch the publisher and have his own publishing company. The artiste who doesn't want to perform live except on special occasions really only has to take into consideration the record company's interests in balance with his own.

Summers is less pessimistic about Leahy's fate and believes that the publisher will now emerge triumphant and more influential than ever in directing Michael's career:

He's got a good relationship with Dick Leahy and I think he'll rely on him more and more as a buffer to bounce ideas backwards and forwards on his music. He always used to do that even when we were looking after him. He'd play the stuff to Dick and say "What do you think of this?" . . . he regards Leahy as a second father figure and he *does* listen to him. Leahy was very involved in his career before we were. He had George's confidence.

The true power of Leahy will be revealed later in 1987 when his music publishing contract with Michael expires. I would not like to wager on the outcome of that epoch.

Looking back over George Michael's troubled business history, Leahy may well suffer several sleepless nights pondering his probable destiny. His star asset greatly resembles a boy *roi*, surrounded by a court of powerful nobles whose loyalty and support he has had to rely upon to maintain his throne. In spite of his youth, the maturing monarch has not been afraid to wield the axe and the list of banished favourites testifies to his ruthlessness. Robert Allan, Mark Dean, Simon Napier-Bell, Jazz Summers and Harvey Goldsmith have all been victims of various purges. If these are the teething whelps of the cub prince, Lord save us from the roar of the lion king. Other kith have drifted from Michael's court to seek new kingdoms; the pretender Andrew Ridgeley was despatched abroad, and a retinue of ladies in waiting including Amanda Washbourn, Dee C. Lee, Shirlie Holliman and Pepsi De Manque have joined smaller households.

Alone among the most powerful nobles, Dick Leahy the lionheart, has emerged as the great survivor and presently enjoys the prestige of a veritable prince regent. He has demonstrated his loyalty and exercised more power and influence in Michael's kingdom than any of his illustrious rivals. Whether he survives the reign largely depends on political astuteness and kingly caprice. The boy king must now decide whether to retain his regent's much used guiding hand or seize complete control and rule alone.

The Day Of The Final

Saturday 28th June, a memorable day in the 1986 rock calendar with no less than three major musical events taking place simultaneously. At Clapham Common, an anti-apartheid benefit is in full swing, the indoor Wembley Arena offers a "reggae sunsplash" and on the hallowed turf of Wembley Stadium, the pop sensation of the 80s is staging its final farewell. The morning tabloids brazenly blazon "Wham! Souvenir" on their front pages, cheekily cajoling fans into purchasing a superfluous newspaper in the vain hope of reading some last minute revelations, prophetic previews or stadia survival tips. No such delicacies are to be found inside. Instead, we are teasingly promised our "souvenir" in the Monday edition *after* the concert. This Chinese box method of presenting a story is only marginally less annoying than BBC Radio One's trick of securing listeners for an entire week by broadcasting an interview with Wham! in brief daily instalments. On the day of the concert, they repeat the interview as a one hour special, cleverly maximizing listening figures in the process. The broadcast ends at 3pm, leaving precisely sixty minutes to reach the stadium before the start of the show.

The majority of the 72,000 fans are already locked inside Wembley's gates, having set out earlier in the day. A foolhardy hundred had even camped out overnight, as if testifying to the chaos Wham! could have wreaked had they chosen a smaller, intimate venue for their display of pop euthanasia. With 4 pm approaching, a few Wham! stragglers can be observed boarding buses and tubes. Their allegiance is detectable in Wham! encrested badges, t-shirts and hats. Occasionally, they burst into an unmelodious "Wham! Rap"or "Wake Me Up Before You Go-Go", but fail to progress beyond the first verse. A couple of commuters at the end of a tube carriage are flanked by a poster innocently proclaiming the importance of a recent Wham! chart topping single. On this particular day, the stark slogan FREEDOM has a significance which the Reed Employment Agency could never have envisaged.

Outside the stadium, souvenir scalpers and ticket touts ply their wares in a doleful manner. Earlier in the week, George Michael promised to scupper these merciless extortioners by holding back several thousand tickets at the box office. Judging from the mood of these would be profiteers, his ruse has proven enormously effective. The first tout I speak to is a dour Scot, badly sunburnt and evidently in need of a stiff drink. His guttural mumblings ("Wan' ticket?") reveal none of the menacing sharpness or barely concealed aggression of the traditional Wembley East End sharpie. He is obviously unconfident and willing to haggle. Rather than the conniving barrow-boy rhetoric of a con man, this fumbling amateur comes straight to the point: "How much do you *want* to pay?" The temptation to take his words literally and proffer £1.50 proves difficult to resist. After insisting he name his price a figure of £25 is suggested. Barely able to contain my laughter, I quickly walk away. Like a recalcitrant puppy, the tout follows uttering a bemused whining sound which emerges as the familiar chorus "But how much do you *want* to pay?" His voice betrays a genuine incredulity, as though no reasonable person could possibly reject so generous an offer. As I turn a corner, I can still hear that old refrain now transformed into a desperate plea: "But the tickets cost £13.50 in the first place. What do you *expect* to pay . . . I don't understand".

Sixty yards on, another tout appears clutching a handful of brightly coloured £13.50 tickets. Without a sign of perturbation, he quietly suggests the eminently sensible asking price of £10. It is, he concludes, "a bad day", and although the concert has yet to begin, he has already despaired of making further profit. An indignant frown greets my accusation of probable forgeries and prompts the stoic tout into a fascinating defence of his integrity. He combs my finger across the perforated surface of a ticket while directing my attention to the tiny silver pictorial representation of the stadium edifice which flashes brightly in the afternoon sun. This demonstration is apparently proof positive that his tickets are genuine. His glib concern is so enticing that I actually hand over a tenner to this toytown tout, ever thankful to the Wham! boys for saving me £3.50 and a probable booking fee.

Inside the stadium, the afternoon sun beats down on a half-naked throng herded together like cattle in an overcrowded pen, ferociously protecting their perpetually infringed body space from unwelcome intruders. But these particular adolescent animals lack the collective sense of a self-protective herd and fail to recognize the urgent need to prevent interlopers from breaking their flanks. In the previous decade, an older, more intelligent crowd realized the importance of organization, and the privileged hundreds who arrived long before Wembley opened its gates learned to establish their patch at the front of the stage by remaining stubbornly seated throughout the day, fanning out their bodies and belongings to ward off selfishly tardy invaders. Maintaining territory meant conserving energy, easing cramped limbs, plotting a visible, if ambitious, route to the lavatories and preventing a disciplined crowd from degenerating into a melee. It was only when the bill toppers began their set that the ever vigilant front line arena platoon would rise as one and remain on their feet for the climactic duration of the evening. But today's Wham! audience is blessed with neither foresight nor common sense. Even before the opening act has taken the stage, an unruly mass is standing and craning its collective neck in the vain hope of spotting a star. Nobody has the charisma or intelligence to tell them to shut up and sit down. Beneath the superficial air of camaraderie lies an absolute lack of shared responsibility, characterized by a maverick mentality and amoralistic absence of utilitarian logic which will shortly be rewarded with ever diminishing foot space and a crush so intense that virtually nobody will be able to sit down for the next five hours. As more people surge forward, the ethos of the crowd is very much along the lines of "every man for himself". Late comers are tolerated and passively encouraged by the naive insularity of child-like revellers whose selfish indiscipline has inadvertantly declared the arena a free-for-all market-place. With persistence and ballet-like feats of dexterity, it is relatively easy to sidle between swaying bodies and forge ahead to the pulsating heart of the crowd.

By the time I reach a suitably central position the first "mystery guest" is already working his way through a non-stop medley of old hits. For many, Gary Glitter symbolizes the early 70s, an age when musical pop talent was less important than a colourful and exaggerated image. Although Glitter does not figure prominently in the list of musical influences that created Wham!, his media omnipresence during their formative childhood years is evidently sufficient credentials to warrant a special invitation to open the show. It might just as well have been Slade or Sweet up there today, but Gary Glitter will suffice. More than any other figure in 70s UK pop, he epitomizes the pop star gone to seed, who miraculously drags his tired body through one more punishing performance. Dressed in an absurd white costume that makes Elvis Presley's garish Las Vegas gear seem tasteful by comparison, Glitter runs gamely across the long catwalks at the side of the stage, almost suffering a cardiac arrest in the process. His physical exertions are punctuated by dramatic stops and manic stares, as though he were a performing rabbit trapped in the mesmerizing glare of a spotlight. At its best, Glitter's performance is beyond parody, but then again so is his life. A frustrated 50s pop singer, unable to chart in spite of a wealth of pseudonyms, he eventually found fame a decade later in the unlikely person that now bestrides the Wembley stage. Bankruptcy and the Grim Reaper have conspired to end the Glitter legend, but after every despairing headline has been exhausted, he returns as of old in an increasingly laughable attempt to retrieve his belated pop crown. Backstage, he is known, not without some affection, as "the leader". Glitter likes to present himself as the Dorian Gray of Rock 'n' Roll and every concert now serves as a testament and celebration of his inexplicable longevity. In reality, he is the complete antithesis of Dorian Gray, for it is the man beneath the make-up that grows grotesquely old while the image, reinforced by a ludicrous black bouffant and carefully applied mascara, remains deceptively youthful. Glitter's attempts to hide the ravages of physical decay are only partly successful, but therein lies his appeal. His futile attempts to forestall the march of time with silly clothes, idle boasts, modest declamations and public buffoonery create a curious mixture of comedy and pathos.

The cries of "Gary, you fat, old bastard" that reverberate around me are ultimately superfluous, for the star openly admits the incongruity of his age, image and performance. At one point he reveals that his last appearance at Wembley Stadium was in 1972, an unsolicited admission which provokes howls of laughter from the assembled teenagers who suddenly realize that this antiquated figure who calls himself "the leader" was performing this same rock 'n' roll set long before they were conceived. The distracting joke betrays a Falstaffian vulnerability which consistently requires Glitter to transform age into commodity. In front of 70,000 Wham! fans, however, his performance seems nothing more than an embarrassing anachronism. Of course, Glitter's music and persona always have been anachronistic and even during his successful peak, in 1972, he seemed a peculiar relic from the 50s, recently arisen from suspended animation like Adam Adamant. At Wembley, however, there are no new hits to replenish his autumnal career, while the old songs sound threadbare and void of even nostalgic interest, for who could be sentimental about the second-hand pop of the early 70s?

At times, Glitter can anaesthetize bad pop by the sheer audacity of his kitsch grandiose gestures, but today his theatricality has left the audience unmoved and the lack of sparkle in his set has been compounded by a sound system which has reduced the leader to the level of a muted cabaret singer crying out his lungs in front of a worn record player. Eventually, a charitable soul presents him with a bouquet of red roses and, like some condescending Hollywood starlet, Gary insists on spending several minutes distributing the flowers to his supposedly adoring fans in the front row.

The Glitter set ends in a blaze of sweltering heat which threatens to melt the sardine packed arena into a molten sepulchre of dehydrated and charred corpses. The tabloids had suggested that "Wham! fatigue" would take its toll on developing adolescents, a prediction that is suddenly made irrefragible by the 95 degree heat and six square inches of breathing space. Fortunately, the St. John Ambulance Brigade have prevented a mass outbreak of fainting by dispensing litre bottles of water which are thirstily consumed or used as baptismal jugs for stadium bathers.

The newly washed are greeted by the diminutive Nick Heyward, who launches into the greatest hits of Haircut 100, augmented by his own triumvirate of major successes: "Whistle Down The Wind", "Take That Situation" and "Blue Hat For A Blue Day". The clarity of sound throughout his set is most impressive and a particularly inspired bespectacled trumpeter receives several justly rewarded appearances on the giant Wembley telescreens. The effervescent and appropriately titled "Fantastic Day" has an almost anthemic quality which effectively captures the celebratory spirit of the afternoon. Not surprisingly, Heyward repeats the song during a well-deserved encore and leaves the stage with a dignity and quiet professionalism surprising in a performer who has not appeared in front of a live audience in over two years. Without breaking sweat, he has made the preceding Glitter spectacle seem like a prehistoric debacle.

The Wembley stewards once more dispense water to the over heated multitude, but on this occasion their thoughtfulness proves ill-advised. Suddenly, there is too much water and the overgrown schoolkids in the crowd have decided to transform Wembley into a giant swimming pool. Their repugnant oafishness and gross vulgarity are scarcely credible. Water fights commence and continue in a tedious and distracting fashion for the rest of the day. The participants indulge in spitting contests, and take inordinate pleasure in drenching themselves and their opponents with warm jets of salivary spray. One youth specializes in soaking the front of girls' t-shirts and the rear of their shorts so that their breasts and bottoms are visible for all to admire or deride. As the water guzzling and spraying continues unabated, you marvel at the capacity of these remarkable young bladders. After further consideration you realize they are so drenched and dripping that it is quite likely that public urination has been added to the fun. Not content with water, several self-professed "lads" revert to their favourite lager, the effect of which amplifies their boorish behaviour to an interminable degree. Swearing, spitting and idiot dancing, they belie the theory that all Wham! fans are extras from a "Club Tropicana" video. Two days after the concert, John Blake of *The Mirror* will inform us that the audience are "the most gloriously glamorous crowd I have seen at a rock concert in my entire life. Golden-skinned girls so beautiful they make you gasp, jostled alongside boys with sun-streaked hair and perfectly cut Italian clothes . . . it was as though the most exotic young people in Europe had been drawn to Wembley to pay homage to the band which, more than any other has provided the soundtrack of our lives in the Eighties."

He must be joking. Most of the girls are, in fact, pale and uninteresting schoolkids whose only excursion to Europe has been on the day ferry to Bologne. The boys are about as Italian as Alf Garnett and their sartorial elegance is unmeasurable since the majority are virtually naked. Blake's flattering prose typifies the view from the press enclosure, reinforced by a quick walkabout through the crowd. Like tourists visiting a zoo, the media are dazzled and amused by bright plumage and monkey tricks, but never enter the cages where the stale smell of urine and undigested food induce involuntary nausea. Even the clean cut, anodyne Wham! have their share of animal aficionados. The latter dress uniformly in denim shorts, specially designed to hide their apparent manhood. Several are branded with degrading tattoos which testify to a puzzling Oedipal fixation. A tall dark haired youth, drenched with water and swaying in a semi-drunken stupor, has the name "Steve" carved on one arm and the letters "MUM" on the other. His companion prefers to couch his maternal obsession in a revelatory riddle: "I'm In Love With Another Man's Wife . . . My Mother."

These mummy's boys are so dependent on matriarchal discipline that, left to their own devices they can do no more than sink into the stench-filled sandpit of infantile degeneracy.

Backstage, the stars and guest stars suffer no such animal mischief, for their behaviour is closer to that of playful fifth formers on their first pub outing. Chief among their retinue is a former head boy whose balding and overweight presence adds a majesterial seniority to the proceedings. As befitting a wealthy, honoured guest renowned for his generosity and extravagance, Elton John has arrived laden with booze and presents. Magnanimously, he sets up his own private bar and tuck shop which is rapidly invaded by the most recently elected prefects of the New Pop, Simon Le Bon and the Frankies, who are egged on by such celebrated alumni as Ronnie Lane and Rod Stewart. As the beer flows, Elton's irrepressible extrovertism unfolds in the form of a synthetic lawn and private swimming pool, which is ostentatiously erected beside his 60 foot mobile caravan. The Wham! boys are grateful for a refreshing mid-afternoon dip before returning to their heavily guarded dressing rooms.

George, as usual, spends the last couple of hours with his hair stylist sister Melanie, who ensures that the superstar's locks are kept firmly in place. The Panayiotou sanctum resembles a cross between a hair salon and an amusement arcade, packed with an array of Battlestations and Space Invaders machines. Between the whirring of hair dryers and simulated explosions of astro debris, George inspects the progress of his support acts on a couple of mini video screens. The elaborate electronic equipment betrays the precise nature of a perfectionist who dutifully charts the course of the day's events for reasons other than dilettante amusement or musical appreciation.

In suitable contrast, Andrew Ridgeley plays the aristocratic host, dutifully entertaining his family and selected friends with a private drinks party and buffet. He too has travelled a long road since those summer evenings at the Three Crowns, Bushey, where the simple pleasures of beer and crisps held unimagined epicurean delights.

Outfront, the audience relieve their growing frustration by watching an unsynchronized display of Mexican World Cup style hand-waving from the packed terraces. The effort is so appalling that even the water-spitting animals are distracted for only a few seconds. High in the sky, an aircraft passes overhead with a long streamer wishing "Jack Kay a Happy 25th Wedding Anniversary". The video screens exploit the air travel motif by informing us that "Wham! Choose British Caledonian". In case there was any doubt about that boast, the roar of a Caledonian jet introduces the long awaited first screening of "Wham! In China! A Cultural Revolution". Since completion, the video has undergone a name change and emerges finally as "Foreign Skies", a title appropriately borrowed from the first line of Wham's "Like A Baby". A "Bad Boys Overseas / CBS" copyright, the project was originally filmed by famed director, Lindsay Anderson, but his involvement ended upon his return to London when he was informed that his services would no longer be required. However, Anderson rightly receives recognition for his direction and, indeed, the credits describe the work as "a Lindsay Anderson Film".

Produced by Martin Lewis and Jazz Summers, the video mixes love songs with "documentary" footage of the historic tour. Unfortunately, the dialogue is inaudible and disappears in the Wembley air amid annoyingly self-conscious screaming whenever Ridgeley or Michael appear on the screen. It would be unreasonable to make any definitive judgement on the aesthetic quality of the video in such restrictive circumstances, but it is difficult to escape the impression that the whole exercise smacks of a glorified home movie. The salivating animal standing beside me announces authoritatively: "It's like watching paint dry", before resuming his watery pursuits. What he misses are the fleeting good bits: the Kung Fu choreography during "Bad Boys"; the backing musicians' hilariously inept version of Del Shannon's "Runaway"; the ironic exposé of upper class smugness at the British Ambassador's drinks party, and the generally impressive additional music courtesy of Richard Hartley. Maybe the drowned dialogue will make entertaining sense of it all. However, if the Wham! boys expect to generate substantial sales from this exclusive preview then they will surely be disappointed. Even the dedicated hundreds crushed closest to the video screens get bored extraordinarily quickly and seem far more interested in talking among themselves or watching the lowlights of the spit/spray contests.

Following *Foreign Skies* there is a deceptively long interval which encourages a mood of hushed expectancy. The stage is empty now, shrouded in a giant black curtain bearing the stark message "The Final". Behind that curtain, a road crew works industriously erecting a podium for the enormous ensemble of musicians and singers whose performance may yet determine whether the concert is a triumph or an anti-climax. Although these outdoor stadium concerts are notorious for their paucity of organization and unapologetic tardiness, The Final has produced no prima donna delays or serious technical hitches to threaten the all important schedule.

As 7.30 approaches, the audience display uncharacteristic signs of impatience with a sprinkling of slow hand claps and shouts of "Come on George". Several people are loading cameras which have spent most of the day hidden inside plastic bags in preparation for a Wham! grand entrance. Other fans fumble nervously and inspect rolls of film which they fear have been damaged irrevocably by the bestial water-spitting louts. Significantly, there are no carefully concealed cassette recorders rearing their sly microphone heads from the bottom of sports bags or food parcels. In spite of its historical significance, The Final is not a musical event to be captured for posterity and enjoyed by tape collectors and pop fans in years to come, but a phenomenon whose ephemeral value lies in its instant obsolescence.

At 7.35, the familiar opening bars of "Everything She Wants" reverberate from behind the black drapes which remain tantalizingly closed. Several minutes pass before the teaser curtain finally swishes open to reveal the feline George Michael prowling across the stage, flanked by two male negro dancers. High pitched adolescent screams of joyful recognition rend the Wembley air, but the star performer shows no emotion whatsoever. Dressed in a fringed black jacket, black singlet, black trousers and dark glasses, he appears both moody and menacing, and his concentration is fixed intently on the carefully choreographed dance steps which impel him hypnotically towards the audience on the left side of the stage. The melodramatic opening engenders an atmosphere of uncertainty and expectancy. Where is Andrew Ridgeley? That should be the question on everyone's lips but George Michael has made such an impression that the whereabouts of his partner seem scarcely relevant. A routine designed to exploit audience expectation by delaying the entrance of one of the artistes appears to have backfired dramatically. The decision to leave Ridgeley waiting in the wings has merely reinforced the old adage "George Michael *is* Wham!" Already, Andrew is on the brink of public humiliation in front of 72,000 people and the concert hasn't even begun! Not surprisingly, this increases the suspense tenfold. Suddenly, I catch myself thinking "Has George dumped his erstwhile companion and transformed The Final into a debut solo performance?" My question is answered immediately.

Enter, stage right, the boy they call "the saddest superstar". Following George Michael's adulation-seeking entrance, Ridgeley has every reason to fall victim to that recent press epithet. Yet, far from appearing overawed or intimidated by his partner's grand ovation, he brushes such considerations aside and oozes enough confidence to sustain the illusion that he can even take George at the height of his powers. Dressed in funereal black, with a long coat and severely cropped hair, he bears little resemblance to the doe-eyed youth whose smiling face decorated the walls of inestimable numbers of teenage bedrooms. Character lines have at last emerged on that visage which now looks older, tougher, and somehow more genuine. His old Lothario image is momentarily reinforced by the presence of Holliman and De Manque, dressed in their notoriously risqué rubber dresses. Barely able to contain their laughter, they embrace the role of Victorian maidservants, coyly yet seductively disrobing their aristocratic master. Seizing the moment, Ridgeley thrusts his fingers forward, and with agonizing slowness, removes his black gloves like a Soho stripper who has been forced to double up for an absent colleague. The entire routine is stagey and ham-fisted but the vaudevillian sexuality produces the desired effect, exciting the crowd to delirium and making Michael's grunt and grind seem pedestrian and unimaginative in comparison.

In those opening minutes, Ridgeley effectively answers the questions that interviewers have been posing for the past few years. The mystery of his contribution to Wham! really does lie in the image and, despite reports to the contrary, that facet of the group personality suddenly seems both convincing and important. Over the years, Michael has dwarfed his partner as a composer, singer, producer and arranger, leaving only the visual image and stage persona to quibble about. Michael has never regarded himself as a natural performer, but even in this area his improvement since the early days has been marked. In narrowing the gap between himself and Ridgeley in terms of stage charisma, Michael has inevitably de-emphasized his partner's sole remaining crucial contribution to the act. But, today, Ridgeley has chosen to remind the world, for one last time, why Wham! succeeded as a duo.

While Michael offers workmanlike choreography, which is not altogether unimpressive, the swaggering Ridgeley seems a much more commanding presence. Admittedly, his self-confidence far exceeds his talent, but stadium concerts demand grandiose gestures to convey emotion, real or manufactured. Ridgeley may now, and probably always has been, acting the part of a pop star, but his performance is far more convincing than that of his younger partner, who is allegedly the real thing. For the remainder of the concert, Ridgeley can afford to take his now customary supportive role since the memory of his emphatic entrance, in the most difficult and testing circumstances imaginable, has provided a much needed mock-heroic epitaph to his flickering pop star career.

The histrionics briefly over, Wham! complete "Everything She Wants" and after a few words from Andrew ("You really look good, you really do") they move into "Club Tropicana". The first big hit of the set produces loud applause which forces George to break his noticeable silence with a well rehearsed speech: "I'd just like to say this is obviously the most important gig we have ever played. And I think that, in front of me now, this is the best thing I've ever looked at. We've got four years of thank yous to say this evening and I know we're going to enjoy saying them. So let's get started."

The Wham! set is nothing if not well paced. With such a relatively small canon of songs it is imperative to surrender the weaker numbers early in the evening before the audience grow weary and impatient. Realizing that they will have to save several of their biggest hits for a spectacular encore, Wham! carefully introduce their remaining chart milestones at potentially weak points in the set. The innocuous "Heartbeat" from *Make It Big* is followed by "Battlestations", the least well known number from the recent E.P. With a lull period approaching, Holliman and De Manque are ushered on for a nostalgic rendition of "Bad Boys". Abandoning rubber dresses for leather jackets and skirts, they sport absurdly high beehive wigs adding a much needed injection of theatrical humour to the proceedings. The song over, they disappear, failing to re-emerge until as late as the second number of the encore.

Without the girls, The Final slips back into middle gear with a cover of the Isley Brothers' "If You Were There", an exuberant "A Ray Of

Sunshine" and the exceedingly dull "Credit Card Baby". Suddenly, I notice a middle-aged woman standing two feet in front of me. Her smile and vaguely apologetic tone indicates that she has been easing her way through the crowd, but has now reached the last impenetrable block of semi-naked bodies. Satisfied with her efforts, she settles down to enjoy the show in the stamina-sapping heat amid the most enthusiastic and physi- cally reckless spectators in the arena. Nobody questions the presence of this small woman, whose seniority alone appears to exonerate her from the verbal lashings usually afforded solitary interlopers at such a late stage of the afternoon. Writhing from side to side, she superficially resembles the generation of younger fans that surround her. It is only on closer inspec- tion that you notice the darkening hair, streaked blonde at the sides, like a middle-aged woman in search of a flatteringly younger fashion. The effect is as simple and unassuming as that expressed by any teenage girl. Her dress is stadium casual: white shorts, white sneakers and a turquoise singlet, the right strap of which slips disobediently from her shoulder whenever she gets carried away, which is often. Whenever one of the boys wiggles his way towards the end of a catwalk the smile of the middle-aged woman widens and her hands ascend towards her face in a display of awe that I find somewhat disconcerting from a person of such mature years.

There is little doubt left in my mind that the woman is Jenny Ridgeley. As George Michael wails his way through "Credit Card Baby", my mind focuses on press cuttings past and a smile and hairstyle that this dancing woman duplicates all too convincingly. From that point on, I determine to stalk her every move with the express intention of buttonholing her for a few exclusive comments after the show. Unfortunately, I overestimate her stamina and interest. When "Credit Card Baby" ends, there is a brief pause, as though Wham! are about to announce a short interval. At that moment, the Jenny Ridgeley look-alike turns heel and pushes her way back out of the crowd, never to return. With the show resuming, it is impossible to follow without losing my prestigious place in the crowd. Fearing, for a moment, that I may have been guilty of wishful thinking or suffering investigative delusions in the hot day sun, I stand my ground. The myster- ious woman, if indeed she was Jenny Ridgeley, will have ended up in the royal enclosure or alternatively faded into the netherworld of also-ran sup- porters at the rear of the stadium. A scoop missed, there is nothing else left but to enjoy the rest of the show.

One of the highlights of the evening occurs as early as 8.35 when a white grand piano is hoisted onto the stage, and speculation mounts as to the significance of this interruption. Michael teases the audience by pointing out that neither he nor Ridgeley will attempt to play the instrument. That honour is to be bestowed upon the fat figure who sidles across the stage dressed in a clown's attire and enormous red wig. It is, of course, Elton John disguised as Ronald McDonald, the infantile character created by the obscenely wealthy hamburger chain which was almost entirely responsible for transforming a sizeable section of the British public into junk food addicts on a par with their American counterparts. John's reasons for donning this distasteful outfit remain unclear, though most suspect that it has less to do with sponsoring hamburgers than distracting attention from the aesthetic imperfections of the body hidden beneath the costume. The extrovert football chairman has always championed camp glitter and on this day, in front of the self-professed hunks of the New Pop, his psychologically self-defensive sartorial excesses are needed more than ever.

While Elton John takes his piano seat, George spends a disproportionate amount of time introducing the audience to a stadium game popularized by Wham! during their last US tour. Like an overfussy schoolmaster with an overlarge class of mixed ability pupils, Michael splits the stadium crowd into three groups, each of which is allocated a "la la la" or "yeah yeah yeah" to be shouted during various points in the chorus. About ten minutes pass while the indulgently patient singer takes the audience through their paces, urging them to learn their lines, synchronize their shouts and raise their arms at precisely the correct times. After endless rehearsals, which make you eternally grateful for not being born a session musician or Wham! producer, the operose *meistersinger* reluctantly announces that he is satisfied.

A guest guitarist appears in the form of David Austin, whose significance in the Wham! story extends far beyond an appearance on the recording of "The Edge Of Heaven". Austin is the silent partner, the friend who preceded Ridgeley and continues to represent the musical muscle and artistic aspiration which the sun-tanned one failed to achieve. It is fitting that he should figure on the last single as a reminder of what might have been if a different Wham! line up had existed.

"The Edge Of Heaven" concludes with loud cheers and the spectators are so pleased with their display of Pavlovian whining that they adopt their various "la la las" and "yeah yeah yeahs" as unimaginative chants to be uttered at impatient moments throughout the remainder of the performance, including the encores. Meanwhile, George bestows further retrospective glory upon David Austin by reminding the world that they were once busking buddies with a repertoire which included the next song, "Candle In The Wind". George points out, with due politeness, that the number was written by the humble clown sitting silently at the piano. His politeness, however, does not extend as far as actually allowing Elton John to sing his own composition. That privilege is reserved for George Michael, solo superstar, who offers a plaintive cover on which Elton is conspicuous for uttering not a single word in harmony or chorus.

With the show moving into top gear, Michael decides to play the sexy suggestive luminary of media notoriety and offers some words on the taboo subject of teenage promiscuity: "How many of you came here unaccompanied and how many are planning to go home with someone of the opposite sex? All I can say is – this number is for you."

What follows can only be described as George Michael invoking the spirit of P.J. Proby and Tom Jones. As the strains of "Love Machine" pulsate from the stadium speakers, the singer struts across the stage and adjoining catwalks, gyrating his backside and thrusting his pelvis forward in such a provocative fashion that he resembles nothing less than an over-sexed monkey involved in a plethoric display of sexual intercourse. At one point, his hand glances perilously close to his genitals, an action which provokes a wave of screaming approval. Only a couple of days before, the soaraway *Sun* had printed a story about a distraught mother fleeing from a Brixton theatre, protectively clutching her teenage daughter after allegedly witnessing George Michael unzipping the flies of his trousers in mime at the climax of the same song. That incident was deemed important enough to warrant a front page headline and, judging from the raucous reaction of the spectators, the report has been widely read.

The "Love Machine" routine has evidently taken its toll on Michael, and after several Gary Glitter style cardiac-inducing runs across the massive stage, he pauses for breath and surveys the fruits of his success with a speech of barely restrained emotion: "This has probably got to be the best moment in my life. In fact, it definitely is. You're fantastic." Still recovering from his pseudo-erotic jerks, George wisely elects to slow the tempo with a slyly placed ballad. While introducing "A Different Corner" he takes the opportunity to thank everyone for granting him a second number one hit and dedicates the song to "One special person" adding somewhat enigmatically "and they know who they are". The use of the plural is most confusing, for it would have been far more natural to conclude "and she knows who she is". Are we to assume the song is dedicated to one person or many, or has George, in his excitement, confused personal pronouns? Later in the show he describes "Freedom" as "a favourite of Andrew's and I's", which causes grave doubts about the grade he achieved at O-level English Language, let alone A-level English Literature. My mind commutes effortlessly back to earlier in the day when, on a radio special, George cheekily ticked off Andrew for his appalling use of grammar in uttering the meaningless reply: "It'll be kept putting off." Surprisingly, Ridgeley takes neither of these golden opportunities to exact a sweet revenge.

Instead, George introduces the seasonably incongruous "Last Christmas", which is greeted with rapturous applause in spite of the 92 degree heat. Not content with inspiring moronic choruses of "yeah yeah yeah" throughout the afternoon, Wham! decide to play another indulgent game with the re-introduction of the tedious Mexican wave. George once more slips into his headmaster persona with eager admonitions to "lift the orange side of your programme" in crest-like formation. In spite of all his coaching, the display is embarrassingly paltry, lacking even the redeeming spontaneity of the afternoon's appalling effort. Confident that he can produce better results, Ridgeley requests the spectators to raise the red side of their £5 programmes and repeat the pointless exercise. This time the wave subsides before reaching even half way across the arena.

Ridgeley's acute embarrassment is small beer in comparison to the result of the next playful diversion. In an act of time-wasting folly, George has decided to inaugurate a cheering contest, as if seeking empirical evidence that he is more popular than Andrew. Poor Ridgeley is forced to drink the cup of humiliation to the dregs as the cries inevitably proclaim Michael a landslide winner. Surprised by the ease of his victory, George suggests, rather diplomatically, that the high pitched squeals in his favour were amplified unfairly by the stage microphone that he was thrusting forward. Few are convinced by his courteously implausible explanation.

In an attempt to restore Andrew's importance, George delves far back into his past and describes the moment "in Mr Ridgeley's front room" when the duo composed their debut single "Wham! Rap". The song still sounds fresh and exciting in live performance, conjuring up the days when Wham! were a more unified partnership. Michael again travels back to 1982 for a surprise rendition of Carly Simon's "Why". This is no mere arbitrary selection for, as every Wham! student knows, Simon's "The Right Thing To Do" was the first record that George ever bought. Her inclusion among the credits today is a fitting tribute.

As the show reaches its latter stages, Andrew chimes in with an arrogant reminder that Was (Not Was)' "Where Did Your Heart Go?" may be "someone else's song, but our record". The mood grows sentimental before the uplifting "Freedom" ends the performance leaving the audience to wait patiently for the inevitable encores.

Having exhausted most of their repertoire during the preceding two hours, there is little mystery about which songs they will play upon their return. No less than three number ones have been held back for a dramatic conclusion, and the only question concerns the order of play.

Cleverly, George commences with "Careless Whisper", the parabolical hit which first prompted rumours of an imminent split. The audience acknowledge his pre-eminence as a soloist, but the true spirit of the evening is evoked in the concluding triumvirate of Wham! classics. "Young Guns" heralds the long awaited return of Holliman and De Manque dressed, appropriately enough, as cowgirls. Once more, their involvement guarantees that the number is a showstopper and makes you wonder why they were used so sparingly on this historic day. As the audience awaits Wham's second encore, George runs around the stage pretending that he is an aeroplane about to crash. The reason for this childish aberration is both unexplained and forgotten as Wham! tackle possibly their most famous song to date. "Wake Me Up Before You Go-Go" would have been the perfect closing number, reminding the 72,000 crowd of that happiest of moments when Wham! returned from self-imposed exile to capture the top of the charts in the spring of 1984. George himself acknowledges that if Wham! are to be remembered by one song then it is likely to be this most infectious of his compositions. Yet, on the day, "Wake Me Up Before You Go-Go" has been relegated to penultimate status, for everybody knows that a more recent number 1 has been inexplicably ignored.

While preparations are underway for the grand finale, a firework display from behind the stage illuminates the arena with green, red and blue flashes of colour. When Wham! return, George introduces the backing group and allows Deon Estes to indulge himself with some long-winded bass playing before the familiar strains of "I'm Your Man" throb through the stadium speakers. As the song begins, the recently bare stage becomes a Wham! fancy dress party, with the girls reverting to leather and Andrew donning a fringed brown jacket in imitation of Buffalo Bill. By far the strangest creature on the podium is Elton John, the self-professed champion of sartorial absurdity, who waddles across the stage in what looks like a pink sack topped off with a mohican wig of similar hue.

Mid-way through the song, Simon Le Bon arrives to share lead vocals with George Michael, as the forlorn Ridgeley stands alone on the opposite side of the stage watching proceedings with a smile of acceptance. The coupling of the two biggest heart-throbs of the New Pop is an interesting spectacle, putting paid to all those rumours of bitchy rivalry between Wham! and Duran Duran. For a few minutes, the audience is transported into a parallel world in which the portly Le Bon played second male lead in the Wham! story. That chillingly convincing image fortunately proves evanescent, for George rightly reunites with his proper partner to bring the evening to a fittingly sentimental and friendly close. Arm in arm, the smiling duo sing out the final notes of their career as Wham!, while threatening green laser lights dazzle the crowd into submission and acceptance. The Wham! story ends in a warm embrace captured poignantly on the giant twin screens and frozen for emphatic effect.

As weary bodies trudge towards the exit gates, the stadium scoreboard flashes a last message: "Thank you and goodbye. Wembley wishes you all a safe journey home". It is already evident that many of the crowd wish they were back at home. Within the arena, a herd of thirsty bodies drink like cattle from taps conveniently signposted "DRINKING WATER". Behind them lies a dark, polluted sea of plastic cups, cans, bottles, discoloured liquid that was once tea or coffee, and the dregs of foul-smelling overheated beer. Wembley is not a pleasant sight after a pop concert, and already helpers are beginning to collect the rubbish, a Herculean task which will continue throughout the night and beyond.

Outside the stadium, anxious parents wait at pre-arranged points for the safe return of their children while police officers and St. John Ambulance staff maintain a low key presence, gently ushering the crowd to the car park and bus and railway stations. Souvenir vendors implore the streaming masses to stop and buy one final momento of the great day, but there is now a discernible note of desperation in their voices. The items still on sale are multifarious: posters and scarves priced at £1; Wham! bags slashed to fifty pence and, strangest of all, several caches of "souvenir cigars". As the pace of the crowd gathers speed, the familiar smell of onions, grease and burnt meat wafts through the air. The hot dog stands and mobile burger parlours are doing a surprisingly roaring trade selling quarter pounders, jumbo sausages and litre packs of "Mr. Juicy" all for £1 each. At this stage of the evening, the vendors want to keep their prices as digitally uncomplicated as possible. Those kids who have managed to dodge the souvenir sellers and junk food merchants next find themselves beset by rapacious reporters. Although tired and dishevelled, a group of girls allow themselves to be photographed while a sprightly newshound reels off a list of quick fire questions.

"Do you think George will go sentimental and middle of the road?" enquires the fresh faced journalist.

"No!" cry the girls in unison before wandering off into the night.

One last solitary assailant salesman still holds court on the road to the station. He claims to be selling Wham! fan club records for a bargain £1.50 each. "Only 7,000 of these have been pressed," he boasts triumphantly. With the engaging patter of a barrow boy, he cajoles passing punters with simple yet irresistible logic: "If you can pay £3 for a lousy poster, you can pay £1.50 for a record."

The street outside Wembley Park Underground station is lined with people crowded together in one huge ugly mass. Mobility has been reduced to single pigeon steps and it takes over twenty minutes to travel as many yards as congestion undermines logic and threatens mob rule. Chaos is postponed long enough to reach the legendary platform 4 which is overrun with an unruly throng destined for Central London. Eventually, the stationary train pulls away, having suffered assault from several latecomers diving through the rapidly closing doors.

My compartment is remarkably uncrowded as though the sudden departure had taken the weary travellers unawares, leaving most of them stranded on the platform. The mood of the passengers is anything but exuberant. Four girls lie slumped across the floor of the compartment like prisoners of war on their way to a concentration camp. Further down the carriage, two pairs of mothers and daughters sit facing each other on parallel seats. While the mothers chat idly about the concert and rummage through their Wham! bags to compare souvenirs, the girls sit in stony silence, too exhausted even to communicate with each other. The tops of their shoulders are sunburnt red and it is evident from their fair complexions that considerable pain will visit them later in the night. As each station passes, their eyes grow tired and you realize that it is already probably way beyond their bedtime. Even fervent 13 year-old Wham! fans have a palpable threshold of exhaustion.

At Finchley Road, half a dozen people cross the adjoining platform from a parallel train and besiege our carriage. Their effort causes them to collapse in a heap. At St. John's Wood, a few baffled commuters get on, unsure of what is causing this sudden disruption to their normally sedate late night journey home. Eventually, the train reaches civilization, passing through familiar place names such as Baker Street, Bond Street, Green Park, and finally Charing Cross. There is a mass exodus at Green Park as dozens of passengers dressed in t-shirts and shorts transfer to the popular Victoria line. Their weariness is betrayed by an uncharacteristic silence broken only by the odd loudmouth still inebriated from his final can of lager.

By the time the train reaches Pimlico, the Wham! contingent is no longer dominant. My final image is of two lads whose personae look uncomfortably familiar. One of them stares intently at a carriage glass window, apparently disturbed by his reflection. He teases his disordered hair which is identical to George Michael's 1984 style, complete with Lady Di swishes and troughs in all the right places. As he leans forward, two partly hidden gold earrings are revealed as if in honour of his pop star hero. The companion seated next to him sports a contemporary Andrew Ridgeley haircut, spoilt only by his unfortunate facial features which are a grotesque distortion of pop star prettiness. True to form, he sings the chorus of "Wham! Rap" in an annoying repetitive tone throughout the final stages of our journey. It is an appropriate epitaph to the two stars who symbolized the unrepentant ephemerality of 80s style New Pop.

While the majority of the arena audience suffers the equivalent of military fatigue and hobbles home to bed in defeat, the Wham! boys are already replenishing lost energies. Not for them the deadened limbs resulting from five hours of standing in one spot where it was impossible even to fall to your knees. Nor did they have to suffer near dehydration and a seven hour fast in order to avoid the horrifying prospect of surrendering their square foot of turf to reach the excruciatingly distant Wembley toilets. Nature repaid the toilet trained beer drinkers in a sadistically painful fashion and their torturous trip to and from the lavatories proved the equivalent of a nightmarishly prolonged game of running the gauntlet. The great lesson of The Final was that the spectators suffered far greater physical exhaustion than the performers.

Backstage, Wham's recovery from their 2½ hour performance is complete and the mood remains buoyant throughout the closing stages of the evening. George Michael sheds a few tears of joy and relief while his partner cracks open a bottle of champagne to share with his parents and the ubiquitous Elton John. After changing their sweat-drenched clothes, the boys descend upon the Hippodrome, a fashionable West End club, where they host a £65,000 party. As they drive towards the club entrance at 12.15, a throng of well wishers greets them with loud cheers. Inside, the club has been specially decorated for the post-gig celebration with silk-covered walls, artificial snow spread across the floor, and hundreds of balloons marooned on the tables and chairs. While disc jockeys play an endless medley of Wham! greatest hits, the boys head towards their V.I.P. lounge, but soon re-emerge on to the dance floor.

Press photographers are overjoyed at the opportunity of snapping some shots of Andrew's girlfriend, Donia Fiorentino, parading around in a sexy off-the-shoulder dress. The *big* news, however, is that George has a new female companion called Kathy Jueng. With their barely disguised under-tones of polite racism, the tabloids will later tell us that Michael has dumped his "long term" girlfriend, the "dusky" Pat Fernandes, in favour of an "oriental beauty". "Love struck George" is evidently besotted with his "China girl" and "romance is definitely on" cry the knowing headline writers. The probable inaccuracy of such conjecture is placed in stark perspective by the tendency of the same papers to resort to cheap unfounded sensationalism, which is demonstrably incorrect. With the headline "Wham II", *The Sun* makes the patently ludicrous suggestion that George is teaming up with David Austin to launch a new group without Ridgeley. Needless to say, virtually every person in the stadium knows that Michael is merely producing his old friend's next disc as he has done before and will no doubt do again. The Austin blunder merely dis-tracts from further speculation about George's romantic entanglements as the singer's worst criticisms of the press are momentarily verified.

The 72,000 fans will surely be neither fooled nor encouraged by talk of Wham! II, let alone George's own fanciful comments on a probable vinyl reunion before the Nineties. For they know that the Wham! story effectively ended at 10.17 pm on 28 June 1986.

Andrew Ridgeley: The Saddest Superstar And Other Media Myths

The press is important in its place on the dartboard, but people don't take it that seriously. You can overexpose something to the extent that you put out a good record and people go "Ugh!" The reason Wham! are not taken seriously is because the media has made them into pop stars. And so have we. We've all been guilty of it, including the boys. What happens is, it gets out of control. You can't control it when you've got two good looking boys making pop songs.

Jazz Summers

It's a game and a lot of people suffer from their policy of not being interviewed. When you're a pop star, you must accept that you can't just be famous for what you do. It's not clever for an artiste to say they won't talk to the press because then they have no hold. They become fair game. There's no reason to hold *anything* back. My responsibility is to my readers. It's not to the musicians. They use us to sell records . . . Andrew Ridgeley became a really snotty superstar who went on and on about how he hated the press. He made his own bed and he had to lie in it.

John Blake

People always said Andrew was less than half of Wham! It's ludicrous. If Andrew hadn't been there Wham! wouldn't have happened at all. It would have been just George as a good singer. The whole image of Wham! was Andrew. It was really two Andrews. The image was two young guys out on life's adventure, having fun, just like "Starsky and Hutch" and "Butch Cassidy and the Sundance Kid" as I've frequently described it. But that was Andrew, not George. George alone wouldn't have been suitable to sing those songs. They were all group songs and needed a lot of gutsy imagery. Andrew provided that imagery right through. He has been consistent. He was never the musical force in Wham! but *always* the gutsy imagery. Andrew's not a pathetic character in any way. He's very self-possessed and together. The press will print in their papers what will sell.

Simon Napier-Bell

The low brow tabloid press reflects its own version of history in regular bulletins from a semi-factional universe in which the public and private lives of pop stars coalesce uneasily to create hybrid characters, whose complexity is surrendered in the pursuit of a clearly identifiable stereotype. It is a landscape in which particular aspects of personality are indiscriminately magnified in order, paradoxically, to reduce the subject to the level of caricature. These caricatures of convenience may be eternal or evanescent for they are governed by simple, self-defining headlines such as "Randy Andy", "Animal Andy", "Bad Boy" or "Bad Boy Makes Good". Steadfast .images can be shed like snake skins in this twilight world of imposed disorder where circulation figures are measured in a continual chaotic mutability; where George Michael can be depicted as an extrovert nightclub habitué on Monday and a miserly introvert on Tuesday; where Wham's sexuality veers from excessive womanizing to near platonic celibacy; where one journalist waxes enthusiastic on Lothario bedroom secrets, while another labours over gay rumours; where Andrew Ridgeley is a happy-go-lucky playboy, but also the saddest superstar of all; where his hard-drinking, hedonic high jinks defines his success, yet also chronicles his downfall; where he is dismissed as a selfish tax exile only to be applauded as a secret philanthropist. It is a fascinating world of myths, legends and kaleidoscopic images that requires no explanation or rational argument. Under the cover of showbiz columns, overpaid pseudo-investigative journalists regularly contradict their own facts and reverse their opinions with an amnesiacal conviction which would be genuinely frightening were it not so absurd. The tabloids are the Ministry of Truth of the modern world, in which pop history is consistently re-written and the past functions merely as a tool of the present.

When the press first bit their teeth into Wham! they discovered the familiar taste of rich, succulent sexuality. Wham! surrendered to their insatiable appetites by basting themselves in the juices of imaginary sexual encounters past, prompting their interrogators to conclude: "It's a waste of time asking George and Andrew how many girls they've slept with – they lost count long ago". This distinctly tabloid prose prefaced by such unimaginative headlines as "Wham! Bam!" and "Wham! Bang!" defined the group throughout 1984 when artificial eroticism sprang from their lips as readily as shuttlecocks popped from their shorts. George Michael sensed the danger in allowing himself to be stereotyped as a teenage Casanova and wrote himself out of the tabloids' script towards the end of the year. Such a feat normally would have proved nigh impossible, but Michael was blessed with a partner whose newsworthiness as a Lothario was unequalled by any contemporary figure in the New Pop pantheon. Like two fleeing foxes hitting a forked path, the Wham! boys diverged and when Michael turned around he saw the relieving spectacle of a pack of newshounds halting momentarily before deciding *en masse* to pursue his partner. Ridgeley was to give them a merry chase.

Long before Michael left him to his tabloid fate, Ridgeley had unwisely concluded a Faustian pact with Fleet Street from which there was no easy release. At the peak of Wham's much publicized "comeback", in the summer of 1984, the tabloids ran a sensational story claiming that Ridgeley had been involved in a brawl and was presently in the hands of a plastic surgeon. Apparently, he had been seriously disfigured with horrendous cuts spreading from nose to ear. Days later, another story emerged insisting that the alleged fracas was a case of playful high jinks involving Wham! compatriot, David Austin, who had supposedly thrown an ice bucket at Ridgeley. Finally, three weeks later, *The Sun* corrected their previous, and now unacknowledged, report by revealing the startling truth – Ridgeley had undergone a cosmetic nose operation. The intrepid sleuthhounds had sniffed him out in a St. Tropez hideaway, and after extracting a full confession forced him to testify to their investigative skill: "We thought we'd got away with it, but trust *The Sun* to find out and come here and nab me." With those words, whether from his own mouth or a copywriter's pen, Ridgeley opened a Pandora's Box of unwelcome scrutiny which was to dog him for the remainder of his Wham! days.

Playing games with Fleet Street by fictionalizing your own life is an extremely dangerous undertaking, for at any moment the pen is likely to be wrenched from your hands and turned against you in the form of prurient tales far beyond your own prosaic imaginings. Having scripted his own sexual adventures for most of 1984, Ridgeley was shortly to fall victim to the lurid prose of unwanted ghost writers and voyeuristic photographers.

While Ridgeley was safely away on a world tour, *The Sun* ran an extraordinary story under the headline "Hands Off My Andy! Pop Star Wars For Two Girls Who Love Wham's Superstar". In the piece, two topless models, Elisha Scott and Jackie St. Clair, *both* claimed they were Ridgeley's sweetkins and as a consequence of their rivalry were presently engaged in what the tabloids referred to as a "catfight". The drama allegedly began when Elisha telephoned Jackie one morning about a modelling assignment, only to be greeted by a voice that she identified as Ridgeley. Seething with jealousy, Ms. Scott deduced: "He'd obviously been sleeping with her, the bitch. I bet she offered it to him on a plate. She's a wicked temptress." She then proceeded to relate her own experiences with the young Don Juan, boasting that on their first night together they failed to reach the bedroom but "made love on the floor." After further astonishingly explicit descriptions of these nocturnal shenanigans, she noted his aversion to her nationalist tendencies: "He certainly didn't want me to lie back and think of England." Apart from his more obvious physical attractions, Ridgeley was apparently blessed with eyes of such burning intensity they actually melted Ms. Scott. Her story, still labouring under that metaphysical conceit, ended in true feline fashion with a threat to her rival: "I'll scratch her eyes out."

Ms. St. Clair evidently relished the prospect of a confrontation and, con-

fidently catalogued her own earthy charms, before purring enigmatically:
"He told me that dark girls brought out the animal in him. His nickname
for me is walnut whip. You'll have to work out why for yourself."

The Sun's vast readership was still pondering over the meaning of the
"walnut whip" metaphor several days later when the story was revived in a
typically titillating tabloid photo session. With their claws encased in a pair
of boxing gloves, the models were shown gamely pairing up against each
other. Their breasts were once more amply displayed.

The intense rivalry between the girls was rapidly replaced by a more
ferocious skirmish between the warring tabloids. *The Mirror* entered the
fray with their own insightful analysis of the impending catfight. Their
money was clearly on Jackie St. Clair who was, by this time, threatening
passionate violence: "If he ditches me in favour of Elisha I'll break his
nose. And I'll give her a black eye." *The Mirror* concluded their research
by noting Jackie's wardrobe of sexy clothes, an evident riposte to Ms. Scott
who had previously announced her intention to win Andrew back by teas-
ing him with her sexy garb. Nor did the story end there. *The Star* belatedly
intervened with the unlikely claim that both girls, unbeknownst to each
other, were flying to New York on 14 February to confront Andrew. An
alarmist news reporter buried his head in his hands and warned of a "St.
Valentine's Day Love Massacre".

Poor old Connie Fillippello, Wham's protective PR lady, was inundated
with requests for Ridgeley's reaction to the serialized catfight. Connie
assured concerned reporters that Andrew didn't know the girls from Eve
and went on to chide the models for their "lively imaginations". Half way
round the world, Jazz Summers learned of the salacious stories after
receiving a copy of the original article:

> I opened up a paper and it showed two topless models fighting over
> Andrew. One of them had her arm around him with her boobs hanging
> out in the middle of *The Sun*. I thought "When did he do *that*?" So I
> walked into the dressing room and said "Andrew?" He looked at the
> paper and I could see him thinking "I didn't do that". They'd made a
> cardboard cut out of him and they actually had written underneath
> "Elisha and cardboard cut out of Andrew Ridgeley". But, of course,
> that was in small print at the bottom.

Ridgeley was astonished by the stories, particularly the "walnut whip"
allusion, which he found highly amusing. He could not recall ever meeting
the girls, which seemed extraordinary in the circumstances. The tabloids
specialize in kiss and tell stories and although they often seem spiced up, at
least the relationships are real enough. But this was a new departure.

The tabloids' feverish pursuit of Scott and St. Clair underlined, most
forcibly, their near obsession with Ridgeley as a symbol of New Pop newsworthiness. For the sake of sanity, it was advisable for the sensationalized
superstar to maintain a low profile and wait for the sleuthhounds to loosen

their clenched toothed grip. Instead, the irrepressible Ridgeley chose this very moment to embark on a series of escapades which would enliven the front pages for months ahead.

One month after *The Sun's* celebrated "catfight", Ridgeley played host to the tabloids' wildest fantasies during two memorable evenings at the Dragonara Hotel in Bristol. In the company of George Michael, he was attending a ball organized by the Bristol Polytechnic Rugby Club. Michael maintained a low profile throughout the visit and fortunately did not figure in *any* of the incidents that supplied the Street of Shame with suggestive headlines and lurid tales for the best part of a week. *The Sunday People* produced arguably the sauciest headline with their "Carry On" style "Oh Andy! What *Were* You Doing With The Girl In Green Knickers?" The girl in question, sociology student Lynn Brown, had set out to seduce the partying superstar whose photograph graced the wall above her bed. Her strategy was spontaneous and provocative. She simply flashed her brightly coloured underwear, an action seemingly guaranteed to arouse Andrew's "animal passion". Before long, the pair were heading for a hotel bedroom to enact scenes that would not have been out of place in a Brian Rix farce. A jealous boyfriend, armed with a fire extinguisher, was determined to douse their passion and continually interrupted their amorous proceedings by hammering furiously on their door. Ironically, it was his own ardour that was cooled when a y-fronted Andrew poured a glass of water over his head. According to the *Sunday People*, the hard-drinking evening ended in disappointment, but the ever incisive *News Of The World* managed to wring some baffling performance gradings from the "college charmer" who coyly cooed: "I'll give him nine out of ten for effort and seven out of ten for style." Her biggest regret, it transpired, was neglecting to secure Ridgeley's by now legendary canary y-fronts as a hunting trophy. It was left to her boyfriend to sum up this quintessentially English farce with the delightfully euphemistic phrase, "She's a naughty girl."

The vampirish tabloids were far from content with one night of naughtiness and despatched their lupine undercover teams to scavage further indiscretions. *The Sun* discovered more than they could have hoped for the following evening when Ridgeley attended an outrageous fancy dress disco. Several scantily-dressed girls were present and *The Sun* duly reported one losing her bra and another whose slacks were surreptitiously unzipped. Ridgeley, of course, had to be featured in this student saturnalia and was portrayed as a drunken reveller twanging suspenders, organizing a "big boobs" competition and indulging in other wanton activities. After reading *The Sun's* exhaustive list of misdemeanours, Andrew was uncharacteristically indignant enough to inform the rival *Daily Star* of his semi-innocence. All he admitted was getting "very merry" and adjudicating a sexy bottom contest. Of course, that in itself warranted a front page headline with the curiously Scottish intonation: "I'm No Randy Andy!" Within the space of two months, Ridgeley's exploits had replaced the space usually reserved for prime ministers and members of the Royal Family. And there was worse to come.

A splurge of Wham! publicity followed within days of the Rugby club incident when the duo was whisked away for their fateful China visit. Ridgeley briefly attempted to placate his Fleet Street pursuers, but lost patience when they returned incessantly to the subject of his recent misconduct. The political implications of the China trip were reduced to a single question which summed up the tabloids' sphere of interest: "What do you think of Chinese girls, Andrew?" The enquiry remained unanswered.

Upon his return to England, Ridgeley wasted no time in attracting more controversy. His latest passion, motor-racing, had journalists scurrying across to Brands Hatch to witness the superstar smashing his practice car in spectacular fashion. One week later, a fresh posse of reporters, swelled by several representatives from the middle brow tabloids, descended upon Snetterton, an obscure Norfolk town which the pop idol had chosen as the setting for his debut race. The media vigilance did not go unrewarded. The following day headlines proclaimed "Wham! Crash No. 2 For Andy". In fact, Ridgeley had only momentarily lost control of his vehicle in a typical off the track spin, before returning to finish 20th in a field of 30. Nevertheless, from that day forward, Ridgeley's motor-racing became synonymous with the word "crash".

Away from the track, Ridgeley re-assumed his mantle of chief nightclub boor with a series of well publicized transgressions. At Stringfellows, a photographer was splashed with lager for displaying too keen an interest in Andrew's movements. Days later, Ridgeley was spotted leaving the Live Aid party at Legends in a drunken state. At Tramp, he grabbed a woman, slung her across his knee and dropped her on the floor while other patrons looked on in amazement. Xenon, a famed nightspot for Wham! drama, was thrown into chaos when Andrew and one of his followers began rolling across the floor. Before long, a playground bundle ensued, which ended in flying fists and overturned drinks. A passing press photographer could not believe his luck when he clicked a bleary-eyed Ridgeley in the midst of the throng. A similar incident occurred at the Hippodrome which featured a special floor show starring Ridgeley and David Austin. The highlight was the unsavoury spectacle of Andrew being dragged across the floor to the incongruous strains of *Swan Lake*. Later, the incorrigible Wham! hell-raiser took an amused, almost philosophical, view of his disgraceful behaviour: "At the Hippodrome I'm usually dead drunk and they shouldn't really throw me out for collapsing in the bar, but they do."

The gormandising tabloids seemed intent on gnawing Ridgeley's flesh to the bone and urgently needed more salacious copy to fill the autumn period when Wham! would be absent in America. A brief lull in Ridgeley's night-life forced them into a bidding war for his uncensored confessions. As ever, *The Sun* proved the most persistent and desperate of the bunch, with a budget of staggering proportions. Nor were they content to haggle with Jazz Summers or even Napier-Bell. They telephoned Morrison/Leahy and requested the publishers to pass on an offer of £50,000 for an exclusive interview. Ridgeley was intrigued by the offer, though he found the prospect of a *Sun* exclusive somewhat disconcerting. He jokingly requested a Rolls Royce in place of the money and, to his amazement, his terms were accepted. When *The Sun* discovered that a Rolls could not be manufactured overnight, the deal was amended and the parties settled on a Ferrari Daytona Convertible. A contract was hastily drafted, but, at the eleventh hour, Ridgeley reconsidered the consequences of surrendering copy approval and backed down. From that point onwards, a new caricature began to take form in the fertile tabloid imagination.

It was not *The Sun*, but *The Daily Star* that first exploited the full horrors of Ridgeley's transmutation from jack-the-lad hell-raiser to spiritual wreck. In a sobering article titled "Punch Drunk! That's The Wham! Star Whose World's Falling Apart", journalist Rick Sky honed in on Ridgeley's familiar excesses, but added a new dimension to his drunken revelry. Far from celebrating his fame and glory, Andrew was apparently blotting out the horrific realization of his increasing redundancy in Wham! Ridgeley's reluctance to talk with the press was used as further evidence of surly evasiveness, replacing his once boisterous *joie de vivre*. The article ended with hints of an impending Wham! split and some contrastingly complimentary remarks on George Michael's work and general attitude. Clearly, Michael was becoming the yardstick by which to measure the depth of Ridgeley's fall.

The Sun was next to draw blood, though they had to wait until Christmas before unearthing another public outburst from their favourite quarry. The setting was a Chinese restaurant in Soho. The headline: "Ridgeley's Four Letter Night Out". It transpired that Andrew was guilty of using appallingly coarse language in an exclusive eaterie which upset some fellow diners. Interestingly, George Michael was also in attendance but not one foul word was heard emanating from his lips. Apparently, not much else happened to write home about. Far from suffering a dressing down from the waiters, Andrew was tolerated, and actually calmed down of his own volition. Nobody was asked to leave the restaurant or even mildly reprimanded. The article ended in anti-climax.

By early 1986, Ridgeley's "bad boy" routine seemed like ancient history. But the tabloids boast the powers of Chronos and their prose can commute effortlessly between the past and the present to lift new perspectives from old news. It was left to John Blake of *The Mirror* to complete the revisionist process by which Ridgeley's activities were transformed from low comedy into tragic pathos. In an "exclusive", poignantly titled "The Saddest Superstar", Blake regurgitated a checklist of Ridgeley's recent public peccadilloes before launching into an astonishing re-examination of the nightclubbing prodigy, whose happy-go-lucky high jinks were magically mutated into a miracle play on the dangers of alcohol. Blake's acerbic catalogue of infamous incidents was reinforced by some two year old drinking tales from Simon Napier-Bell, which, in their new context, provided a damning resonance. History had been transformed into a knife which was now firmly lodged in the back of the faltering superstar. After describing Ridgeley's drinking persona as "vicious and unpleasant", Blake concluded that the "saddest superstar" of all was poised to become "another rock 'n' roll casualty".

In retrospect, Blake perceives the piece as an inevitable backlash caused by Ridgeley's antipathy towards Fleet Street and his haughtiness as a "snotty superstar":

> You've got to be clever to be a pop star today. You've got to think about other people's feelings and motivations. If you use people for publicity and then you become famous and sell records and say those people are shit, you must expect they're not going to take kindly to you. And I think you're doing a service to the reader to tell him how this person really isn't very nice and has been swayed by success. I was attempting to show what happened in Wham! and why it disintegrated. If they'd been prepared to speak to the press, one wouldn't have to use old quotes. You can't whip up all this hysteria and then say, "I'm not talking". You create a vacuum. The result is a rehash . . . I'd have much preferred to speak to Andrew Ridgeley.

From Blake's testimony, it seems perfectly clear that hell hath no fury like a tabloid spurned. Looking back, Ridgeley was probably no worse than any of his contemporaries in the New Pop, just less cautious, less gracious, and considerably less unctuous in his PR relations. Only Boy George, who played the media game for far bigger stakes, was destined to receive a greater comeuppance.

Ridgeley's unrestrained high jinks transformed him into a figure of ridicule and, arguably, the most boorish superstar of the 80s New Pop. But it took the mass resentment of the tabloids to distillate that boorishness into a pathos which fermented into the saddest superstar vitriol. It was, of course, a completely erroneous image. Far from being a spiritual wreck seeking sanctuary in the artificial security of celebrity nightclubs, Ridgeley was leading a rather settled life in Monaco. He confessed his boredom with constant nightclubbing and seemed far more interested in spending time with his steady girlfriend, Donia Fiorentino. He drank less, lost weight, and actually worked at his French Formula III motor racing with an industry that suggested it was a passion rather than an ephemeral interest. When he returned to England, in preparation for Wham's final concert, he resembled anything but the pathetic, defeated character of media infamy. On the contrary, he was obviously in excellent physical shape and had lost none of his confidence or arrogance.

By mid-1986, a few commentators were still moaning about his lack of creativity in Wham! But the criticisms now had a hollow ring, rather like an old joke told once too often. Everyone agreed that since *Make It Big* his importance in Wham! had been mainly historical. Many felt that any good looking boy might have replaced him and got away with it, but Wham! themselves disagreed. Even so, wasn't his arrogance galling and unwarranted? Maybe so, but it was also his greatest strength and saving grace.

Contrary to what his detractors will allege, Ridgeley has not milked Wham! to the full. He could have knocked off a couple of dull tunes and pushed for a greater share in the songwriting credits, or forced himself into the spotlight as an occasional singer. Michael would probably have welcomed the chance of a break. In fact, it is amazing that Ridgeley allowed himself to be overshadowed so willingly, so uncaringly. The consequences do not appear to have bothered him in the least, and that attitude has continued to this day. Far more talented artistes than Ridgeley have left successful groups, gone away, licked their wounds ar d returned with their own equivalent of "Wham! II" or "New Wham!" The more cynical and heretical superstar will often argue that the original membership of the group wasn't that important anyway. Consider how easily Ridgeley could pluck another budding George Michael from the legions of would-be blue-eyed soul stars that have emerged in Wham's wake. With a commissioned songwriting team, name producer and PR push, Ridgeley could easily rest on past laurels. Yet, he has so far declined these opportunities. The pop star career that is his for the taking (and make no mistake, record companies would sign him tomorrow on the strength of his Wham! pedigree and image alone) is ominously overdue. Instead, Ridgeley pursues his dreams as a racing driver and future movie actor. Most critics will tell you that he's living in cloud cuckoo land and will fall flat on his face in both these spheres. Maybe they're right, but that's not the point. What is important is that poor deluded Ridgeley still retains the arrogance to try something new and far more ambitious than retreading the boards as a pop idol. For a person who has always taken a lazy approach to superstar life, Ridgeley appears to be making things unnecessarily difficult for himself. By the time his acting and racing ambitions have been exhausted, or exploded, he may well have missed the massive record company advance and guaranteed Top 10 album/single which the early euphoric aftermath of Wham! promised so unreservedly. Yet, he doesn't give a damn. For that, if nothing else, he deserves a sneaking admiration.

George Michael: Image, Politics And Contradictions

George always knew what he wanted, but he wasn't always sure how to get it. The first time I photographed Wham! they were happy to have a cheese sandwich and a coca-cola. One of the last sessions I did with them Andrew said he'd like a smoked salmon sandwich and a glass of claret. Their expectations had changed completely.

Chris Craymer
(*Wham! Photographer*)

Pop stars don't lead normal lives. They're very sheltered. They can't do what they want, can't dance in a club or go where they want, just like that. They're harassed wherever they go by photographers and start to see the world very narrowly. If you want them to resolve their contradictions, you've got to send them off somewhere where they can read and learn to be natural. They don't develop naturally, that's why there are a lot of casualties, and that's why they need protecting. They're emotional people.

Jazz Summers

We thought that if they were going to write rubbish about us, we might as well know what kind of rubbish it was. So we made most of it up and we had quite a laugh until we realized that we were making fools of ourselves by letting them print it at all.

George Michael

One month I'd be a fat, facist, homosexual, with a huge Georgian house somewhere in Essex. The next I'd be a lean, virile left winger.

George Michael

Image, politics and contradictions. For George Michael, the trouble began in 1984, a period of intense competition between the children of the New Pop. Sex and politics determined status and news space as perhaps never before. The anti-Reaganite stance of Frankie Goes To Hollywood and the sexual politicizing of Holly Johnson and Paul Rutherford filled showbiz columns and spawned many articles in the serious music press. Self-confessed homosexual Jimmy Somerville admitted indulging in sexual practices which, eighteen years before, would have rendered him liable to imprisonment under British law. That did not stop Bronski Beat from scoring several major hits on the appropriately named Forbidden Fruit label. But the redoubtable queens of the ball were the gender-bending Boy George, and his colourfully effete media partner, Marilyn, whose exploits provided an inexhaustible source of copy for Fleet Street gossip columnists. Culture Club even adopted a quasi-political stance with the protesting "War Song" and catch-all anthem "Karma Chameleon". The sexual/political mix was proving an irresistible pop attraction.

Wham! had already secured a degree of short-lived "political credibility" in 1983 with their song trilogy of unemployment, young marriage and teenage rebellion. In 1984, they turned their attention to sex. An intense PR campaign to promote their "comeback" from litigious exile revealed the duo pandering to the sexually-fixated tabloids. Wham! allowed themselves to be presented as insatiable womanizers and their new, sexier image was used as an antidote to Culture Club and their ilk. Suddenly, George Michael found himself being asked how a girl might best lure him into bed. His reply was couched in the style of traditional tabloid prose: "They've got to be subtle, like stroking my hair and caressing my chest". Other enquiries were more pointed, and the answers more outrageous.

Wham's fictional bed-hopping adventures seemed nothing more than a passing summer fad, but by late winter the sun-tanned holiday snaps from "Club Tropicana" still featured heavily in the colour sections of the Sunday press. An opening paragraph from the *News Of The World* underlined how dangerously clichéd and stereotyped Wham! had already become:

> They started looking glum the moment the girls wouldn't take off their clothes. But then, it had been a bad day. A very bad day. It was almost midnight and neither George Michael nor Andrew Ridgeley from Wham had been chatted up, groped or stripped by a girl, much less been dragged off feet first to a bedroom. For pop's sexiest duo, there aren't many days when that happens.

The image was way out of hand and Wham! had only themselves to blame. They had allowed themselves to become paste-board pop stars rather than flesh and blood figures. Realizing his error, Michael attempted to break the stereotype by stressing the romantic side of his nature. He expressed a distaste for promiscuity and assured prying reporters that Wham!, unlike other older groups, did not exploit their fans for sexual favours. On the contrary, they studiously avoided the excesses of touring life and were extremely careful in choosing their friends and partners.

In spite of George's bathetic declamations, Fleet Street still enjoyed its role as media matchmaker. During the next couple of years, the press linked his name with a number of women, ranging from "constant companion" Pat Fernandes, to Hazel O'Connor, Brooke Shields, and even the two girls in the "Careless Whisper" video. Predictably, all attempts to uncover some furtive liaison proved fruitless and silly. As a result, the press grudgingly conceded that the Wham! star was telling the truth – he was *not* promiscuous.

In promoting his non-promiscuity, Michael was not whitewashing his fictional tabloid past entirely. He still related the problems of sleeping with a girl whilst wearing contact lenses and spoke unusually frankly about his emotional interactions in several interviews with the serious music press. He prided himself on keeping his private and public lives separate, while somehow managing to avoid the glare of Fleet Street at its most intense. Only occasionally did he throw PR caution to the wind. His interviews with *New Musical Express* were sprinkled with offensive four letter words, and he confessed to indulging in pre-marital sexual relations. The press, apparently used to such behaviour from pop stars, provided no moral commentary.

The tabloids also perceived Michael as a rather liberal young man, whose loss of innocence was regarded as unexceptional. However, certain journalists used that liberality to scurrilous effect by introducing the question of homosexuality. The "gay" theme was evident in several Wham! interviews under such titles as "Gay? I'm Not Even Happy – Says George". All they told us was that *every* person ever asked about the subject, who had even the remotest contact with Wham!, regarded the innuendo as not only inaccurate but laughable. One Wham! associate pondered perplexedly: "I don't know where these gay rumours began . . ." The answer, no doubt, was at the news desk of an imaginative editor in search of a new angle. All it takes is one journalist to enquire, in mock innocence, "You're not gay by any chance", and even an emphatic and angry denial will be turned into an unwanted headline. After that, every article is destined to include at least one curious question on the matter, "just to put the record straight". Michael, to his credit, has attempted to transcend it all, even arguing that a so-called "androgynous image" may work to his advantage in the pop world, as it has done for other stars, such as David Bowie. Although surprisingly willing to talk about the media's unwholesome interest in his sexuality, he refuses to be badgered into quashing rumours and broadcasting denials. He confesses a fear that the press' morbid fascination with his sex life might encourage a certain salacious tabloid to invent a contumelious tale brimming with damaging falsities and unfounded insinuations. In such circumstances, the newly litigious Michael would sue unhesitatingly. His firm belief that none of his former associates, even the disgruntled ones, would countenance a "gay story" ("it could never happen") and their frequent testimonies to his heterosexuality ought to put the tedious and untenable gay question to rest, once and for all.

Although Michael has successfully re-written his media sexual history, finally convincing the tabloids that he wasn't a promiscuous womanizer, he has been less fortunate with his political revisionism. Certain sections of the serious music press still tend to see him as the unacceptable face of Thatcherite pop, a view that can be traced back to 1984. The rapid transition from dole queue reject to Club Tropicana playboy has left a nasty taste, particularly in the mouths of those critics who had championed Wham's early songs extolling "fun of the dole". In the context of Club Tropicana, such sentiments betrayed a depressingly hollow ring, with previously unforeseen connotations of an almost Tebbetian "Get On Your Bike" insensitivity. Wham! consistently dismissed such criticism as naive, and fell back on environmental theory, claiming that their songs were honest reflections of their changing position on the social ladder. What they failed to resolve was the peculiar trichotomy between their attitudes, lifestyle and art. Their once consistent image ultimately appeared curiously lopsided.

In spite of his new "serious" image, George Michael has failed to shrug off completely the stigma of the 1984 Wham! For many, he still tends to be regarded as a pools winner pop star, coining absurdly large amounts of money for penning lightweight pap. This is the unwanted legacy of Wham! Even today, the name George Michael is still inextricably linked in the public imagination with sun-tans, shorts and *nouveau riche* crassness. The image of Wham! at their peak is a powerful icon which transcends Michael's earnest revisionism and defies the logic of retrospective argument.

Image is the arbitress of prejudice, for it encapsulates its own version of truth in a freeze frame whose iconographical potency resists change, in the same way that a portrait belies the ravages of time. Look at all the great pop idols of the past and you see image consistently overcoming contradiction, subjugating logic, ignoring complexity and ultimately disregarding literal truth. Elvis, the archetypal anti-authoritarian teenage rebel, was actually a home-loving kid who adored his mother and called his father "sir"; The Beatles were loved for their zany but clean humour though, in reality, their sordid exploits in Hamburg were reprehensible; The Stones were crude, loutish and degenerate, yet Jagger had attended the London School of Economics and was undoubtedly one of the most articulate and self-disciplined figures in 60s pop. For several of these stars, their original "true" selves later mutated into their self-created images. The mask became the face.

There are many more examples of images establishing myths that transcend dull truth. Even the anti-star philosophy of punk created its own immutable icon in The Sex Pistols. For the music press, the perceived image was a neo-Hogarthian portrait of a downtrodden, snotty-nosed, working-class kid, landing a well aimed kick into the backside of a long-haired, self-satisfied American a'n'r rep in a satin bomber jacket, who himself symbolizes the bland artifice of somnabulistic soft rock, FM-controlled heavy metal music and the whole stinking capitalist enterprise that is the record industry. Like punk itself, The Sex Pistols were full of contradictions, but their attitude represented such an important backlash against the prevailing malaise that particular foibles were swept under the carpet. The Sex Pistols were radical, even though the individual members held some extremely reactionary views, occasionally indistinguishable from the average "Oi" outfit. It is amusing to read back copies of the music press and watch the Pistols receive a patronizing slap on the back for their radicalism, while their more distasteful and ideologically suspect views are ignored or, even worse, paraded as ironic and clever. As ever with pop icons, image and attitude are all important, no matter how questionable the artistes involved become when placed under scrutiny.

With Wham!, image again overcame contradiction and revisionism. They remained the hard drinking, club loving *nouveau riche* bad boys, though according to Summers, they were never the nightclub habitués of media imagination. It was simply that the more prosaic aspects of their lifestyle went unrecorded, while their every social outing was a *paparazzi-circus*. Wham! fully realized the strength of the consumerist image when their vaguely left wing political platitudes fell on deaf ears or were dismissed as downright hypocritical. Like punk at its peak, the dictates of the New Pop, as represented by Wham!, Spandau Ballet and Duran Duran, allowed little ambiguity in its political orientation. Spandau also called themselves socialists, but for the music press and the public, lifestyle spoke louder than words. So with Wham!, image overruled argument and even actions. And the image suggested embourgeoisement, lower middle class Toryism, designer clothes, imminent tax exile in exotic climes, and jack-the-lad disregard for the poor sods not lucky enough to make the grade. It was no matter that Wham! criticized Margaret Thatcher or supported the miners or paid taxes – the image remained unalterable. Even their extravagant support for various charities, which might have totally transformed their "Tory" image somehow conjured up the unfortunate vision of nineteenth-century factory owners performing their social duties as philanthropists. For the Wham! boys, such images must have seemed like horrible and perverse distortions, yet they sneakily transcended mundane truths. At present, Michael has to live with the galling realization that his *truer* self, the thoughtful singer songwriter occasionally revealed in self-analytical interviews, is still overshadowed by the Wham! icon of 1984. His battle to re-invent himself in the public eye is an awesome task which will only be achieved when his attitude, lifestyle and art are forced into alignment. Michael intends to achieve that fusion with his songwriting and solo career. Whether he will succeed is another question.

Epilogue: Happy Christmas...
War Is Over

Simon Napier-Bell still spends most of his waking hours in the spacious front room of a large Georgian house in the opulent setting of Bryanston Square. There, he can be found sitting in a comfortable cream armchair issuing instructions into the mouthpiece of a lightweight telephone that seldom ceases to ring. Between calls, Simon conducts business meetings and press encounters with an engaging smile and sprightly tone. His dress is smart but calculatedly casual and there is something about the room which is vaguely disconcerting. The ceiling is high, the pastel colours soothing, the prints tasteful, the metal table inappropriately modern, but something seems strangely missing. It is only as you get up to leave that you fully realize how ludicrously spacious that room is. The pervasive whiteness merely exacerbates the effect. But there is no time to relish the mystery for you have already stayed far longer than your busy host intended. After the outstretched hand of a middle-aged entrepreneur wishes you farewell, you move towards the door and, if alert, your eye catches the reflection of a suddenly more serious looking man returning to his ringing telephone in what momentarily seems a sparsely furnished exhibition hall, with all the warmth of a Harley Street surgery. As you close the newly painted white twin front doors, you walk into the bright sunshine of a privileged London street, full of expensive parked cars, but eerily void of pedestrians. Inevitably, Napier-Bell's mellifluent words recur in your mind as you briskly cross the road. A convenient wooden bench, avenues away from the intrusive noise of London traffic, allows you to check another invaluable tape recording which has captured the confessions and revelations of a disarmingly frank and occasionally cynical music business veteran. You fast forward the second side of the tape, sigh with relief at the audibility of the voice and linger over a particularly interesting quote which will enliven the text that has already taken form in your head. The disembodied voice speaks warmly of George Michael, of Jazz Summers and of the split that has reduced the Wham! phenomenon to the stark level of boardroom politics. The voice says it has no regrets. You rewind to review the final words of the tape, only to discover an expert self-publicist busily at work. He now speaks of having discovered another act from the mountains of unsolicited cassettes that arrive every week. "Two kids as good as Hall and Oates," he enthuses, barely able to suppress his disbelief at stumbling upon such a find. Groups come, groups go, but there are always hopeful young men in search of stardom and Napier-Bell is happy to be travelling back to the pleasurable point of discovery. Soon, no doubt, a new set of faces will be seen in the emptiness of that white, spacious room.

Jazz Summers, at the time of writing, still runs his business from a company which bears the mirrored Christian name of his former partner. Nomis Management no longer exists and Summers will soon be vacating his first floor headquarters at the end of Gosfield Street. He will walk away with the few remaining Nomis acts, still intent on realizing his dream of establishing a corporate management structure on an international level. For the moment, he sits at a cluttered desk in an office that would barely accommodate Napier-Bell's settee. He still attends long business meetings and enjoys the time-consuming pressure of music business management. When that pressure becomes too great, he reminds himself of earlier working days as a malcontented radiographer and congratulates himself for having had the courage to leave a guaranteed job for life. Once known for his aggression and inflexibility, he now waxes philosophic, even wistful, as he tucks into an unidentifiable meal, while ably displaying a dextrous employment of chop sticks. His diet, like everything else in Jazz' life, reflects his new start. "I'm macro-biotic now," he confides, "it means big life." The Summers diet provokes considerable discussion from his faithful secretary Jane, who marvels at her employer's reformed temperament since ingesting sea-weed, brown rice and little else. Even fruit and dairy produce are rigorously prohibited. Jazz has recently signed a Scottish group, appropriately named the Soup Dragons, one of whose members commits the cardinal sin of demanding sugar in his coffee. Another meeting over and Jazz has at last found a company name befitting a macro-biotic mogul. Welcome: Big Life Management.

Mark Dean has dissolved the Innervision label and most of the bad memories associated with its brief history. He now runs the self-referential MDM Records based in a Portobello Road office owned by Virgin Records. In spite of his image as a tough, young mogul, Dean remains ingratiatingly polite, occasionally betraying the air of a man who has done too much too quickly. The psychology and style of this overreacher manifest themselves in curiously comic ways. On a hot summer's day, Dean's secretary, Miranda, proffers a refreshing drink of water in a glass so ludicrously large and unwieldy that it demands two hands to control. Compare Napier-Bell's tastefully small china cups and you begin to realize the

significance of the inversion. Small receptacles in a big room, big receptacles in a small room – the old mogul and the young tycoon are as studiously opposed as different coloured chess pieces. In contrast to Napier-
Bell's white room and cream sofa, the centrepiece of Dean's office is a strik-
ingly jet black settee. Strangely, there is no desk in Dean's sanctuary and
important paper work is conspicuous by its absence. His conversation is
buoyant with a decidedly stoic tone, typical of a young man who has
suffered and survived the rigours of litigation and near liquidation. With a
much improved licensing deal Dean appears more secure than ever before
and his persistence has already been rewarded with a Top 10 hit, courtesy
of Pete Wylie. Proof enough, perhaps, that he has not lost the Midas touch.
In 20 years time he'll probably be on the board of directors at CBS.

Siobhan Bailey survived the sinking Nomis to retain her prestigious position as George Michael's personal assistant. Engaging and efficient, she can
still be contacted directly on a personal hotline, saving callers from the perpetual vacillation of over-protective secretaries. Her route to George
Michael is equally direct and her ability to extract vital information at a
moment's notice is a rare and worthy asset.

Connie Fillippello, the exotically named Italianate PR, still works for
George Michael and betrays the same professional solicitude that characterized her glory days with Wham! With her high heels, large round earrings and extraordinarily long gaberdine coat, Connie resembles an off
duty fashion model fresh from a visit to the hairdresser and manicurist.
Her mood is seldom brusque and she displays a genuine concern for secretaries and other such inferiors which transcends normal PR grace. It's hard
to believe that her soft spoken feline demeanour and irritatingly regular use
of the word "darling" is not mere affectation, but the image is ingeniously
maintained and her guard never drops. She is the consummate 80s public
relations officer.

Bryan Morrison still works in a Hyde Park flat less than five minutes away
from Napier-Bell's Georgian house. The Morrison/Leahy organization is
well protected from unwanted visitors and gaining admittance requires the
pluckiness of a seasoned explorer. The first hurdle is an imposing intercom, answered by Patricia Rowley, an alert personal assistant who dili-
gently requests the nature of your business like a sentry seeking an esoteric
password. The recognition of your name coincides with a sharp buzzing
sound which drowns her brief words of welcome. Suddenly, you are in an
intimidatingly plush vestibule, confidently walking forward in a determined attempt to avoid the suspicious glance of an alert house porter who

studiously feigns uninterest. Having progressed this far, the final hurdle is both unexpected and momentarily baffling. In a scene reminiscent of *Alice in Wonderland* your eyes fix upon a sign which explains that the offices of Morrison/Leahy are inaccessible by stairs. Potential pop stars suffering from claustrophobia turn back at this point, inevitably abandoning their dreams of stardom, for the next stage of the odyssey will propel them into a manually operated lift with heavy zigzag gates that open and close like a concertina. This wondrous device is actually a tradesman's elevator converted by fresh paint and gold polish into a quaint symbol of *nouveau riche* luxury. While you struggle to unlock the sturdy lift gates at the third floor, Patricia appears and like a native guide in an unfamiliar jungle beckons you towards the safety of an adjacent waiting-room. That room is magnificent in its spacious opulence with an impressive selection of recording equipment taking up the entire length of the far wall. Soon, Bryan Morrison wanders through eyeing you curiously, yet too courteous to demand your business. For a second you are overwhelmed by the temptation to acknowledge his presence, but the whim passes. As he leaves the room, you concede the opportunity of demanding an impromptu interview. The possibility of unravelling the true history of the once outrageous Pretty Things or unlocking the secrets of another renowned 60s entrepreneur pass, probably forever. Morrison will appear again later in another room. His countenance is vaguely reminiscent of Napier-Bell, with a hint of cynicism couched beneath a rather smug smile. His sun-tan and elegantly smart clothes advertize a subtle affluence which is rounded off more ostentatiously by the large cigar that he puffs with deep satisfaction. In that moment, he represents nothing less than an old fashioned caricature of the successful music business mogul. He struts impatiently across the room, disinterestedly dictating a self-indulgent letter to a quality newspaper objecting to an unfavourable report concerning some exclusive rural club that he frequents. Months later, you learn that he has opened an exclusive polo club in Hampshire. The music press, ever prone to hyperbole, add a scarcely believable footnote that the membership fee is £4,500 a year with an additional levy of £800 a game. Naturally, Wham! are spotted at the grand opening, apparently sipping champagne . . . The secretary finishes typing Morrison's disgruntled missive. The letter will be despatched on elegantly headed Morrison/Leahy notepaper in a thick vellum Morrison/Leahy envelope and the recipient will wish that his employers could afford such superior quality parchment.

Dick Leahy looks more worn and haggard than his partner, and the years spent behind a record company desk can almost be chronicled in the lines indelibly imprinted across his forehead. Like Morrison, he enjoys the ostentatious luxury of a big Churchillian cigar, no doubt equating the aroma with memories of boardroom meetings past. His other distinctive feature is a perpetual sun-tan with a pigmentation that arguably excels both his well-travelled partner and the cosmopolitan Napier-Bell. If ultra-violet rays really can seriously damage your health then the time that Leahy has spent in foreign climes will likely be repaid with suffering in his old age. Such thoughts are far from his mind as he sits forward in his chair, carefully surveying his long history in the record business. Mark Dean still likes to portray him as the secret force behind Wham! and who am I to argue with him? Unlike Dean, Napier-Bell, Summers, Allan or Innervision, Leahy has retained the confidence of George Michael and ultimately emerges as the surprise survivor in this 80s pop parable. His strength lies partly in his overt caution and discretion. He refuses to submit to a taped interview, discourages the jotting down of surreptitious notes, and finally insists verbally, and twice more in writing, that *everything* is off the record. He has nothing to say to me, but still spends three hours going through the motions. Far from saying anything good or bad about anyone, he prefers to offer no opinion at all.

Shirlie Holliman and Pepsi De Manque have retained their slinky stage apparel for a new career as a vocal duo. Their chart hopes rest on Wham!-style upbeat ballads of which their debut "Heartache" is a typical example. Ironically, it was their old employer (duetting with Aretha Franklin) who prevented them from achieving a number 1 hit at the first attempt.

Andrew Ridgeley now lives in Monaco, surrounded by rich and titled friends who endlessly discuss the rituals of Formula One motor racing. Once a media favourite who boasted more column inches than the Royal Family, the *enfant terrible* of pubescent pop has found to his pleasure that prying journalists seldom infiltrate his Monaco eyrie. Yellowing pages of Ridgeley high jinks can still be found in dusty press files but present day despatches betray a more prosaic tone speculating with unrecognizable politeness on his Thespian activities or the likely date of his wedding to long-time girlfriend Donia Fiorentino. Andrew, typically, is telling his inquisitors nothing.

George Michael took a long-overdue rest following Wham's final concert and is presently completing work on his first solo album. This is the release which his former manager confidently predicts will sprout ten hit singles and outdo Michael Jackson's *Thriller,* becoming one of the most commercially successful albums of all time. George has wisely resisted such premature hyperbole preferring to await the day with quiet confidence. Meanwhile, he trusts that Wham! will be remembered as one of the more interesting teenage phenomena in the history of pop, though not to the extent of belittling his solo career by onerous comparison.

Discography

WHAM!

SINGLES

Wham! Rap (Enjoy What You Do)/Wham! Rap (Enjoy What You Do)
Club Mix   *Innervision IV LA 2442*
Young Guns (Go For It)/Going For It   *Innervision IV LA 2766*
Bad Boys/Bad Boys (Instrumental)   *Innervision IV LA 3143*
Club Tropicana/Blue   *Innervision IV LA 3613*
Club Fantastic Megamix/A Ray Of Sunshine (Instrumental)
                                           Innervision IV LA 3586
Wake Me Up Before You Go-Go/Wake Me Up Before You Go-Go
(Instrumental)   *Epic A4440*
Freedom/Freedom (Instrumental)   *Epic A4743*
Last Christmas/Everything She Wants   *Epic GA 4949*
Everything She Wants (Remix)/Last Christmas   *Epic QA 4949*
I'm Your Man/Wham! (Do It Right)   *Epic A 6716*
The Edge Of Heaven/Battlestations/Where Did Your Heart Go?/
Wham! Rap '86   *Epic FINET 1*
Last Christmas/Where Did Your Heart Go?   *Epic 650-2697*

ALBUMS

Fantastic   *Innervision IVL 25328*
Bad Boys; A Ray Of Sunshine; Love Machine; Wham! Rap (Enjoy What
You Do); Club Tropicana; Nothing Looks The Same In The Light; Come
On; Young Guns (Go For It).

Make It Big   *Epic EPC 83611*
Wake Me Up Before You Go-Go; Everything She Wants; Heartbeat; Like
A Baby; Freedom; If You Were There; Credit Card Baby; Careless
Whisper.

The Final   *Epic EPC 88681*
Wham! Rap (Enjoy What You Do) 12″ version; Young Guns (Go For It)
12″ version; Bad Boys 12″ version; Club Tropicana; Wake Me Up Before
You Go-Go; Careless Whisper 12″ version; Freedom; Last Christmas 12″
version; Everything She Wants 12″ version; I'm Your Man (Extended

Stimulation); Blue (Armed With Love); A Different Corner; Battlestations; Where Did Your Heart Go?; The Edge Of Heaven.

The Final (Boxed Set)   *Epic WHAM 2*
Includes *The Final* double album on gold discs, t-shirt, notebook, pencil, calendar and numbered certificate.

Cassette Exclusive

The 12" Tape   *Epic EPC 450 125-4*
Wham! Rap; Careless Whisper; Freedom; Everything She Wants; I'm Your Man.

VIDEOS

Wham! The Video   *CBS/Fox VHS 3048-50*
Wham! Rap; Club Tropicana; Wake Me Up Before You Go-Go; Careless Whisper; Last Christmas.

Wham! '85   *CBS/Fox VHS 3075-50*
Everything She Wants; Freedom; I'm Your Man.

Wham In China – Foreign Skies   *CBS/Fox VHS 7142.50*
Documentary film, including selections from Wham's performances in China.

Wham! The Final   *CBS/Fox VHS 3846.50*
The Edge Of Heaven; A Different Corner; Where Did Your Heart Go?

GEORGE MICHAEL

SINGLES

Careless Whisper/Careless Whisper (Instrumental)   *Epic A 4603*
A Different Corner/A Different Corner (Instrumental)   *Epic A 7033*
I Knew You Were Waiting/I Knew You Were Waiting (Instrumental)
         Epic DUET 2

Omnibus Press

No.1 for Rock & Pop books.

Omnibus Press and Bobcat Books have published books on the following rock and pop stars:

AC/DC ... Bryan Adams ... A-Ha ... The Alarm ... The Beatles ... Pat Benatar ... Chuck Berry ... Big Country ... Black Sabbath ... Marc Bolan ... David Bowie ... Boy George & Culture Club ... Kate Bush ... Eric Clapton ... The Clash ... Phil Collins ... Elvis Costello ... Crosby, Stills & Nash ... The Cure ... Dead Or Alive ... Deep Purple ... Def Leppard ... Depeche Mode ... The Doors ... Duran Duran ... Bob Dylan ... Eurythmics ... Bryan Ferry & Roxy Music ... Fleetwood Mac ... Frankie Goes To Hollywood ... Peter Gabriel ... Marvin Gaye ... Genesis ... Jimi Hendrix ... Human League ... Billy Idol ... Julio Iglesias ... Michael Jackson ... Mick Jagger ... The Jam ... Japan ... Billy Joel ... Elton John ... Howard Jones ... Quincy Jones ... Journey ... Joy Division ... Judas Priest ... James Last ... Led Zeppelin ... John Lennon ... Madness ... Madonna ... Barry Manilow ... Marillion ... Bob Marley ... Paul McCartney ... Gary Moore ... Jim Morrison ... Ozzy Osbourne ... Jimmy Page ... Pink Floyd ... The Police ... Elvis Presley ... The Pretenders ... Prince ... Queen ... Quiet Riot ... Ratt ... Lou Reed ... Rolling Stones ... David Lee Roth ... Rush ... The Sex Pistols ... Sigue Sigue Sputnik ... Simon & Garfunkel ... Simple Minds ... Siouxie & The Banshees ... Slade ... The Smiths ... Bruce Springsteen ... Status Quo ... Cat Stevens ... Sting ... Supertramp ... Talking Heads ... Tears For Fears ... Thompson Twins ... Pete Townshend ... UB40 ... U2 ... Ultravox ... Van Halen ... The Velvet Underground ... Wham! ... The Who ... Stevie Wonder ... Paul Young ... Frank Zappa ... Z Z Top.

Omnibus and Bobcat titles on all the above are available from good book, record and music shops. In case of difficulty, contact Book Sales Ltd., Newmarket Road, Bury St. Edmunds, Suffolk IP33 3YB.